GUIDE TO THE W...
North West
& the Pennines

Recommended by
British Waterways

Nicholson
An imprint of HarperCollins*Publishers*

Also available:

Nicholson/Ordnance Survey Guide to the Waterways
1. **London, Grand Union, Oxford & Lee**
2. **Severn, Avon & Birmingham**
3. **Birmingham & the Heart of England**
4. **Four Counties & the Welsh Canals**
6. **Nottingham, York & the North East**
7. **Thames, Wey, Kennet & Avon**

Nicholson/Ordnance Survey Inland Waterways Map of Great Britain

First published in 1997 by
Nicholson
An imprint of HarperCollins*Publishers*
77-85 Fulham Palace Road
Hammersmith, London W6 8JB
and
Ordnance Survey
Romsey Road, Maybush
Southampton SO16 4GU

Text © Nicholson 1997
Waterways information © Nicholson 1997

© Crown copyright 1997

The mapping in this publication is based upon Ordnance Survey® Pathfinder®,
Outdoor Leisure™ and Explorer™ maps.

Ordnance Survey and Pathfinder are registered trade marks and Outdoor Leisure and
Explorer are trade marks of Ordnance Survey, the National Mapping Agency of Great Britain.

The representation in this publication of a road, track or path is no evidence of the existence of a
right of way.

Researched and written by David Perrott, Jonathan Mosse and Jane Mosse.
Design by Bob Vickers.

The publishers gratefully acknowledge the assistance given by British Waterways
and its staff in the preparation of this guide.

Photographs reproduced by kind permission of the following picture libraries:
British Waterways Photo Library pages 17, 40, 60, 97, 114, 120, 131, 136, 171;
Bill Meadows Picture Library pages 36, 120, 141, 160; Derek Pratt Photography pages 37, 108.

Thanks is also due to CAMRA representatives and branch members.

Great care has been taken throughout this book to be accurate, but the publishers
cannot accept responsibility for any errors which appear, or their consequences.

Printed in Italy.

ISBN 0 7028 3300 2
JN 8537
97/1/15

The canals and river navigations of Britain were built as a system of new trade routes, at a time when roads were virtually non-existent. After their desperately short boom period in the late 18th and early 19th centuries, they gracefully declined in the face of competition from the railways. A few canals disappeared completely, but thankfully most just decayed gently, carrying the odd working boat, and becoming havens for wildlife and the retreat of the waterways devotee.

It was two such enthusiasts, L.T.C. Rolt and Robert Aickman who, in 1946, formed the Inland Waterways Association, bringing together like-minded people from all walks of life to campaign for the preservation and restoration of the inland waterways. Their far-sightedness has at last seen its reward for, all over the country, an amazing transformation has taken place. British Waterways, the IWA, local councils, canal societies and volunteers have brought back to life great lengths of canal, and much of the dereliction which was once commonplace has been replaced with a network of 'linear parks'.

The canals provide something for everyone to enjoy: engineering feats such as aqueducts, tunnels and flights of locks; the brightly decorated narrowboats; a wealth of birds, animals and plants; the mellow unpretentious architecture of canalside buildings; friendly waterside pubs and the sheer beauty and quiet isolation that is a feature of so much of our inland waterways.

It is easy to enjoy this remarkable facet of our history, either on foot, often by bicycle, or on a boat. This book, with its splendid Ordnance Survey mapping, is one of a series covering the waterways network, and gives you all the information you need.

CONTENTS

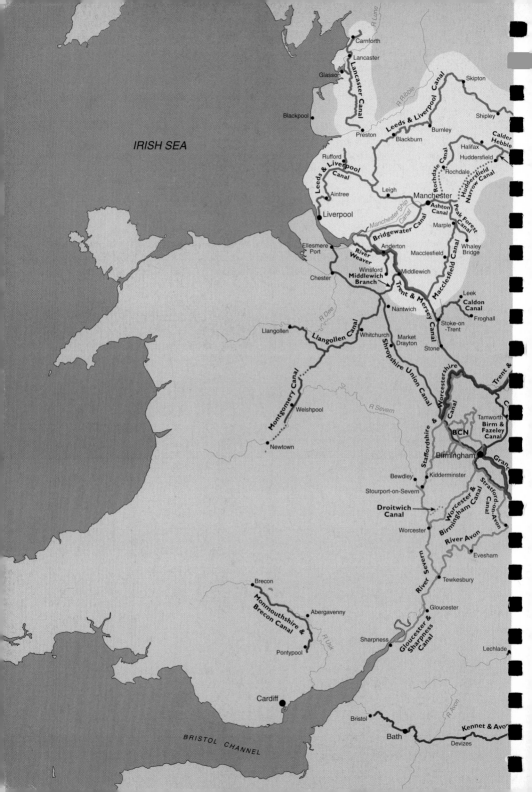

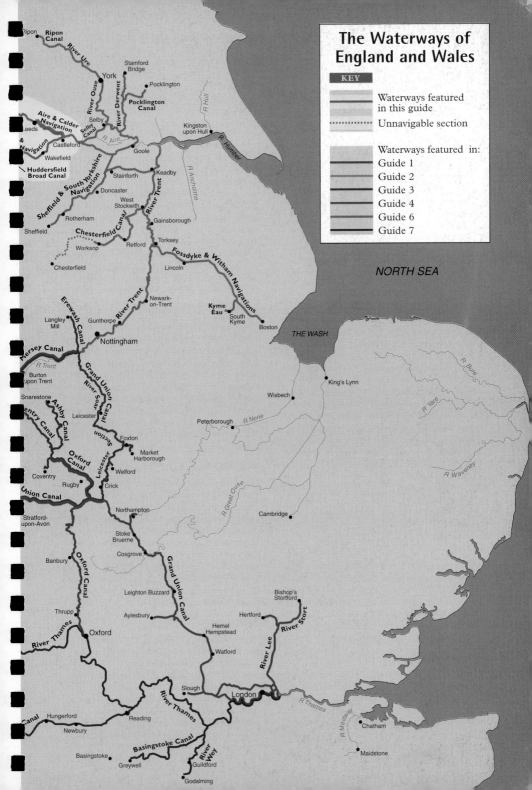

The Waterways of England and Wales

KEY

Waterways featured in this guide

Unnavigable section

Waterways featured in:
Guide 1
Guide 2
Guide 3
Guide 4
Guide 6
Guide 7

NORTH SEA

THE WASH

Ripon
Ripon Canal
River Ure
Stamford Bridge
York
Pocklington
Pocklington Canal
R Hull
River Derwent
River Ouse
Selby
Selby Canal
Kingston upon Hull
R Humber
Aire & Calder Navigation
Leeds
R Aire
Goole
& Navigation
Castleford
Wakefield
Stainforth
Keadby
Huddersfield Broad Canal
Doncaster
R Ancholme
River Trent
West Stockwith
Sheffield & South Yorkshire Navigation
Rotherham
Gainsborough
Sheffield
Chesterfield Canal
Worksop
Retford
Torksey
Fossdyke & Witham Navigations
Chesterfield
Lincoln
River Trent
Newark-on-Trent
Kyme Eau
South Kyme
Boston
Erewash Canal
Langley Mill
Gunthorpe
Mersey Canal
Nottingham
R Trent
Burton upon Trent
Snarestone
Grand Union Canal
River Soar
Leicester
King's Lynn
Wisbech
R Bure
R Yare
Ashby Canal
Oxford Canal
Leicester Section
Foxton
Market Harborough
Peterborough
R Nene
Coventry
Welford
R Waveney
Rugby
Crick
Union Canal
Northampton
R Great Ouse
Stratford-upon-Avon
Cambridge
Stoke Bruerne
Cosgrove
Oxford Canal
Banbury
Grand Union Canal
Leighton Buzzard
Bishop's Stortford
Aylesbury
Hertford
River Stort
Thrupp
Hemel Hempstead
Oxford
River Lee
River Thames
Watford
Slough
London
R Thames
R Medway
Canal
Hungerford
Reading
River Thames
Chatham
Newbury
Basingstoke Canal
Basingstoke
River Wey
Maidstone
Greywell
Guildford
Godalming

The slogan 'Waterways For All' was aptly coined to take account of the wide diversity of people using the inland waterways for recreation.

Today boaters, walkers, fishermen, cyclists and 'gongoozlers' (on-lookers) throng our canals and rivers anxious, in one way or another, to share in the enjoyment of our quite amazing waterway heritage. British Waterways, along with other navigation authorities, is empowered to develop, maintain and control this resource in order to maximise its potential: namely our enjoyment. It is to this end that a series of guides, codes, and regulations have come into existence over the years, evolving to match a burgeoning – and occasionally conflicting – demand. Set out below are the key points as they relate to everyone wishing to enjoy the waterways.

LICENSING – BOATS

The majority of the navigations covered in this book are controlled by British Waterways and are administered on first a regional and then on a local basis. Individual Waterway Managers are detailed in the introduction to each waterway and hold considerable autonomy. All craft using BW waterways must be licensed and charges are based on the length of the craft. This licence covers all navigable waterways under BW's control and in a few cases includes reciprocal agreements with other waterway authorities (as indicated in the text). Permits for permanent mooring on the canals are also issued by BW. Apply in each case to:

Customer Services
British Waterways
Willow Grange
Church Road
Watford WD1 3QA
Telephone: 01923 226422
Facsimile: 01923 226081

Since 1st January 1997 BW and the Environment Agency have introduced the Boat Safety Scheme, setting technical requirements for good and safe boat-building practice. A safety certificate will be necessary before applying for a craft licence.

Other navigational authorities relevant to this book are mentioned where appropriate.

LICENSING – CYCLISTS

Cyclists using BW towpaths are no longer required to purchase an annual licence. However they must apply for a free permit which in turn should be attached to their bicycle. Permits are obtainable from the address above; from Waterway Offices and, in many cases, from cycle shops near a waterway.

TOWPATHS

Few, if any, artificial cuts or canals in this country are without an intact towpath accessible to the walker at least. However, on river navigations towpaths have on occasion fallen into disuse or, sometimes, been lost to erosion. In today's leisure climate considerable efforts are being made to provide access to all towpaths with some available to the disabled. Notes on individual waterways in this book detail the supposed status of the path but the indication of a towpath does not necessarily imply a public right of way or mean that a right to cycle along it exists. If you are in any doubt, check with the latest published Ordnance Survey Map before you proceed. Motorcycling and horse riding are forbidden on all towpaths. Where bicycling is forbidden, exceptions may apply to boat crews 'lock-wheeling' to set locks ahead of their boats.

BW NAVIGATION GUIDE

Previously known as the Boaters Guide this publication has for many years set out the operating details of individual canals, listing everything from bridge and lock availability times through to telephone numbers for Regional and Waterway Offices. It is essential reading to accompany any guide to the navigable rivers and canals of this country. It is regularly updated and a copy may be obtained, free of charge, from the address above. It should be read in conjunction with the General Canal Bye-laws, also free from BW.

INDIVIDUAL WATERWAY GUIDES

No national guide can cover the minutiae of the individual waterway and more recently Waterway Managers have been producing guides to specific navigations under their charge. Copies of individual guides (where they are available) can be obtained by phoning the Waterway Office detailed in the introduction. It should be noted that times – such as operating times of bridges and locks – do change year by year and from winter to summer. Therefore your copy of a BW waterway guide should be regularly updated.

STOPPAGES

British Waterways works hard to programme its major engineering works into the winter period when demand for cruising is low. To this end it publishes a National Stoppage Programme and Winter Opening Hours leaflet which is sent out to all licence holders, boatyards and hire companies. Inevitably emergencies occur necessitating the unexpected closure of a waterway, perhaps during the peak season. Water shortages – particularly prevalent during recent dry summers – lead to restrictions and occasionally closure. Details are published on lockside noticeboards or by telephoning Canalphone on 01923 201401 for North West, North East and Midlands & South West Regions; 01923 201402 for Midlands & South West and Southern Regions.

STARTING OUT

If you are hiring a canal boat for the first time, the boatyard will brief you thoroughly. Take notes, follow their instructions and *don't be afraid to ask* if there is anything you do not understand.

GENERAL CRUISING NOTES

Most canals are saucer-shaped in section so are deepest at the middle. Few have more than 3-4ft of water and many have much less. Keep to the middle of the channel except on bends, where the deepest water is on the outside of the bend. When you meet another boat, keep to the right, slow down and aim to miss the approaching craft by a couple of yards: do not steer right over to the bank or you are likely to run aground. If you meet a loaded commercial boat keep right out of the way and be prepared to follow his instructions. Do not assume that you should pass on the right. If you meet a boat being towed from the bank, pass it on the outside. When overtaking, keep the other boat on your right side.

Speed

There is a general speed limit of 4 mph on most BW canals. This is not just an arbitrary limit: there is no need to go any faster and in many cases it is impossible to cruise even at this speed: if the wash is 'breaking' against the bank or causing large waves, slow down.

Slow down also when passing moored craft, engineering works and anglers; when there is a lot of floating rubbish on the water (and try to drift over obvious obstructions in neutral); when approaching blind corners, narrow bridges and junctions.

Mooring

Generally speaking you may moor where you wish on BW property, as long as there is sufficient depth of water, and you are *not causing an obstruction*. Your boat should carry metal mooring stakes, and these should be driven firmly in with the mallet if

there are no mooring rings. Do not stretch mooring lines across the towpath. Always consider the security of your boat when there is no one aboard. On tideways and commercial waterways it is advisable to moor only at recognised sites, and allow for any rise or fall of the tide.

Bridges

On narrow canals slow down and aim to miss one side (usually the towpath side) by about 9 inches. *Keep everyone inboard when passing through bridges*, and take special care with moveable structures – the crew member operating it should hold the bridge steady as the boat passes through.

Tunnels

Make sure the tunnel is clear before you enter, and use your headlight. Follow any instructions given on notice boards by the entrance.

Fuel

Hire craft usually carry fuel sufficient for your rental period.

Water

It is advisable to top up every day.

Lavatories

Hire craft usually have pump-out toilets. Have these emptied *before* things become critical. Keep the receipt and your boatyard will usually reimburse you for this expense.

Boatyards

Hire fleets are usually 'turned around' on a Saturday, making this a bad time to call in for services. Remember that moorings at popular destinations fill quickly during the summer months, so do not assume there will be room for your boat. Always ask.

LOCKS AND THEIR USE

A lock is a simple and ingenious device for transporting your craft from one water level to another. When both sets of gates are closed it may be filled or emptied using gate or ground paddles at the top or bottom of the lock. These are operated with a windlass.

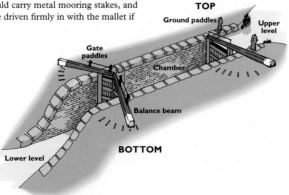

TOP

Ground paddles

Upper level

Gate paddles

Chamber

Balance beam

BOTTOM

Lower level

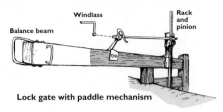

Lock gate with paddle mechanism

Labels: Balance beam, Windlass, Rack and pinion

General tips:
- Make safety your prime concern. *Keep a close eye on young children.*
- Always take your time, and do not leap about.
- Never open the paddles at one end without ensuring those at the other are closed.
- Never drop the paddles – always wind them down.
- Keep to the landward side of the balance beam when opening and closing gates.
- Never leave your windlass slotted onto the paddle spindle – it will be dangerous should anything slip.
- Be wary of fierce *top gate* paddles, especially in wide locks. Operate them slowly, and close them if there is *any* adverse effect.
- Always follow BW instructions, if these are given.

PLANNING A CRUISE

Many a canal holiday has been spoiled by trying to go too far too fast. Go slowly, don't be too ambitious, and enjoy the experience.

A *rough* calculation of time taken to cover the ground is the 'lock-miles' system:

Add the number of *miles* to the number of *locks* on your proposed journey, and divide the resulting figure by three. This will give you a guide to the number of *hours* it will take. But don't forget your service stops (water, shopping, pump-out), and allow plenty of time to visit that special pub!

TIDAL WATERWAYS

The typical steel narrow boat found on the inland waterways system has the sea-going characteristics of a bathtub, which renders it totally unsuitable for all-weather cruising on tidal estuaries. However the more adventurous will inevitably wish to add additional 'ring' cruises to the more predictable circuits within the calm havens of inland Britain. Passage is possible in most estuaries if careful consideration is given to the key factors of weather conditions, crew experience, the condition of the boat and its equipment and, perhaps of overriding importance, the need to take expert advice. In many cases it will be prudent to employ the skilled services of a local pilot. Within the text, where inland navigations connect with a tidal waterway, details are given of sources of both advice and

pilotage. This guide is to the Inland Waterways of Britain and therefore recognizes that tideways – and especially estuaries – require a different skill and approach. We therefore do not hesitate to draw the boater's attention to the appropriate source material.

GENERAL

British Waterways manages and cares for more than 2000 miles of Britain's rivers and canals. Other substantial lengths of waterway are administered by the Environment Agency and by individual Canal Authorities and Trusts. Whilst BW strives for consistency in what they do and how they do it – their objectives are enshrined in the Citizen's Charter – other organisations work within differing sets of parameters. The boater, conditioned perhaps by the uniformity of our national road network, should therefore be sensitive to a need to observe different codes and operating practices. Similarly it is important to be aware that some waterways are only available for navigation today solely because of the care and dedication of a particular restoration body, often using volunteer labour and usually taking several decades to complete the project. This is the reason that, in cruising the national waterways network, additional licence charges are sometimes incurred. The introduction to each waterway gives its background history, details of recent restoration (where relevant) and also lists the operating authority.

British Waterways is a public body, responsible to the Department of the Environment and, as subscribers to the Citizen's Charter, they are linked with an ombudsman. Problems and complaints should, in the first instance, be addressed to the local Waterway Manager as listed in the introduction to individual waterways. The current management structure is well suited, in the majority of cases, to providing swift and effective remedy. If satisfaction cannot be gained at this level then the ombudsman can be contacted as follows:

Waterways Ombudsman
2 Paper Buildings
Temple
London EC4Y 7ET
Telephone: 0171 582 0377
Facsimile: 0171 820 9429

FREEPHONE CANALS

This is available if you need help from British Waterways outside normal office hours on weekdays and throughout weekends. Simply dial 100 and ask for Freephone Canals. This service is completely free of charge. You should give details and location of your problem so that you can receive help as soon as possible. If you have a mobile telephone dial 01384 240948.

AIRE & CALDER NAVIGATION

MAXIMUM DIMENSIONS

River Lock to Leeds Lock
Length: 143'
Beam: 17'
Headroom: 12'

Leeds Lock to Castleford
Length: 200'
Beam: 20'
Headroom: 12'

Castleford to Wakefield
Length: 140'
Beam: 17'
Headroom: 12'

MANAGER

(01977) 554351

MILEAGE

LEEDS to:
Castleford: 10 miles, 5 locks
Wakefield: 17¹/2 miles, 10 locks including
Fall Ing

SAFETY NOTES

BW produce excellent Cruising Notes for
the pleasure boater using this waterway,
obtainable by ringing the manager's office.
This is both a commercial waterway and one
developed from a river navigation: both pose
their own disciplines highlighted in the notes.
Each lock on the waterway has a set of traffic
lights both upstream and downstream of the
lock chamber. The purpose of these lights is
to convey instructions and advice to
approaching craft.

Red light
Stop and moor up on the lock approach. The
lock is currently in use.

Amber light *(between the red and green lights)*
The lock keeper is not on duty. You will need
to self-operate.

Green light
Proceed into lock.

Red & green lights together
The lock is available for use. The lock keeper
will prepare and operate the lock for you.

Flashing red light
Flood conditions – unsafe for navigation.

Most lock approach moorings are immediately
upstream and downstream of the lock
chamber however, **please note:**

1 Ferrybridge Lock upstream approach
mooring is located on the river side of the
lock island.

2 Knostrop Lock downstream approach
mooring is located alongside the lock
bulnose.

3 Locks at Leeds, Lemonroyd, Castleford,
Woodnook and Broadreach allow access
to river sections of the navigation. For
interpretation of river level gauge boards
see Safety Notes in the introduction to the
Calder & Hebble Navigation on page 41.

4 There is a safe haven mooring immediately
upstream of Lemonroyd Lock.

All locks between Leeds and Wakefield
(except Fall Ing Lock) are equipped with
VHF Marine Band Radio. They monitor and
operate on channel 74.
In an emergency non-VHF users contact the
manager's office or out of office hours dial
100 and ask for Freephone Canals. Mobile
phone users dial 01384 215785.

The River Aire was first made navigable to Leeds in 1700, and rapidly became a
great commercial success, taking coal out of the Yorkshire coalfield and bringing
back raw wool, corn and agricultural produce. Improvements were then made to
the difficult lower reaches, with first Selby and later Goole becoming Yorkshire's
principal inland port. The opening of the New Junction Canal in 1905 further
secured its suitability for commercial traffic, which today still amounts to some
2¹/2 million tonnes, mainly coal, sand and petroleum.

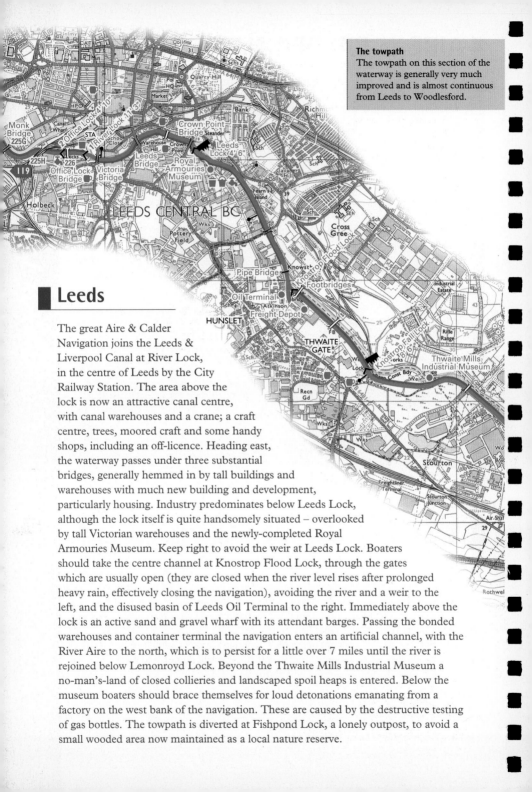

Leeds

The great Aire & Calder Navigation joins the Leeds & Liverpool Canal at River Lock, in the centre of Leeds by the City Railway Station. The area above the lock is now an attractive canal centre, with canal warehouses and a crane; a craft centre, trees, moored craft and some handy shops, including an off-licence. Heading east, the waterway passes under three substantial bridges, generally hemmed in by tall buildings and warehouses with much new building and development, particularly housing. Industry predominates below Leeds Lock, although the lock itself is quite handsomely situated – overlooked by tall Victorian warehouses and the newly-completed Royal Armouries Museum. Keep right to avoid the weir at Leeds Lock. Boaters should take the centre channel at Knostrop Flood Lock, through the gates which are usually open (they are closed when the river level rises after prolonged heavy rain, effectively closing the navigation), avoiding the river and a weir to the left, and the disused basin of Leeds Oil Terminal to the right. Immediately above the lock is an active sand and gravel wharf with its attendant barges. Passing the bonded warehouses and container terminal the navigation enters an artificial channel, with the River Aire to the north, which is to persist for a little over 7 miles until the river is rejoined below Lemonroyd Lock. Beyond the Thwaite Mills Industrial Museum a no-man's-land of closed collieries and landscaped spoil heaps is entered. Below the museum boaters should brace themselves for loud detonations emanating from a factory on the west bank of the navigation. These are caused by the destructive testing of gas bottles. The towpath is diverted at Fishpond Lock, a lonely outpost, to avoid a small wooded area now maintained as a local nature reserve.

NAVIGATIONAL NOTES

1 All the locks on the Aire & Calder operate mechanically and, although controlled by lock keepers, can be boater operated out of hours. Obey the traffic light signals.

2 Remember that this is a river navigation. Many of the locks are accompanied by large weirs, so keep a sharp lookout for the signs which direct you safely into the locks.

3 When the river level rises after prolonged heavy rain, the flood gates will be closed. Pleasure craft should stay put until they are advised by a lock keeper that it is safe to proceed.

4 This is a commercial waterway, used by 600-tonne tanker barges and push-tow coal pans. Keep a lookout for them, and give them a clear passage. Moor carefully, using bollards or fixed rings rather than mooring stakes, since the wash from these craft can be substantial.

Boatyards

Ⓑ **Yorkshire Hire Cruisers** 26 Canal Wharf, Leeds (0113 245 6195). 🛒 🔧 D Pump-out, overnight mooring, dry dock.

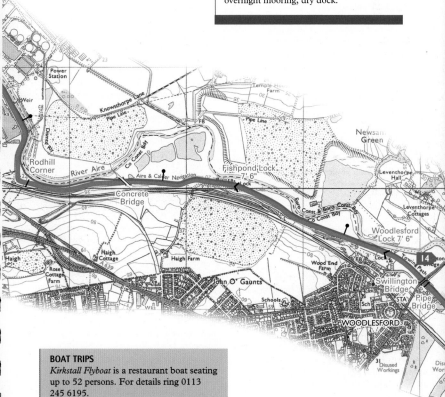

BOAT TRIPS

Kirkstall Flyboat is a restaurant boat seating up to 52 persons. For details ring 0113 245 6195.

● Leeds

W. Yorks. MD Tue, Fri, Sat. All services.
A vast industrial city that was a wool centre
in the Middle Ages and has continued to
grow to prosperity under the textile and
clothing trades; indeed Marks & Spencer
started business here with a stall in the
market. Montague Burton also became
established here, building what was to
become, by 1921, the largest clothing
factory in the world. However the last few
years have brought substantial changes,
with old industries being replaced by new,
and the atmosphere is one of growth and
prosperity.

The great Town Hall in Victoria Square
(walk north from Victoria Bridge and turn
left at Great George Street) stands as a
magnificent monument to Victorian civic
pride. Recently cleaned, it was designed by
Cuthbert Brodrick and opened in 1858.
Looking at the Corinthian columns on all
sides and the clock tower some 255ft high, it
is hard to believe that Brodrick was only 29
years old when he submitted his plans. As a
measure of this man's self-confidence, note
that he also designed the organ, installed in
1859, which itself weighs almost 70 tonnes,
has 6,500 pipes and stands 50ft high. The
light and airy Corn Exchange (north of Leeds
Bridge along Call Lane and now a shopping
arcade) built in 1861 is also Brodrick's work.
Always the cultural centre of Yorkshire, the
city hosts an international concert season and
an international piano competition. It has
several splendid theatres, including The
Grand in Briggate, modelled on La Scala,
Milan; the City Varieties, the oldest surviving
music hall in the country; and the Leeds
Playhouse Repertory Theatre. Also impressive
is the way, perhaps unique in the development of northern industrial towns, that
contemporary and Victorian buildings stand
harmoniously side by side. There are several
splendid parks and rich museums, and
excellent shopping facilities, including the
ornate Victorian Queens and County arcades.
Headingley, until recently the home of
Yorkshire cricket and a test match venue,
attracts an enthusiastic following in the area,
and of course the city's association with football and rugby teams is known worldwide.
Boaters should try to spend a day here if they
possibly can – there are good moorings on the
Leeds & Liverpool Canal by Office Lock, or
above Leeds Lock. See also page 119 (Leeds
& Liverpool Canal) for information on
Armley Mills Industrial Museum and Abbey
House Museum.

Metro. The area is well served by an excellent,
cheap bus and train service which offers a
variety of 'Day Rover' tickets. Phone 0113
245 7676 for details.

Tourist Information Centre City Station
concourse, Leeds (0113 242 5242). The
usual mine of free information and the first
place you should visit. You can obtain a free
guide to all the museums and galleries in
West Yorkshire, and for £1.00 the useful
Museum of Leeds Trail Guide is a must. *Leeds
Nights* (also free) details local pubs, eating
houses and night clubs.

Art Gallery and Henry Moore Sculpture Centre
The Headrow, Leeds (0113 247 8248). Walk
north from Victoria Bridge. A large collection
of mainly 19thC paintings, drawings and
prints. Sculpture by Henry Moore, Barbara
Hepworth and Jacob Epstein. *Open all day
Mon–Sat, & Sun afternoons.* Free.

City Museum Calverley Street, Leeds (0113
247 8275). Walk north from Victoria Bridge.
Archaeology, natural history, ethnography,
coins – exactly what you would expect in a
large city museum. *Closed Sun & Mon.* Free.

Granary Wharf The Canal Basin, Leeds (0113
244 6570). Below Office Lock. 30 craft and
food shops set under the vaults of the old
wharf warehouse, *open daily 10.00–17.30. At
weekends and B. Hol Mon* there are additional
stalls, special events, street entertainment and
music. Also a range of refreshments. Free.

Leeds – Settle – Carlisle Line From Leeds City
Station. The 70 miles from Settle to Carlisle
is said to be one of the most memorable rail
journeys in the world, so this would make an
excellent day trip away from the boat. *Every
Sat & Sun from May–Oct* there are free
guided walks from trains on the line. Coach
tours around the Yorkshire Dales also
connect. Details from leaflets at the station or
Tourist Information Centre.

Middleton Railway Tunstall Road, Leeds
(0113 271 0320). Built in 1758 to link
Leeds with the Middleton Colliery, this is
considered to be the world's oldest railway.
It operates at *weekends Easter–end of year* from
the industrial suburb of Hunslet, where steam
engines were once built.

Royal Armouries The Waterfront, Leeds
(0113 220 1999). Beside Leeds Lock with
moorings in Clarence Dock, adjacent to the
complex. The emphasis is on participation in
this massive, inter-active museum reputed to
be Britain's largest, post-war leisure development. Five themed galleries unfold stories of
weapons, battles, tournaments, falconry and
the wild west. See, touch, smell and handle
before retiring to watch the skills of an
armourer or experience the tranquillity of a
Japanese tea garden. *Open daily Apr–Oct,
10.00–18.00 (last admission 16.00) &*

Nov–Mar, 10.00–17.00 (last admission 15.00).
Closed Xmas Eve, Xmas Day & New Year's
Day. Two cafés and a bistro. Full disabled
access. Charge.
Tetley's Brewery Wharf The Waterfront,
Leeds (0113 242 0666). Just downstream
from Leeds Bridge. A trip through the history
of the English pub. Optional brewery tours.
Open Apr–Oct, Tue–Sun 10.30–17.00.
Oct–Mar, Wed–Sun 10.30–16.30. Charge.
Thwaite Mills Industrial Museum Thwaite
Lane, Leeds (0113 249 6453). A canalside
flint and china stone-grinding mill built in
1872 and powered by two waterwheels until
1975, when they were washed away, bringing
closure a year later. Visitors are able to see the
working conditions in the mill, as well as a

Marshall engine and various artefacts. *Open
10.00–17.00 Tue–Sun.* Charge.
Tropical World and Roundhay Park Roundhay,
Leeds (0113 266 1850). A wide selection of
buses from the city centre serve this tropical
paradise featuring butterflies, exotic blooms
and colourful fish. This is also one of
Europe's largest parks with a boating lake,
woodland walks, scented gardens (including
National Collections) and canal gardens and
waterfalls. *Open 10.00 to dusk every day except
Christmas.* Free.
● **Woodlesford**
W. Yorks. PO, tel, stores, garage, station. Good
moorings above the lock, and nearby pubs
make this a popular stopping place for
boaters.

Pubs and Restaurants

A fine city such as Leeds has many pubs and
restaurants. The following are a selection of
those fairly close to the navigation.
✕ ♀ **Hansa's Gujerati Vegetarian Restaurant**
72–72 North Street, Leeds (0113 244 4408).
Worth seeking out for excellent, home-cooked
dishes with an Indian flavour. Families warmly
welcomed.
✕ ♀ **Hereford Beefstouw** 38 The Calls, Leeds
(0113 245 3870). Airy establishment, not
limited to its excellent steaks, offering snacks
and a children's menu and overlooking the
river.
✕ ♀ **The Italian Job** 9 Bridge End, Lower
Briggate, Leeds (0113 242 0185). Well-loved
Italian favourites and a warm welcome dished
up in this busy pizzeria.
✕ ♀ **Whan Hai** 20 New Briggate, Leeds (0113
243 5019). Good value for money in a
Pekingese restaurant. *L & D. Closed Mon.*
🍺 **Grove** Back Row, Leeds (0113 439 254).
South of Victoria Bridge. Small traditional pub
with a choice of rooms. John Smith's,
Courage, Ruddles, Bass and guest real ales,
lunchtime food (*not Sat*). Folk *Fri* and live
music *most nights.* Outside seating.
🍺 **Adelphi** Hunslet Road, Leeds. South of
Leeds Bridge. A superbly restored and very
grand Edwardian pub, with lots of etched glass
and mahogany. Tetley's real ale, food *lunchtime*
(Mon–Fri).
🍺 ✕ **Whitelock's** Turk's Head Yard, Briggate,
Leeds (0113 453 3950). North of Leeds
Bridge. An unspoilt Edwardian pub, one of the
first buildings to have electricity. Younger,

Theakston, Flowers and McEwan real ales,
together with excellent fresh traditional bar
food *all day.* Restaurant *open lunchtimes and
Mon–Thur evenings.* Children in restaurant or
family room. No electronic machines.
🍺 **Duck & Drake** Kirkgate, Leeds (0113 246
5806). North of Crown Point Bridge, near the
church. Simply decorated pub with an open
fire and a choice of 15 real ales at weekends
(only 13 *during the week!)* These include
Theakston, Old Mill, and Timothy Taylor and
are served together with bar snacks *lunchtime.*
Live music *Sat & Thur.* No children.
🍺 **Palace** Kirkgate, Leeds (0113 244 5882).
Straight forward, no-frills pub dispensing Ind
Coope, Marston's, Tetley's and guest real ales,
open all day. Food available *lunchtimes and
evenings (not Sun evening) until 20.00.* Outside
seating and pub games.
🍺 **Crooked Billet** Thwaite Gate, Leeds (0113
271 7841). Comfortable Tetley's and
Theakston real ale pub with beams and
brasses. *Lunchtime* bar food *Mon–Fri.* No
children. Disco *Fri.* Garden.
🍺 **Two Pointers** Church Street, Woodlesford
(0113 282 3124). Up the hill from the lock. A
smart pub serving Boddingtons, Castle Eden
and Whitbread real ales. *Lunchtime bar food.*
Children and vegetarians catered for. Patio.
🍺 **White Hart** Church Street, Woodlesford
(0113 282 2205). Just past the Two Pointers.
A snug and comfy Tetley's real ale pub.
Family room, large garden and live music
*Fri. Post office, shops and Chinese take-away close
by.*

Castleford

The navigation continues along its straight course with the River Aire just to the north, its meanderings having endowed it with a series of oxbow lakes. All around are the remains of disused coal workings, some landscaped into smooth grassy banks, others a gaunt pale grey. At Woodlesford a

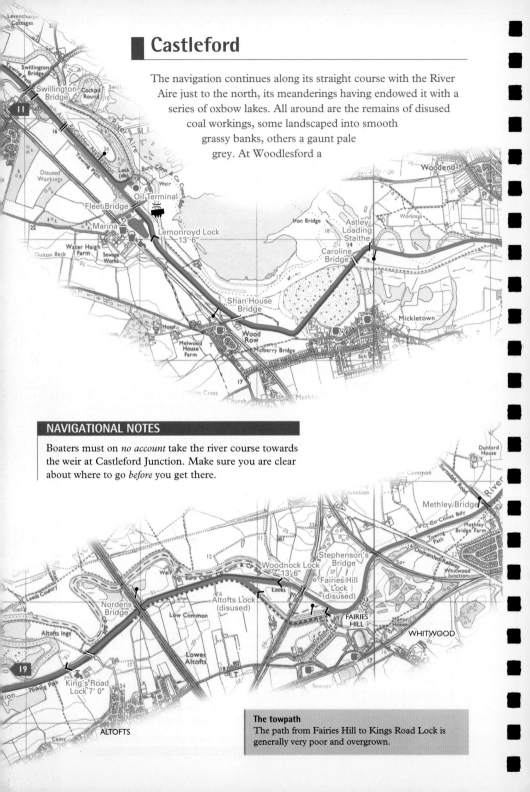

NAVIGATIONAL NOTES

Boaters must on *no account* take the river course towards the weir at Castleford Junction. Make sure you are clear about where to go *before* you get there.

The towpath
The path from Fairies Hill to Kings Road Lock is generally very poor and overgrown.

path up from the lock leads to two pubs, a post office, and shops. There is a supermarket and off-licence. Just before Fleet Bridge an arm branches off to the north. A disused lock here once used to connect with the river. Enclosed by the arm is an oil terminal – notice how the storage tanks have been colonised by house martins. The river by Fleet Lock was the site of a disastrous breach which occurred in March 1988, when the ground separating it from the adjacent St Aidens open-cast mine collapsed and the water poured in. Apparently the river below the breach flowed backwards for half a day, such was the volume of water consumed, and the workforce only just managed to rescue the large cranes. With the new alignment of the navigation it will be possible to re-commence mining, once the workings have finally been pumped out. The area under the old river bed will also come into production and hopefully the staithe at Caroline Bridge will again be busy, loading regular trains of compartment barges with coal for the huge Ferrybridge Power Station downstream.

continued in Book 6

Rejoining the river at the new Lemonroyd Lock (combining the old Lemonroyd Lock with the now vanished Kippax Lock) the mining village of Allerton Bywater appears at the end of the newly constructed section of waterway. There is a welcome waterside pub here, but make sure you moor securely if you stop, since passing commercial craft cause a considerable wash. There is a waterways 'crossroads' at Castleford. Navigators heading towards Sowerby Bridge should turn right here and must on no account go straight across – since that way leads to the huge Castleford Weir. To the left, through the Flood Lock, are a sanitary station, showers and good moorings, beyond which lies the route to Sheffield (see Book 6), Goole, Hull, York, the River Trent and ultimately the North Sea. The large commercial craft which trade to Leeds emerge from here, so boats travelling downstream on either the Rivers Aire or Calder, though not entering the flood lock, must still observe the traffic signals to avoid collision with vessels leaving the lock. Entering the River Calder, navigators will notice that its course here has been straightened, as the oxbow lakes either side will testify. After ducking under a large road bridge and two railway bridges a path which gives access to two fine pubs at Whitwood can be seen to the south. Your nose will also tell you there is a large sewage works here. Pressing on, the large, deep mechanised Woodnook Lock is reached. This replaced the earlier Fairies and Altofts locks (now disused) to the south. By comparing the sizes of the locks, an impression of the improvements carried out on the navigation during the last 100 years can be gained. Beyond the large motorway bridge is King's Road Lock (also mechanised) and paths from here lead to Altofts, although there is little reason to walk the half mile or so, except for supplies.

Pubs and Restaurants

United Kingdom Station Road, Wood Row (01977 555840). Up the path from Lemonroyd Lock, just over the level crossing. John Smith's real ale. Inexpensive food available *lunchtime (not Sat) and evenings, 7 nights a week. Open all day Mon & Fri-Sun.*

New Bay Horse Mickletown (01977 553557). Turn right out of Pit Lane, up from Caroline Bridge (do not moor anywhere near the staithe). Family pub with a restaurant serving Tetley's, Friary Meux and guest real ales. Food available *L & D (not Sun D).* Children and vegetarians catered for. Family room, large garden and children's play area. Quiz *Tue,* darts and dominoes.

Boat Riverside, Allerton Bywater (01977 552216) . An attractive Bass and Worthington, Yorkshire pub with a waterside garden. Bar meals available *lunchtimes, Wed–Sat in the winter and lunchtime and evenings 7 days a week in summer.* Children's room and outdoor play area. Quiz *Thur and Sun.* Take care when mooring here, as passing commercial craft can create a sizeable wash.

Victoria Hotel Main Street, Allerton Bywater (01977 516438). Tetley's, John Smith's and Theakston real ales together with bar food served *lunchtime, evenings and all day at weekends* in this friendly, modernised local. Carvery *Mon– Fri.* Children and vegetarians catered for. Garden and quiz *Sun.*

Old Mill Castleford (01977 557034). Just south of Castleford Junction, at the Barnsdale Road Bridge. Theakston, Younger and guest real ales in a friendly local with two landlords: one the uninvited ghost of the 1928–41 incumbent. Disco and quiz *Fri.* Post office and stores close by.

Griffin Castleford (01977 557551). Opposite The Old Mill. John Smith's real ale. Outside drinking area. Quiz *Wed.*

Ship Castleford (01977 552036). Immediately south of the River Aire. Tetley's and John Smith's real ales dispensed in this comfortable and welcoming, traditional brewery pub with stained glass and a tiled exterior. Inexpensive bar food *lunchtime* and outside seating overlooking the river. Children welcome and quiz *Sun.*

Garden House Castleford (01977 552934). Downstream from The Ship. An ideal, comfortable, family pub with food available *lunchtime and evenings 7 days a week.* The Goole packet boat used to leave from outside but now the friendly landlord is more concerned with serving Vaux, Thorne, Samson and guest real ales. Vegetarian and children's menu. Outside seating and *Thur* quiz.

Bridge Inn Whitwood (01977 550498). A most interesting pub, newly built but with old bricks and timbers. There is a lofty ceiling over the bar, with more intimate drinking and eating areas off to the sides. Good bar meals (*lunchtime and evenings except Sun evening),* friendly staff and Theakston, Black Sheep, John Smith's, Tetley's and guest real ales. Patio, children welcome. B & B.

New Wheatsheaf Whitwood (01977 553052). Large, brightly decorated traditional pub, where someone clearly takes a great pride in their flower arrangements. Tetley's and John Smith's real ales, and a wide range of interesting and appetising food served *L & D (not Sun D)* in both bar and restaurant. Children welcome, vegetarian menu. Quiz *Sun.* Patio.
Between these two pubs is the Castleford & Whitwood Greyhound Racing Stadium (01977 559940), where there are races *every Mon, Wed & Fri at 19.30.*

Temple Newsam House (0113 264 7321). Walk north from Swillington Bridge, fork left after the river – 2 miles. A superb Tudor/Jacobean house in 900 acres of parkland. Magnificent Georgian and Regency interiors. Rare breeds centre in Home Farm, walks in park and woods, magnificent displays of roses and rhododendrons in gardens. *Open 13.00–17.00 Tue–Sun, Apr–Oct; 14.00–17.00 Sat & Sun only, Nov–Mar.* Tea room, shop, estate and gardens *open all year.* Charge for House admission, Home Farm and Estate free.

Mickletown
W. Yorks. PO, tel, stores. Claimed by the locals to be the second largest village in England – it is suggested that Wroxham in Norfolk is the largest – Mickletown has clearly had its problems since the neighbouring colliery closed. The next-door village of Wood Row is very close by, and the *pub, store and post office* there can be easily reached via a path from Caroline Bridge.

Allerton Bywater
W. Yorks. Stores, tel. A mining village, but the pit is now closed. Coal was once loaded from wagons onto barges from a small staithe here.

Castleford
W. Yorks. EC Wed. MD Mon, Fri, Sat. All services. Once the Roman settlement of Lagentium, now a busy industrial town which has grown up at this important waterways junction. The Waterway Manager's Office can be seen by the Flood Lock, and Allinsons mill is situated by the huge weir – here they produce their popular stoneground flour.
Castleford Museum Carlton Street, Castleford (01977 722085). Victorian Castleford theme exhibition. *Open daily during library opening times.* Free.

Altofts
W. Yorks. PO, tel, stores. Originally a mining village and now a suburb of Wakefield, with a pick-your-own fruit farm at the western end, but little else. There was once a pub by the river, but it is now a private house. There are still two pubs in the village.

Stanley Ferry Aqueduct (see page 18)

Wakefield

Birkwood Lock was for a long time the last mechanised lock when travelling upstream. At Stanley Ferry the canal is diverted over the new aqueduct, which stands alongside the original and was opened in 1981. The original aqueduct was thought to be at risk from the large craft which can now navigate here. There is a British Waterways repair yard and lock gate building workshop immediately before the aqueduct, and a marina with a pub beyond. This has been built in a defunct loading basin beside the splendid, stone wharf office. It was here that empty 'Tom Puddings' were hauled onto railway wagons and, after loading at the nearby colliery, re-launched en route for Goole.

After Ramsden's Swing Bridge (*sanitary station, pump-out and showers*) the navigation continues in a dead straight line, passing Broadreach Flood Lock and Heath Old Hall before turning west to join the Calder & Hebble at Fall Ing Lock. There are craft moored here by an old loading chute, a picnic area, boatyard and convenient pub. Below Wakefield Flood Lock the river is navigable for a short distance towards the weir, giving access to a boatyard. Leaving Wakefield you pass under a splendid curving brick railway viaduct known locally as 'the 99 arches'. A careful count will reveal only 95.

Stanley Ferry Aqueduct

It is a good idea to moor at Stanley Ferry Marina and walk to the road bridge for a full view of this fine structure – a trough suspended from a two-pin cast-iron arch – built on the same principle as the Sydney Harbour Bridge, which it predates by 100 years. Nearly 7000 tons of Bramley Fall stone and 1000 tons of cast iron were used in its construction. The first boat to pass across it was the *James*, a schooner of 160 tons drawn by three grey horses, on 8th August 1839. The 700 men who worked on it were fed at the nearby public houses, one of which, The Ship, still stands. Designed by George Leather, the strength of the structure was severely tested when, soon after opening, the largest flood for 20 years caused the river below to actually flow into the trough. The towpath is carried on a separate wooden breakwater designed to protect the aqueduct during such floods. The concrete aqueduct was built in 1981, and the original, by its side, is still in water.

NAVIGATIONAL NOTES

1 Take heed of the notices and flood indicator boards at the locks. Pleasure craft should only proceed if the water level is in the *green* or *amber* sectors.

2 Most locks on the Calder & Hebble have a unique type of paddle gear, consisting of a small perforated wheel which is turned using a 'handspike'. These are obtainable from boatyards on the navigation, and from Castleford Lock. Or a piece of 3" x 2" hardwood, 3ft long, will do just as well.

3 When coming downstream (from Sowerby Bridge direction) keep a sharp lookout for the entrance to Wakefield Flood Lock. There is a large weir on the river, a short distance beyond the boatyard, by the bridge.

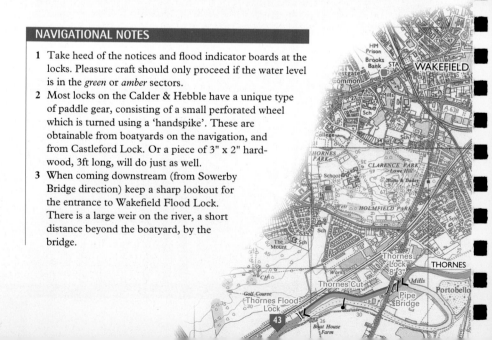

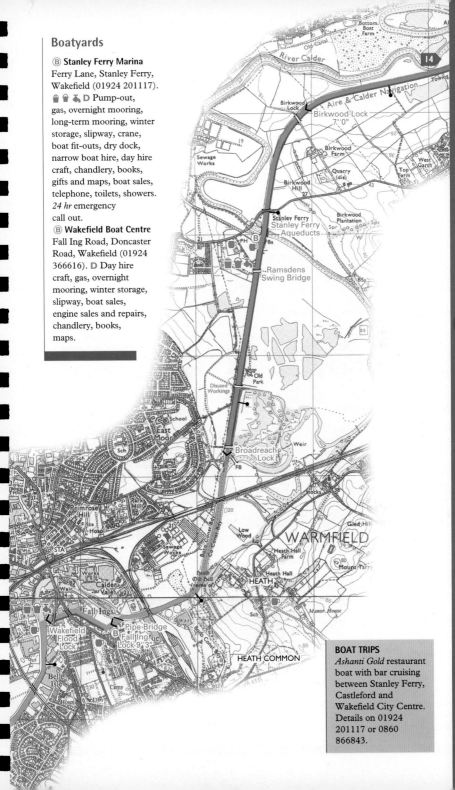

Boatyards

Ⓑ **Stanley Ferry Marina**
Ferry Lane, Stanley Ferry,
Wakefield (01924 201117).
🚿 🚽 ♿ D Pump-out,
gas, overnight mooring,
long-term mooring, winter
storage, slipway, crane,
boat fit-outs, dry dock,
narrow boat hire, day hire
craft, chandlery, books,
gifts and maps, boat sales,
telephone, toilets, showers.
24 hr emergency
call out.

Ⓑ **Wakefield Boat Centre**
Fall Ing Road, Doncaster
Road, Wakefield (01924
366616). D Day hire
craft, gas, overnight
mooring, winter storage,
slipway, boat sales,
engine sales and repairs,
chandlery, books,
maps.

BOAT TRIPS
Ashanti Gold restaurant
boat with bar cruising
between Stanley Ferry,
Castleford and
Wakefield City Centre.
Details on 01924
201117 or 0860
866843.

● **Wakefield**

W. Yorks. MD Mon, Tue, Thur, Fri, Sat. All services. The city centre is north of the navigation. The regional capital of West Yorkshire, it gained city status in 1888 when the cathedral was granted its charter. Mainly 15thC Perpendicular in style, the cathedral's 247ft spire is a landmark for miles around. On a much smaller scale, but perhaps of equal interest, is the Chantry Chapel of St Mary, a rare 14thC example of a bridge chapel, just a short walk north of Fall Ing, by the weir. Industrial pollution has meant that the entire front of the building has had to be replaced twice in the last two centuries: the original now graces the entrance to a boat house at Kettlethorpe. The city itself is set on a hill, and still contains some quiet streets and dignified Georgian houses, notably those in St John's Square, with its delightful church and handsome council buildings. There has been a settlement at Wakefield since Saxon times, and the strategic importance of this site on the River Calder is confirmed by the remains of the 12thC Sandal Castle. The Battle of Wakefield, a significant conflict in the Wars of the Roses, was fought near here in 1460, and resulted in the death of Richard, Duke of York. Wakefield's prosperity was founded on the textile and engineering industries, both of which have taken a battering in recent years. However, the city has been successful in attracting new industry, such as Coca Cola/Schweppes; and the vast and spectacular Ridings shopping complex has created many new jobs. The Theatre Royal & Opera House provides a lively programme of entertainment, and the Yorkshire Sculpture Park at Bretton Hall displays some important works by Barbara Hepworth and Henry Moore, both local artists.

Tourist Information Centre Town Hall, Wood Street, Wakefield (01924 305003). North-west of the cathedral.

Wakefield Museum Wood Street, Wakefield (01924 305350). Local history and archaeology, excavations from Sandal Castle, and the Waterton collection of exotic birds and animals. The building, designed in 1820, was originally a music saloon. *Closed Sun morning.* Free.

Wakefield Art Gallery Wentworth Terrace, Wakefield (01924 305350). Sculpture by local artists Barbara Hepworth and Henry Moore, plus contemporary paintings, prints and drawings. Also **Elizabethan Gallery** showing a wide range of temporary exhibitions. *Closed Sun morning.* Free.

Heath Village 2 miles east of Wakefield. A beautifully preserved village with some 18thC merchants' houses amongst other substantial buildings. Heath Hall is a fine Georgian house by John Carr (1753) with carved woodwork and moulded plaster ceilings. The gas-lit pub is a gem (see below).

Pubs and Restaurants

◗ ✕ **Ferryboat Inn** Ferry Lane, Stanley Ferry (01924 290596). Stones, Whitbread and guest real ales in one of the old, converted wharf-side buildings. Carvery food available *lunchtime, evenings and all day Sun.* Vegetarian menu. Children's room and extensive outdoor play area, patio. *Open all day during summer.*

◗ ✕ **Ship** Stanley Ferry (01924 372420). Close to the marina. Comfortable, family pub, pleasantly decorated. There must have been much merriment here on the day in August 1839 when the new aqueduct opened. Webster's, Ruddles and guest real ales together with an interesting bar and restaurant menu served *lunchtime and evenings.* Vegetarians and children catered for. Garden and outdoor play area.

◗ ✕ **King's Arms** Heath Village (01924 377527). Overlooking the common, originally built as houses in 18thC and converted into a pub in 1841. Tetley's, Timothy Taylor, John Smith's and Clark's real ales in an exceptional old pub with a gas-lit, wood-panelled bar; full of antiques. Open fire, excellent bar and restaurant food *lunchtime and evenings.* Children and vegetarians catered for. Garden. Quiz *Tue.*

◗ **Graziers** Doncaster Road, Wakefield (01924 376788). Just south of Fall Ing Lock. Tetley's real ale pub with some outside seating. *Take-away pizzeria opposite.*

◗ **Henry Boon's** Westgate, Wakefield (01924 378126). West of the cathedral, next to the prison. Fine traditional brewery tap for Clark's Brewery. A real ale enthusiasts' pub, with live music *Thur.* Sandwiches available *lunchtime and evenings.*

✕ ◗ **Clock Tower Restaurant** Town Hall, Wood Street, Wakefield (01924 305130). A unique venture offering superb à la carte and bar meals in a suite of rooms under the Town Hall clock. Excellent views and walls decorated with the plans entered for the competition to design the present structure, combined with an imaginative (and thoroughly affordable) menu. Where else have you seen the Les Routiers sign affixed to the portals of a municipal building? *Open lunchtime 12.00–13.30 (not Sat) and Fri & Sat evenings 19.30–21.00.* Appetising vegetarian menu.

◗ **Jolly Sailor** Thornes Wharf, Wakefield (01924 374172). Opposite Wakefield Flood Lock. Tetley's and guest real ales together with inexpensive, home-made bar meals served *lunchtime (not Sun).* Garden and children's play area. Pub games and quiz *Wed and Sun.*

BRIDGEWATER CANAL

MAXIMUM DIMENSIONS
Length: 70'
Beam: 14' 9"
Headroom: 8'
Draught: 2' 6"

LICENCES
Manchester Ship Canal Company, Land
Planning, Quay West, Trafford Wharf Road,
Manchester M17 1PL.
Enquiries: 0161 872 2411 extn 326.
All craft using the canal must be licensed.
They must also be insured against third party
risks which should include the cost of salvage
and removal of wreck. Any boat holding a
British Waterways canal & river licence may

cruise on the Bridgewater Canal for seven
consecutive days free of charge.

MILEAGE
PRESTON BROOK to
Lymm: 10$\frac{1}{2}$
Waters Meeting, junction with
Leigh Branch: 22
CASTLEFIELD JUNCTION, start of
Rochdale Canal: 23$\frac{1}{2}$
No locks
DUCIE STREET JUNCTION, start of
Ashton Canal: 25 (Rochdale Canal, 9 locks)
Preston Brook to Runcorn: 5$\frac{3}{4}$, no locks
Leigh Branch: 10$\frac{3}{4}$, no locks

The Bridgewater Canal, which received the Royal Assent on 23 March 1759, was
the forerunner of all modern canals, following a route that was independent of all
existing natural watercourses. It was built by Francis Egerton, third Duke of
Bridgewater, to enable coal from his mines at Worsley to be transported to
Manchester and sold cheaply. His agent was John Gilbert and his engineer James
Brindley, who designed a lockless contour canal which crossed the River Irwell on
a stone aqueduct – a revolutionary concept and one that was ridiculed by many
sceptics. However, the line was open to Stretford by the end of 1765.

While the canal was under construction, there began the excavation of a remarkable
system of underground canals to serve the Duke's mines, reached through two
entrances at Worsley Delph. Eventually 46 miles of underground canal were built,
some on different levels and linked by an ingenious inclined plane built along a
fault in the sandstone. The craft used in the mines were known as 'starvationers',
double-ended tub boats which could carry up to 12 tons of coal. This whole system
remained in use until the late 19thC.

In 1762 the Duke received sanction to extend his canal to the Liverpool tideway at
Runcorn – this was later amended in order to connect with the new Trent & Mersey
Canal at Preston Brook. The route between Liverpool and Manchester was opened
in 1776, although Brindley did not live to see its completion. In 1795 the Duke,
then 60 years old, received the Royal Assent for the final part of the network, which
linked Worsley to the Leeds & Liverpool Canal at Leigh.

The coming of the railways did not initially affect the prosperity of the canal. In 1872
the newly formed Bridgewater Navigation Company purchased the canal for
£1,120,000, and they in turn sold it to the Manchester Ship Canal Company in
1885. The building of the new Ship Canal meant that Brindley's original stone
aqueduct over the River Irwell was replaced. Its successor, the Barton Swing
Aqueduct, was no less outstanding than the original, being a steel trough closed by
gates at each end, pivoting on an island in the Ship Canal. The moving structure
weighs 1450 tons, including 800 tons of water.

The Bridgewater Canal is a tribute to its builders in that it continued to carry
commercial traffic until 1974 – indeed its wide gauge, lock-free course and frequent
use of aqueducts makes many later canals seem retrograde.

Preston Brook

Although the main line of the Bridgewater once locked down to the Mersey in Runcorn, this is now a dead end, with the locks being closed in 1966. What is now the main canal route to Manchester bears to the right immediately after the big M56 motorway bridge, and its direct course to the south of the Mersey affords good views of the Manchester Ship Canal. Industry keeps its distance, and only the landscaped grounds of the Daresbury Laboratories intrude. The canal frontage at Moore is attractive, with moored boats, a shop and a phone right by the canal.

Boatyards

Ⓑ **Claymoore Navigation** The Wharf, Preston Brook (01928 717273). 🚽 🛢 [Evenings] Pump-out, gas, narrow boat/day hire craft, overnight and long-term mooring, groceries, shop, boat/engine repairs, public telephone nearby, toilets.

Ⓑ **Preston Brook Marina** Preston Brook (01928 719081). 🚽 🛢 🛠 Gas, overnight mooring, long-term mooring, slipway, boat sales, toilets, showers.

Boat and Butty Company Ringway Road, Runcorn (01928 733522). The Wooden Canal Craft Trust, a dedicated group, restore historic wooden craft here.

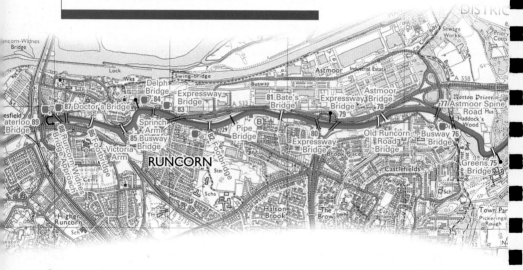

● **Preston Brook Tunnel**
1239yds long and forbidden to unpowered craft. A notice indicates when you may enter.

● **Preston Brook**
Ches. PO, tel, stores. A village which grew to serve the canal, where goods were transhipped from wide beam craft of the north west to narrow boats of the Midlands. Unfortunately, little remains of this activity, and the M56 dominates. **Norton Priory** (01928 569895). Only the undercroft survives from the 11thC. A recorded commentary describes points of interest. Pleasant gardens. *Open Mon-Fri 12.00–17.00; Sat, Sun and public holidays 12.00–18.00.* Charge.

● **Runcorn**
Ches. EC Wed. MD Tue, Thur, Sat. All services. The old town is to be found down by the docks, where the elegant curved 1092-ft single span of

the steel road bridge (built 1961), with the railway beside, leaps over the Ship Canal and the Mersey. The massive flight of 10 double locks which connected the canal to the Mersey was finally abandoned in 1966, and filled in, much to the dismay of industrial archaeologists and canal enthusiasts. Since 1964 Runcorn has been a 'new town', its rapid growth being carefully planned. **Runcorn Tourist Information Centre** 57–61 Church Street (01928 576776).

● **Daresbury**
Ches. Tel, stores. Half-a-mile up the road from Keckwick Bridge. Birthplace of Charles Lutwidge Dodgson, better known as Lewis Carroll. The church has a pretty Lewis Carroll memorial window, where he is shown with characters from *Alice in Wonderland*. Viewing is by prior appointment only – ring the Vicarage on 01925 740348.

Pubs and Restaurants

 ✕ **Red Lion Hotel** Chester Road, Preston Brook (01928 701174).
Greenalls and Bass real ale and meals *lunchtimes & evenings every
day (except Sat lunchtime* only).

 Ring O' Bells Chester Road, Daresbury (01925 740256).
Quiet pub with a Lewis Carroll theme. Real ale and meals
lunchtimes and evenings. Garden.

 Red Lion Runcorn Road, Moore (01925 740205).
A few minutes walk west of bridge 7. Real ale and
food *lunchtimes and evenings*.

There are plenty of pubs in Runcorn, including:

 Waterloo High Street (01928 572149).
Between bridges 88 & 89. Greenalls real
ale and bar meals *Mon– Fri and Sun
lunchtime* only.

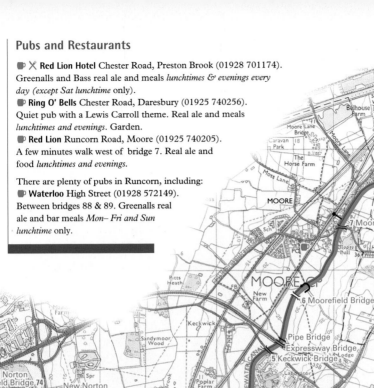

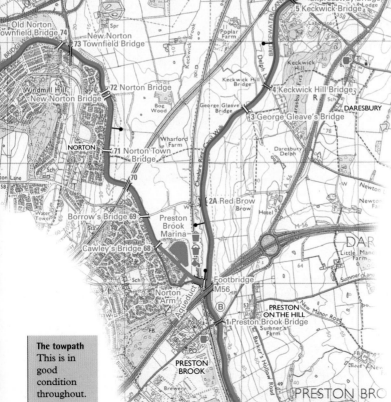

The towpath
This is in
good
condition
throughout.

Stockton Heath

A short rural stretch is interrupted by the estate village of
Higher Walton, which can be seen among trees,
and this is followed by a secluded tree-lined
length in a shallow cutting before the
outskirts of Stockton Heath
are approached. There
follows a pleasant
example of
urban

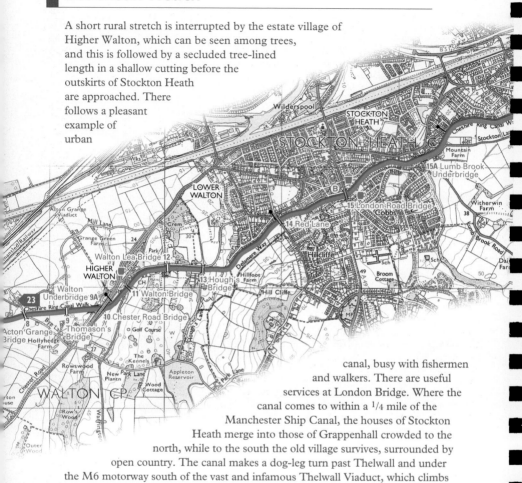

canal, busy with fishermen
and walkers. There are useful
services at London Bridge. Where the
canal comes to within a 1/4 mile of the
Manchester Ship Canal, the houses of Stockton
Heath merge into those of Grappenhall crowded to the
north, while to the south the old village survives, surrounded by
open country. The canal makes a dog-leg turn past Thelwall and under
the M6 motorway south of the vast and infamous Thelwall Viaduct, which climbs
laboriously over the Ship Canal.

Boatyards

ⓑ **Thorn Marine** London Bridge, Stockton
Heath (01925 265129). 🛉 🛠 , **D** *nearby*. Gas
(Shell), groceries, chandlery, books and maps,
boat and engine sales, engine repairs, toilets,
gifts, books and maps, coal and other solid fuels.
Public telephone and shopping centre *nearby*.

● **Higher Walton**
Ches. PO, tel, stores. A pretty, late-Victorian estate
village among trees.
Walton Hall Higher Walton (01925 601617). 20
acres of parkland and gardens *open from dawn to*
dusk. Facilities include children's zoo, outdoor
games, heritage centre, play area, café and
Ranger Service organising activities for the
public and groups (ring for details). Charge for
facilities only.

● **Stockton Heath**
Ches. EC Thur. Shops and services north of
London Bridge. An outer suburb of
Warrington, England's centre for vodka
distilling and a useful place for supplies.
Stockton Quay Bridge 15. The terminus of the
canal from 1771 to 1776, before the Duke of
Bridgewater completed his route from
Manchester to Runcorn, and consequently a
major transhipment point with stables, yards,
wharves, warehouses and a canal company
office. Passenger packet boat services also ran
from here from 1771 to the mid 1880s, one of
the craft being the renowned *Duchess-Countess*.

● **Grappenhall**
Ches. PO, tel, stores. A fine group of buildings
on cobbled streets survive around the church
of St Wilfred, where the village stocks
remain. There are two excellent pubs, which
makes a stop here very worthwhile.

● **Thelwall**
Ches. A short walk north from Thelwall
underbridge will bring you to a ferry where,
for a minimal charge, you will be carried
across the Ship Canal. Ring for details on
01925 824798.

Pubs and Restaurants

▣ ✕ **Walton Arms** Chester Road, Higher
Walton (01925 262659). Hudsons, Greenalls
and guest real ales in a comfortable and
friendly pub, decked with flowers. Food,
steak restaurant, *lunchtimes & evenings daily.*
Outside seating. Regular entertainment.

▣ **London Bridge** Stockton Heath. By Bridge
15. A homely and welcoming pub with a
canalside terrace, offering Stones and
Greenalls real ales. Food *lunchtimes &
evenings daily.*

▣ **The Rams Head** Grappenhall. A comfortable old-fashioned pub serving Greenalls real
ales and a wide range of food. B & B.

▣ **Parr Arms** Church Lane, Grappenhall
(01925 267393). A comfortable and homely
pub, right beside the church, serving
Greenalls real ale. Food *lunchtimes & evenings
(not Sun evenings)*, with a vegetarian menu,
in a large eating area. Children welcome at
publican's discretion. Outside seating and
regular entertainment.

Lymm

There are fine views of the distant Pennines to the north before the canal makes a very pleasing passage through the heart of Lymm, where the streets come right down to the water's edge. There are

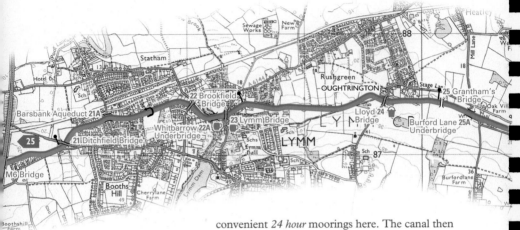

convenient *24 hour* moorings here. The canal then passes the village of Oughtrington to the north and a row of smart new houses to the south before entering surroundings which are surprisingly rural. Rows of moored boats, some in an advanced state of decay, announce the presence of two useful boatyards and a new pub. The fields then gently fall away into the valley of the River Bollin, which the Bridgewater crosses on a large embankment, with fine views of the Manchester Ship Canal and Dunham Park. Dunham Underbridge is a new concrete and steel construction, built to replace the original stone trough which breached disastrously in August 1971 and resulted in a 2-year closure and repairs amounting to £250,000. There are good moorings by Dunham Town Bridge.

● **Lymm**
Ches. PO, tel, stores, banks, fish & chips, laundrette. The l7thC Lymm Cross stands just a few yards from the canal in the centre of this hilly and attractive little town. The dam at the back of the town was built to carry the turnpike road over a sharp ravine, thus creating a pleasant lake in the process.

● **Oughtrington**
Ches. PO, tel, stores. A good place for supplies.

● **Bollington**
Ches. PO. A compact and attractive village, with a fine old pub and a converted mill.
Dunham Massey Hall (0161 941 1025). Until recently the seat of the Earl of Stamford, but now owned by the National Trust. The beautiful 18thC house by John Norris stands in a wooded park, landscaped by George Booth, the Second Earl of Warrington. It contains an 18thC orangery, an Elizabethan mount and a

well-house. Concerts are staged in the gallery; exhibitions, fairs and services are held in the house and chapel; and there is a short programme of interesting conducted walks. Access is via Bollington, over the footbridge near the Swan with Two Nicks pub. *House open Apr–Oct, Sat–Wed 12.00–17.00; garden open daily 11.00–17.30.* Admission charge. Restaurant and shop.

● **Dunham Town**
Gt Manchester. PO, tel, stores. A small, scattered, farming village with a pub.

BOAT TRIPS
A wide beamed party boat with bar and music is available for groups of up to 60 people. Ring the Admiral Benbow pub on 01925 754900 to book.

Boatyards

Ⓑ **Hesford Marine** Warrington Lane, Lymm (01925 754639).
⚓-charge[evenings] Gas, overnight mooring, long-term
mooring, winter storage, slipway, crane (16 ton),
dry dock, chandlery, books and maps, boat
building, boat sales, engine sales and
repairs, toilets.
Ⓑ **Lymm Marina Boat Sales**
Warrington Lane, Lymm (01925
752945). 🏠 ⚓ [evenings]
Gas, long-term

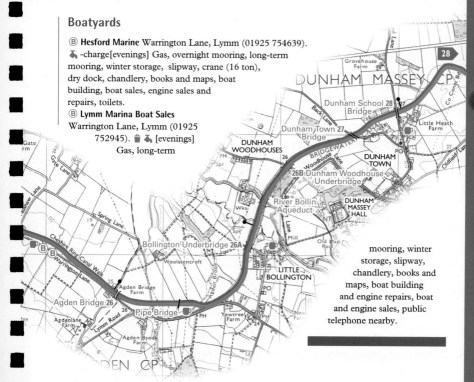

mooring, winter
storage, slipway,
chandlery, books and
maps, boat building
and engine repairs, boat
and engine sales, public
telephone nearby.

Pubs and Restaurants

🍺 **Golden Fleece Hotel** The Cross, Lymm
(01925 755538). By bridge 23. A variety of
real ales are served in this picturesque canalside
pub. Food *lunchtimes only,* with a vegetarian
menu. Children welcome, garden with swings.
🍺 **Bull's Head** Lymm (01925 752831). By
bridge 23. A cosy red plush local pub serving
Hydes' real ale and bar meals *lunchtimes only*
with vegetarian options. Children are welcome
during the day. Small courtyard.
🍺 ✕ **Admiral Benbow** Agden Wharf,
Warrington Lane (01925 754900). Between
bridges 25 & 26. A newish pub serving a
variety of real ales including Bass. Food
*Mon–Fri lunchtimes, Sat lunchtime & evening,
and all day Sun.* Vegetarian options. Children
welcome. Garden. Regular entertainment.
🍺 **Ye Old No. 3** Lymm Road, Little Bollington
(01925 756115). Between Pipe Bridge and
Bollington Underbridge. Attractive former
coaching inn which now has a selection of
special nights, including live music. Bar meals
Mon–Sat lunchtimes & evenings, Sun all day,
vegetarian and à la carte menu. Canalside
garden. Children welcome.

🍺 ✕ **Swan With Two Nicks** Park Lane, Little
Bollington (0161 928 2914). By Bollington
Underbridge (26A), and just a few minutes
walk into the village. A very fine, comfortable
and cosy pub with a friendly atmosphere, serving Boddingtons, Flowers, Castle Eden and
guest real ales. Extensive menu for upmarket
bar food and à la carte *Mon–Sat lunchtimes &
evenings, and Sun all day.* The name of the pub
harks back to times when swans were taken as
food: unmarked birds belonged to the monarch,
who could dispense them at will. The nicks
indicated ownership. It is all very similar to
'Swan Upping' on the River Thames, a ceremony
which still continues today. Restaurant open
for *D only.* Collections of key rings, bottles and
bottle openers. Large garden. Children welcome.
🍺 **Axe and Cleaver Hotel** School Lane,
Dunham Town (0161 928 3391). Village pub
serving Theakston's and Webster's real ale and
food *Mon–Sat lunchtimes & evenings, Sun all day,*
with vegetarian menu. Family room, garden
with play area and bouncy castle. Regular club
meetings take place here including Harley
Davidson, MG, Triumph and Stag owners.

Sale

Beyond Seamons Moss Bridge buildings close in upon the canal, and the countryside rapidly disappears from view. Among the many industrial buildings, both old and new, stands the superb Victorian Linotype Factory, dated 1897, where metal printing type was manufactured. The Metrolink tramway closes in from the south east and escorts the canal all the way through Sale and on into Stretford – as the trams pass by you can enjoy a more relaxing 3 mph. There is a handy canalside pub before the canal is crossed by the M63 motorway, and then itself crosses the River Mersey. A large expanse of graves opposite the Watch House Cruising Club heralds the entrance to Stretford. *PO, stores, fish and chips* are to be found south of Seamons Moss Bridge.

Pubs and Restaurants

Bay Malton Seamons Road, Dunham Massey (0161 928 0655). By Seamons Moss Bridge, no 29. Food with vegetarian option *daily, lunchtimes only*, and Thwaites real ales. Overnight mooring nearby. Children welcome until *19.00*, garden with play equipment.

Bridge Inn Dane Road, Sale. By bridge 36 (0161 969 7536). A comfortable canalside pub offering Boddingtons and OB real ale and bar meals *lunchtimes and evenings, (12.00–20.00 daily)* with vegetarian menu. Garden with children's play area. Regular entertainment with live bands.

● **Altrincham**
Gt Manchester. PO. A few black and white half-timbered buildings remain in the market square of what was once a small market town. Later in the 18thC it became a textile manufacturing centre, and is now, inevitably, a dormitory town for Manchester.

STRETFORD

38 Edge Lane Bridge

Watch House C.C.

Cut Hole Aqueduct
Flood Gates

Playing Fields

Hawthorn Road

Barfoot Bridge

Barfoot Aqueduct

Crossford Bridge

37 M63 Motorway
Water Park

36 Dr Whites Bridge

Allot Gdns

35 Sale Bridge

Offices

Brooklands

● **Sale**

Gt Manchester. All services. A residential
suburb of Manchester, transformed
from a farming community by the
building in 1849 of the Altrincham to
Manchester Railway – hence most of its
buildings are Victorian or later. St
Martin's Church is, however, 18thC
and has a hammerbeam roof. The clock
tower of the town hall, built in 1914, is
a prominent landmark. Look for the
plaque in the wall commemorating the
work of James Prescott Joule, who was
born in Salford and calculated the
mathematical relationship between heat
and electrical energy. The northern
part of Sale merges without boundary
into Ashton upon Mersey, which is
unremarkable except as the birthplace
of Stanley Houghton (1881–1913) who
wrote *The Dear Departed* in 1908 and
Hindle Wakes in 1912.

ARTERIES OF INDUSTRY

A growing economy demands transport and power. The Romans
recognised these needs and built the Caer-dyke, a part of which
still survives as the Fossdyke Navigation, to the west of Lincoln.
They realised a horse can pull only 2 tons on a good road, but up
to 100 tons on a waterway.

Edward the Confessor ordered improvements on the Thames,
Severn, Trent and Yorkshire Ouse, and it was about this time that
an artificial cut, a revolutionary idea at the time, was made to
improve navigation on the Itchen. The development of the 'flash'
lock, where a weir was used to build up a head of water which was
then released to propel craft over an obstruction, was eventually
superseded by the 'pound' lock, still in use today.

But the forerunner of all modern canals, which heralded the
start of the Canal Age, was the Bridgewater Canal, built to serve
the Duke's mines at Worsley and still in use commercially until the
1970s.

Central Manchester

At Waters Meeting the original main line of the canal is joined – to the north west is Barton, Leigh and the connection with the Leeds & Liverpool Canal, which crosses the Pennines to Leeds; to the east is the centre of the Manchester & the Rochdale Canal, which itself, as the name implies, once crossed the hills to Rochdale, before it fell into disuse. It is currently undergoing extensive renovation. The Bridgewater's route is now hemmed in by factory walls and fences, passing close to the Manchester United football ground. The new stand of this famous club towers above the canal, which passes between the ground and Salford Quays. Old Trafford cricket ground, the home of Lancashire Cricket Club and a Test Match venue, is a little further south. By bridge 95 there is a fine mural, painted in 1993, but amongst all the means of transport featured, there is no single reference to a canal! More empty docks are passed before reaching the nicely painted Throstle Nest Footbridge. The Ship Canal is now very close – indeed just across the towpath – with good views of the new City Park buildings and the distant city centre. This is then followed by the connection to the Ship Canal via the new Pomona Lock. Have a look on the towpath side for the circular overflow weir by bridge 97, and notice the disused basins beyond the towpath. This is followed by a railway bridge, more overgrown basins and the Hulme Lock Branch, which was the original junction between the Bridewater and Ship Canals. The excitingly restored Castlefield Junction is then reached. It is well worth stopping here to explore the basins under the railway bridge, and to visit the pubs and restaurants. Moor on the stretch below Grocers Warehouse. The first of the nine wide locks of the Rochdale Canal is right beside the restored Merchants' Warehouse. The gear is anti-vandal locked so you will need to use the British Waterways key. The canal now passes between the backs of tall buildings and beneath elaborate railway arches, all of which have a certain faded grandeur. Tantalising glimpses of Victorian buildings invite exploration, but be wary of mooring away from Castlefield. Finally the canal crawls under an 18-storey office block where a rather desolate lock lurks amidst concrete pillars. The

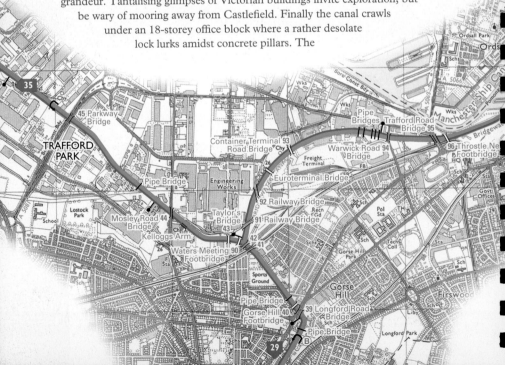

Rochdale Canal Office is next to the top lock, so if you haven't already done so, you must pay your licence fee here, or at the third lock down. Ahead lies an abandoned part of the Rochdale Canal. Sharp right and sharp left turns bring you to the start of the Ashton Canal, and the climb to Fairfield Junction (see page 146).

LICENCES
Rochdale Canal Company, 75 Dale Street, Manchester (0161 236 2456). By the top lock. A licence must be purchased in advance or on the day for this important 2 miles of canal, which are usually open during the cruising season (*beginning of March to end Oct*) *from 09.00–17.00 every day.*

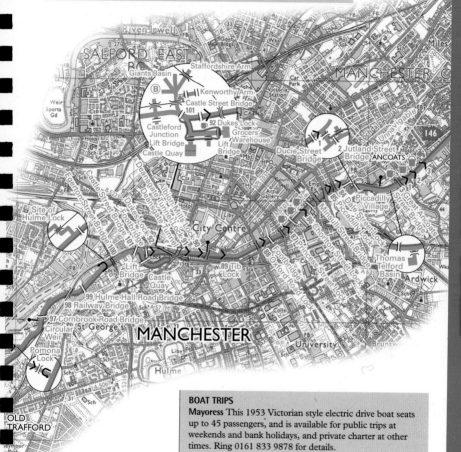

BOAT TRIPS
Mayoress This 1953 Victorian style electric drive boat seats up to 45 passengers, and is available for public trips at weekends and bank holidays, and private charter at other times. Ring 0161 833 9878 for details.

Boatyards

ⓑ **Rathbones** South of bridge 39, offside (0161 865 1880). 🛠 Boatbuilding and repairs. ⓑ **Egerton Narrowboats** The Arches Boatyard, Potato Wharf, Castlefield (0161 833 9878). 🚽 ⛽ 🛠 D Pump-out, gas, day boat hire, overnight mooring, long-term mooring, winter storage, crane (by arrangement), chandlery, engine sales, boat repairs, engine repairs, gifts, books & maps, toilets.

Manchester

All services. One of Britain's finest Victorian cities, a monument to 19thC commerce and the textile boom, Manchester can trace its origins to the Roman fort of Mamucium, built at Castlefield during the first century. The city's early prosperity came with weaving, and its size increased remorselessly with the building of the canals, and later railways, as raw materials could more easily be brought to the city, and finished goods moved out. Unfortunately virtually no early buildings survived the city's rapid growth, although there is an incredible wealth of Victorian buildings surviving, in spite of redevelopment. The Town Hall and surrounding streets are a particularly rich area (north of Oxford Street Bridge). St Peter's Square, by the Town Hall, was the site of the 'Peterloo Massacre' in 1819, when a meeting demanding political reform was brutally dispersed by troops carrying drawn sabres. Eleven people were killed and many more were injured. The Free Trade Hall, once the home of the Hallé Orchestra, is a little further along the road. Built in 1856 on the site of the original Free Trade Hall, it was badly damaged in World War II, but was subsequently re-built to its original Palladian design. It has been converted into a hotel and the Hallé has moved to the new Bridgewater Hall. The old Central Station has now been converted into a £20 million conference and exhibition centre called GMex. There is theatre, ballet and cinema, art galleries, and a wealth of interesting buildings as well as Victorian shopping arcades, many pubs with an excellent choice of good beer, and many excellent restaurants all a short walk from the canal.

Museum of Science and Industry Liverpool Road, off Deansgate, to the north of the bottom lock (0161 832 2244). Located on the site of the world's first passenger railway station, this exciting 'hands-on' museum has 14 galleries covering everything from steam to space, transport to textiles, and includes a working steam train, a reconstructed Victorian sewer (complete with smells!) and an interactive science centre. *Open daily (except 24–26 Dec) 10.00–17.00.* Charge. Coffee shop.

Granada Studios Water Street, close to the Museum of Science and Industry (0161 833 0880). An extremely popular attraction, where you can visit Coronation Street, 'Baker Street', '10 Downing Street', The Giants Room, 3D shows, Motion Master cinema and many other highlights. Restaurants and shops. Disabled facilities. *Open summer Tues–Sun, winter Wed–Sun. Admission for tours from 09.45–15.00, closes at 17.30.* Charge.

Metrolink The new electric 'supertram'. Deansgate is the station closest to the canal, near to the second lock, if you fancy a ride. Information on 0161 228 1228.

Manchester Tourist Information Centre Town Hall Extension, Lloyd Street, to the north of Oxford Street Bridge (0161 234 3157/8).

Manchester Ship Canal

The Harbour Master, Manchester Ship Canal Company, Eastham Locks, Queen Elizabeth II Dock, Eastham (0151 327 1461). The canal was opened in 1894 at a cost of £15$\frac{1}{2}$ million and carries ships up to 15,000 tons displacement. It is 36 miles long and connects the tidal Mersey at Eastham to Manchester. The Weaver Navigation, the Bridgewater Canal and the Shropshire Union Canal connect with it. All craft using the canal must be licensed. They must also be insured against third party risks which should include the cost of salvage and removal of wreck. Any boat holding a British Waterways canal & river licence may cruise on the Bridgewater Canal for seven consecutive days free of charge.

Pubs and Restaurants

There are many fine pubs in Manchester. Those close to the canal include:

Dukes '92 Castle Street (0161 839 8646). Serving a fine selection of beers, including Boddingtons, on an excellent site by the lock. Food, cheese and paté *all day.* Outside seating. Children welcome. Gallery of prints downstairs.

New Union Princess Street (0161 228 1492). Towpath side by Princess Street Lock. A comfortable pub serving food *lunchtimes only,* with vegetarian option. Children welcome *during the day.* Regular cabaret style entertainment. B & B.

Rembrandt Hotel Sackville Street (0161 236 1311). Towpath side between the Princess and Chorlton Street Locks. A friendly gay pub serving J.W. Lees real ales, brewed locally at Middleton Junction. Bar meals *Mon–Fri lunchtimes, Sat snacks only.* Outside seating. B & B.

The Churchill Chorlton Street (0161 236 5529). Towpath side by Chorlton Street Lock. A dark friendly pub serving Greenalls ales and food *lunchtimes, Mon–Sat.*

Jolly Angler Ducie Street, Manchester (0161 236 5307). Near the junction. A small, plain and friendly pub visited by Mike Harding, the folk singer, and offering Hydes' real ale and snacks *at all times.* Regular folk music sessions (*Fri & Mon*). Moorings nearby, but don't leave your boat here overnight.

MANCHESTER SHIP CANAL

Harbour Master, Queen Elizabeth II Dock, Eastham, Wirral (0151 327 1461). The ship canal currently carries an increasing annual tonnage of approximately 2,500 vessel movements per year. A great deal of it is hazardous, petro-chemical traffic and therefore a no smoking régime is enforced. The canal company is happy to allow pleasure boat use on the understanding that certain conditions are adhered to. It is not a navigation for the novice boater and should be viewed as a transit corridor for the experienced boat owner (not hire boater) to access the River Weaver, the River Mersey and the Shropshire Union Canal. In essence the company's requirements are as follows:

1 The boat must carry a £1 million third party insurance cover.
2 The boat is subject to an annual Certificate of Seaworthiness. (At some later date this may be met by a Certificate of Compliance).
3 The appropriate fee is paid, currently set at £13.75 for each lock used.
4 The boater must contact the harbourmaster in advance of passage to obtain copies of:
   a) Pleasure Craft Transit Notes
   b) Port of Manchester Navigation Bylaws
   At this juncture he can discuss appropriate times of arrival and departure to coincide with scheduled shipping movements.
5 At all times the boater is required to act in a responsible manner and be aware that this is a *daytime* transit route only, with no lay-by facilities. He should familiarise himself with the geography of the canal before setting out.
6 VHF radio equipment is desirable (The Manchester Ship Canal Company call and operate on channel 14) and if not available a mobile phone should be considered essential.

The above synopsis is a brief note of the essential requirements and should be read in conjunction with **The Transit Notes** and **Navigation Bylaws** referred to in 4 above.

Weston Marsh Lock

Access to the River Weaver via Weston Marsh Lock is during the following duty hours and only after prior notice to BW at Northwich (01606 723900):
Mon-Thur 08.00-16.00, Fri 08.00-15.00. The lock may be available on *some summer weekends (end of May B. Hol-Sep).* Contact BW for further details.

Ellesmere Port Bottom Lock

Entry into the Shropshire Union from the Manchester Ship Canal is restricted by a swing bridge over the first lock (adjacent to the Holiday Inn) which is not under the control of BW. Boaters wishing to enter the canal must first contact Neston Borough Council (0151 356 6433) to make arrangements for the bridge to be swung. Any difficulties in obtaining assistance should be referred to the BW Chester office on 01244 390372.

Worsley

This is a very interesting section of waterway, well worth visiting for its own sake and a useful link with the Leeds and Liverpool Canal. What was the original line of the canal leaves Waters Meeting through the vast Trafford Park Industrial Estate to cross the Manchester Ship Canal on the impressive Barton Swing Aqueduct. There is an incongruous landscaped pagoda to the south of the aqueduct, and a useful boatyard just to the north. Curving through the suburbs of Salford and the leafy expanse of Broadoak Park the navigation reaches the village of Worsley and the entrance to the underground mines which provided its *raison d'être*. It is well worth stopping to take a look around the Delph, to see at first hand what brought about the canals' construction. You will also notice that dissolved iron ore colours the water bright ochre around here. After Worsley the M62 motorway and its attendant slip roads cross the canal, which then heads west through open country now only hinting at its industrial past, thanks to a vast clearing-up operation. There is, however, more solid evidence of the areas' mining connection at Astley, where it's worth stopping for a short while to visit the Pit Museum.

Boatyards

Ⓑ **Worsley Dry Docks** The Boatyard, Worsley. By bridge 51 (0161 793 6767). Moorings, dry dock only.
Ⓑ **Lorenz & Co** Worsley Road, Worsley. By bridge 46A (0161 794 1441). Based just north of the Barton Swing Aqueduct at Barton Yard. ⚓-charge [evenings]. Boat building and repairs, engine repairs (and call outs), long-term moorings, public telephone.

Ⓑ **Brinks Boats** Boothstown Basin, Worsley. By bridge 54 (0161 728 1184). 🚽 🚿 ⚓ D Pump-out, gas, narrow boat hire, day hire craft, overnight and long-term mooring, winter storage, slipway, boat and engine repairs, telephone, toilets, showers, chandlery, books and maps, gifts, groceries.

BOAT TRIPS
Bridgewater Packet Boat Service Ring 0161 748 2680 for details.

● **Salford**
Gt Manchester. All services. Although now merged with Manchester, Salford was granted its charter in 1230, 80 years before that of its now larger neighbour. It has a fine new university, built in 1967, and a Roman Catholic cathedral dating from 1855. It is, however, most widely known as being the subject of many paintings by the artist L.S. Lowry (1887–1976). It is less widely known that he gained his inspiration by walking the streets of Salford for many years as a rent collector, only painting in the evenings and at weekends – a fact to which he would never willingly admit. There is a wonderful collection of his work in Salford Art Gallery, Peel Park.

● **Salford Art Gallery and Museum** Peel Park (0161 736 2649). One of the largest exhibitions of the work of Lowry, and a re-created Victorian street, are just two of the attractions here. Coffee shop. *Open all year round Mon–Fri 10.00–16.45 and Sun 14.00–17.00.* Free.

● **Barton upon Irwell**
Gt Manchester. Tel, stores, garage. In an interesting position overlooking the two canals. The richly decorated Catholic Church of the City of Mary Immaculate is by Pugin, 1867, and is considered to be one of his best works. Indeed the architect can be found featured in a painting on the south wall of the chancel.

● **Barton Aqueduct**
One of the wonders of the waterways, it carries the Bridgewater Canal over the Manchester Ship Canal. Designed by Sir Edward Leader Williams, it was built in the early 1890s in a bold style comparable to contemporary railway engineering. Gates seal off the 235ft-long 1450-ton section that swings at right angles to the Ship Canal over a central island. It replaced Brindley's earlier aqueduct, built in 1761 and carrying the canal in a trough over 660 ft long and 39 ft above the Irwell, truly a wonder in its day. The aqueduct operates *Summer Mon–Thur 09.15–18.30, Fri–Sun 09.15–20.30. Winter daily 09.15–16.30.*

Patricroft

Gt Manchester. All services. Here are the Bridgewater Mills, established in 1836 by Nasmyth, who invented the steam hammer.

Eccles

Gt Manchester. EC Wed. All services. The town peaked as a cotton and silk weaving centre between 1870–90, and little has happened since, although its name will always be remembered in connection with the famous cakes – round pastry filled with currants. The Church of St Mary has its origins in the 10thC, although the present sandstone building dates from the late 15thC.

Monks Hall Museum Wellington Road contains an important collection of Nasmyth machine tools and relics. *Closed Sun.*

Worsley

Gt Manchester. EC Wed. PO, tel, stores, garage. Originally an estate village dating from the 18th-19thC, but now recognised as the birthplace of British canals. Coal had been mined in Worsley since the 14thC, originally from the surface, and later by sinking shafts. It is thought that a drainage sough, common in underground workings, may have provided the germ of the idea for an underground canal network which could be used to bring the coal out. John Gilbert, the Duke of Bridgewater's agent, probably designed the system, which included an inclined plane on a 1 in 4 gradient 453 ft long and 60 ft wide. Work started at the same time on the building of the canal to Manchester, and eventually 46 miles of tunnels were hewn out. A particular kind of simple double-ended tub boat was used under-ground, called a 'starvationer'. These carried up to 12 tons of coal. The old canal basin at Worsley Delph, with its entrance tunnels to the mines, is still intact, and information boards help to explain its workings. On the canal, look out for the Boathouse, built by Lord Ellesmere to house the royal barge, prepared for Queen Victoria's visit in 1851, and Duke's Wharf, an old oil store. Close-by is Worsley Old Hall, the half-timbered Court House and The Old Reading Room, which was originally a nailers shop, shown on a plan of 1785 and painted on a Wedgwood dinner service presented to Queen Catherine II of Russia. The church, by George Gilbert Scott, 1846, has a spire decorated with crockets and gargoyles – inside there is a rich collection of monuments to the Dukes of Bridgewater.

Astley Green

Gt Manchester. PO, tel, stores. Canalside mining village dominated by a gaunt red-brick Victorian church.

Astley Green Pit Museum To the north of the canal. Being restored by the Red Rose Steam Society, this pit remains as a valuable reminder of life and work in this area in the recent past. Various pit relics to explore, plus a superb engine house containing a 3000HP twin tandem compound engine by Yates & Thom of Blackburn. This once wound the 8 ton lift which transported the miners to their work 873 yards underground, at a maximum speed of 82 feet per second (55 mph!). *Open Tue, Thur & Sun 10.00– 21.00. Steam engines operate on the first Sun each month.* No fixed charge, just give as you wish.

Traditional canal boat decoration

Bridgewater Canal/Leigh Branch **Worsley**

Worsley

Pubs and Restaurants

🍺 **Dutton Arms** Barton Road, Barton (0161 789 5789). A large canalside pub which features original plans for the Manchester Ship Canal. Boddingtons real ale and bar meals *lunchtimes*.

🍺 **Packet House** Liverpool Road, Eccles (0161 789 0047). By bridge 47. A corner pub serving Boddingtons real ale and *lunchtime* bar meals with a vegetarian menu. *Special lunches* of wholesome Lancashire fare for groups, but you must book. Family room and garden with swings. Live music at weekends, and singing contests.

🍺 **The Wellington** Church Street, Eccles. Between bridges 48 & 47. Local pub serving Holts ales.

🍺 ✕ **Barge Inn** By bridge 50. (0161 788 8788). A cosy pub offering food *lunchtimes Mon–Fri & Sun, also evenings Tue–Fri.* Hartleys and Robinson's real ales. Children's play area and canalside patio. Regular entertainment.

🍺 **Barton Arms** Stablefold (0161 794 9373). Brand new pub serving Marstons, Tetleys and a guest real ale, along with food *12.00–21.00 daily*, including vegetarian meals. Quiz nights and other games are featured.

🍺 **Bridgewater Arms** Worsley. Nearby 🏨 🧺. By bridge 51. Large comfortable pub serving Boddingtons real ale and food *Mon–Sat lunchtimes & evenings (17.30–19.30) & Suns 12.00–18.30*. Garden.

✕ 🍷 **Tung Fong** Worsley Road, Worsley (0161 794 5331). Smart Chinese restaurant. *Open lunchtimes & evenings (evenings only Sat & Sun)*.

🍺 **The Moorings** Boothshall Way, Boothstown (0161 702 6251). By bridge 54. A pleasant, large, new pub in a lovely spot overlooking open country and the canal, on the corner of the Bridgewater Park Nature Reserve. It serves Boddingtons real ale, bar meals and snacks with a vegetarian option *all day*. Children welcome, play area. Outside seating.

🍺 **The Old Boathouse Inn** By bridge 58. A comfortable canalside pub with a garden, serving Greenalls real ales.

🍺 **Ross' Arms** Higher Green Lane, Astley (01942 874405). Serves a great variety of real ales, plus food *all day*, and includes a vegetarian menu. Children welcome. Garden. Regular entertainment. B & B.

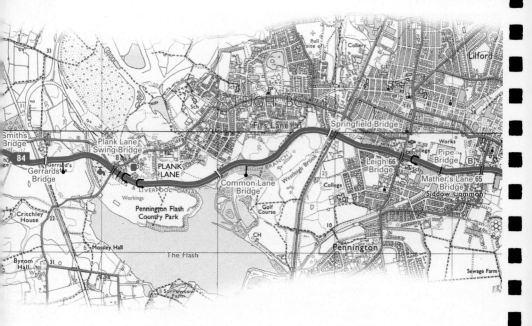

Leigh

After the excitement and interest of Barton, Worsley and Astley Green, the canal now passes through pleasant open land towards the mill town of Leigh, where it transforms into the Leeds & Liverpool Canal, continuing the route to Wigan. Raised canal banks reveal past problems of subsidence in this area, caused by old mine workings. At Leigh the canal passes a sturdy warehouse by bridge 66 before it becomes the Leeds & Liverpool – the familiar stop plank cranes of the Bridgewater finish here, and signs announce you are back in British Waterways territory. Wigan is 7¼ miles away (see page 85).

● **Leigh**
Gt Manchester. EC Wed. All services. Once the archetypal mill town, most of the tall buildings and chimneys have now been demolished to be replaced with ubiquitous new developments. However, in the market place you can see the fine Edwardian baroque Town Hall, built 1904–7, facing the battlemented church of St Mary.

Boatyards

Ⓑ **Lorenz Canal Services** Bedford Basin, Henry Street, Leigh (01942 679690). **D** Long-term mooring.

Pubs and Restaurants

🍺 **Bull's Head** Butts Bridge (64), Leigh (01942 671621). Towpath-side local serving John Smith's real ale and snacks *all day*. Garden. Children welcome. B & B.

🍺 **The Wheatsheaf** Chapel Street, Leigh (01942 671640). Sociable pub on the corner of Warrington Road, serving Tetley's real ale by gravity. Children welcome during the day. Garden. Weekend entertainment. Nearby 🛁 B & B.

LEIGH

Blackmoor

Bedford
Hodge

Lark Hill

High
Green

Cemy

Bedford

Butts Basin

63 Hall House Bridge

Marsland Green

Town
Lane

Peel
Hall

Pipe
Bridge

Astley
Green

Butt's 64
Bridge

BRIDGEWATER CANAL

Rec
Gd

Hooten Gardens

Great 62
Fold
Bridge

61

Marsland Green
Bridge

60

East-Lancs Road
Bridge

59 Lingard's
Footbridge

Morley's
Hall

Sewage
Works

Sewage
Works

Crompton
House

99

Black or Moss Brook

Moss Side

Grange Farm

Sandy Pool
Farm

Sales
House

Bedford Bridge

Magpie's
Nest

A VISIT TO THE MINES AT WORSLEY

'Arrived at Worsley, passing athwart the river Irwell, over
which the canal runs, being raised on arches not less than
fifty feet in height above that stream. Sent compliments to
Mr Gilbert, the steward, asking the favour of seeing the
duke's underground works, which was granted, and we
stepped into the boat, passing into an archway partly of
brick and partly cut through the stone, of about three and a
half feet high; we received at entering six lighted candles.
This archway, called a funnel, runs into the body of the
mountain almost in a direct line three thousand feet, its
medium depth beneath the surface about eighty feet; we
were half an hour passing that distance. Here begins the
first under-ground road to the pits, ascending to the wagon
road, so called, about four feet above the water, being a
highway for wagons, containing about a ton weight of the
form of a mill-hopper, running on wheels, to convey the
coals to the boats.

Arrived at the coal mine, which appearing about five
feet through the roof, was supported by many posts, the
area being about twenty feet square and the height scarce
four. A hundred men are daily employed, and each turns
out a ton a day; the miners' wages two shillings, and the
laborers' about one shilling.'

Samuel Curwen, *Journal and Letters*, 7th June, 1777.

Horbury Bridge (see page 42)

CALDER & HEBBLE NAVIGATION
HUDDERSFIELD BROAD CANAL

CALDER & HEBBLE NAVIGATION

Wakefield to Broad Cut
Length: 120'
Beam: 17'
Headroom: 12'

Broad Cut to Sowerby Bridge
Length: 57' 6" (or 60' narrowboat)
Beam: 14'
Headroom: 9' 6"

HUDDERSFIELD BROAD CANAL
Length: 57' 6" (or 60' narrowboat)
Beam: 14'
Headroom: 9' 6"

MANAGER
(01977) 554351

MILEAGE
WAKEFIELD to:
Cooper Bridge: 13 miles, 13 locks
Sowerby Bridge: 23½ miles, 27 locks
including Fall Ing
Huddersfield Broad Canal: 3¾ miles, 9 locks

SAFETY NOTES

Where locks give access onto river sections of the navigation river level gauge boards are located at each lock chamber indicating conditions as follows:

Green band – Normal river levels safe for navigation.

Amber band – River levels are above normal. If you wish to navigate the river section you are advised to proceed on to and through the next lock.

Red band – Flood conditions unsafe for navigation. Lock closed.

In an emergency telephone the manager's office or out of office hours dial 100 and ask for Freephone Canals. Mobile phone users dial 01384 215785.

The construction of the Aire & Calder resulted in pressure to improve the Calder above Wakefield. After much opposition, the Calder & Hebble was built, with boats finally reaching Sowerby Bridge in the 1770s. Never as successful as the Aire & Calder, it did, however, benefit from trade coming in from the Huddersfield Broad Canal and later, in 1811, from the Huddersfield Narrow. Commercial traffic ended in 1981, when the last coal barges unloaded at Thornhill Power Station. Becoming increasingly popular and yet still uncrowded, this waterway has much to offer, with great industrial interest and, in many places, considerable charm.

The Huddersfield Broad Canal was built to serve the rapidly expanding woollen industry of the 18thC. Completed in 1780, and costing £12,000, the waterway gave local textile manufacturers access to markets throughout Yorkshire as well as coal to feed the steam-driven mills. Despite the inevitable amalgamation with the competing railway company (the London and North Western Railway in 1847) the waterway remained a profitable concern until the late 1940s. It was conceived as a broad gauge canal to accommodate square-rigged, sailing Keels or 'Yorkshire craft' – 58' 0" in length and 14' 0" beam. Due to the navigation's low bridges these had to be de-rigged at Cooper Bridge and bow hauled the remaining 3¾ miles. The Huddersfield Narrow Canal, completed some 30 years later, was built as a narrow gauge waterway unable to accept traffic from the Broad Canal; consequently warehousing and transhipment facilities were developed at Aspley Basin. The problem was partially overcome with the introduction of the West Riding narrow boat: a specially shortened craft able to negotiate locks on both systems.

Horbury Bridge

At Thornes Lock only one of the two chambers is now in use – you will need a Calder & Hebble 'handspike' to operate this, and subsequent locks. Here the navigation enters a short cut and rejoins the River Calder at Thornes Flood Lock, before passing under the M1 motorway. Ahead is the tall spike of Elmley Moor television transmitter. The beautifully kept Broad Cut Low Lock marks the start of a 5-mile-long canal section with 8 locks. There was regular trade on this stretch until 1981, when West Country barges took coal from the British Oak Colliery to Thornhill Power Station. Remains of loading staithes can be seen opposite the Navigation Inn. There are good moorings at Horbury Bridge, and a post office and farm shop are close by. A short arm here used to connect with the river and this has now become an attractive long-term mooring with showers and the usual facilities. Beyond the bridge a tree-lined cutting leads to Figure of Three Locks. There are two locks on the navigation with another now disused which used to connect with the river. Is it this, or the fact that the river here makes the shape of a '3', which gives these locks their unusual name? Experts seem unable to agree. The towpath from Broad Cut to Dewsbury is good, having been improved in 1986–7. After Mill Bank look out for a milestone marked 'from FALL ING 7 miles' on

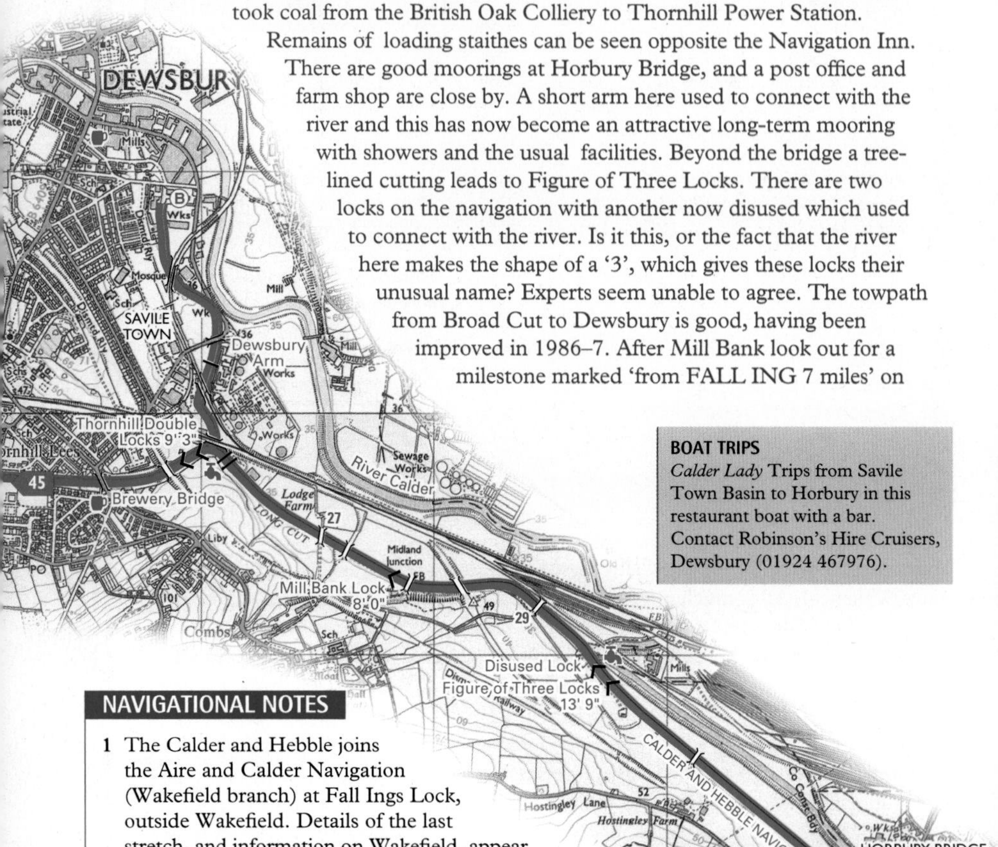

BOAT TRIPS

Calder Lady Trips from Savile Town Basin to Horbury in this restaurant boat with a bar. Contact Robinson's Hire Cruisers, Dewsbury (01924 467976).

NAVIGATIONAL NOTES

1 The Calder and Hebble joins the Aire and Calder Navigation (Wakefield branch) at Fall Ings Lock, outside Wakefield. Details of the last stretch, and information on Wakefield, appear on page 19 in the Aire and Calder section.
2 When ascending Broad Cut Low Lock both ground paddle and gate paddle outlets may be above the water level. Exercise caution when opening to avoid flooding your boat.

Boatyards

Ⓑ **Robinson's Hire Cruisers** Savile Town Wharf, Dewsbury (01924 467976). 🚽 🚿 ♨ D E Gas, pump-out, overnight mooring, long-term mooring, slipway, winter storage, boat building, boat and engine repairs, boat sales, crane, excellent museum, chandlery, books and maps, showers, laundry, toilets, telephone.

the towpath side, by the next bridge. Thornhill Double Locks mark the junction with the Dewsbury Arm, which branches off to Savile Town Basin. This is a worthwhile diversion where Robinson's Hire Cruisers maintain a small but interesting museum in the old stables. Climbing Thornhill Double Locks (good moorings here) the navigation enters a deep secluded cutting spanned by tall bridges.

Pubs and Restaurants

🍺 **Navigation** Calder Grove (01924 274361). Broad Cut Top Lock, by the railway viaduct. Canalside pub serving Tetley's, Timothy Taylor and guest real ales. Inexpensive snacks and bar meals available *lunchtimes and evenings (not Sun evening)*. Garden, children's play area and bouncy castle. Quiz nights on *Sun*. Good moorings here; *post office and fish & chips* just a short distance to the south.

🍺 **Bingley Arms** Horbury Bridge (01924 281331). Tetley's real ale in another fine looking pub. Pub games and pool.

🍺 **Ship** Horbury Bridge (01924 272795). Comfy local with a restaurant serving John Smith's, Bass and Worthington real ales. Excellent value food available *lunchtimes except Mon*. Quiz *Sun & Tue* with live entertainment *Fri*. Children *lunchtimes only*.

🍺 **Savile Hotel** Turn left out of Savile Town Basin and follow Mill Street East to the traffic lights (5-minute walk). Webster's and John Smith's real ales in a large hotel. *Lunchtime* food, sheltered garden. B & B.

✕ **Agra** Warren Street, Savile Town, Dewsbury (01924 467365). Turn left out of the basin, left again, over the bridge and bear left. Superb inexpensive Asian take-away. *Open Mon–Thur & Sun to 23.30, Fri & Sat to 00.30. PO and grocers* close by.

🍺 **Nelson** Slaithwaite Road, Dewsbury (01924 461685). Scramble up the bank at Brewery Bridge. Whitbread, Tetley's and Boddingtons real ales and bar food available *12.00–19.00. Tue–Fri*. Children welcome. Outside seating and games room.

● **Horbury**
W. Yorks. EC Wed. PO, tel, stores, take-away. A small town up a steep hill from the bridge. The hymn 'Onward Christian Soldiers' was written and first sung here by the Reverend S. Baring-Gould as a marching song for children.
Yorkshire Mining Museum Caphouse Colliery, New Road, Overton, Wakefield (01924 848806). On the A642, 2 miles south west of Horbury Bridge (bus service) and accessible by bus 263 from Huddersfield and Wakefield. Go 450ft underground to visit old- and new-style coalfaces. Audio visual show, cafe, shop, picnic area. Wear warm clothes; not suitable for children under 5. *Open 10.00–17.00 Mon–Sun.* Charge.

● **Dewsbury**
W. Yorks. EC Tue. MD Wed, Sat. All services, station. The compact and attractive town centre is a mile away from Savile Town Basin.
Dewsbury Arm Extending for 3/4 mile to Savile Town Basin.

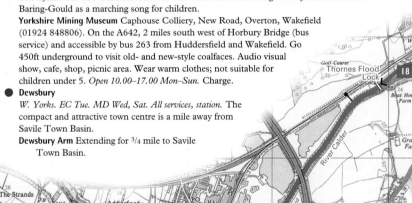

Cooper Bridge

Before long the deep cutting gives way to an open industrial waste-
land (for which there are large-scale redevelopment plans)
around the site of Thornhill Power Station, where barges
once used to unload coal. Between Thornhill Flood
Lock and Greenwood Lock a short, wide, river
section intervenes before the navigation
enters another artificial channel to the
south of Mirfield. There is plenty
of interest around the pub
and boatyard here, and
landscaping and
pretty water-

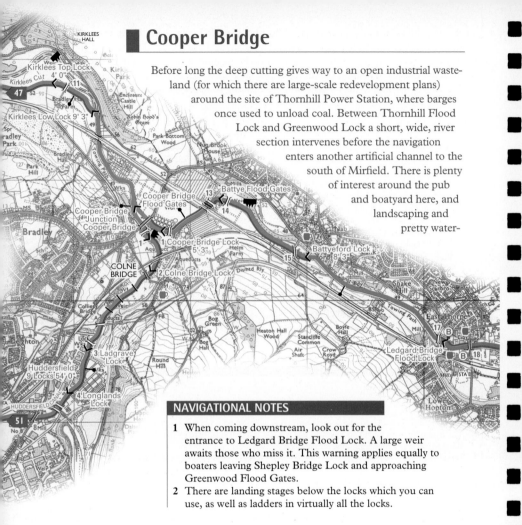

NAVIGATIONAL NOTES

1 When coming downstream, look out for the
   entrance to Ledgard Bridge Flood Lock. A large weir
   awaits those who miss it. This warning applies equally to
   boaters leaving Shepley Bridge Lock and approaching
   Greenwood Flood Gates.
2 There are landing stages below the locks which you can
   use, as well as ladders in virtually all the locks.

Pubs and Restaurants

Bull's Head Huddersfield Road, Ravensthorpe,
Dewsbury (01924 496920). 300yds from
Greenwood Flood Lock. Bar meals *lunchtimes and
evenings* and Tetley's and guest real ales served
in this pub set in 2 acres of parkland. Children
welcome.

Ship Inn East of Shepley Bridge Lock (01924
493364). Large, smart and comfortable pub
dispensing Whitbread, Boddingtons, Flowers and
Ruddles real ales. A carvery restaurant serves food
all day until 22.00, 7 days a week. Vegetarians and
children catered for. Garden and play area.

Swan Inn Huddersfield Road, Mirfield (01924
492054). Above Shepley Bridge Lock. Smart

Tetley's real ale pub with a roadside patio. Bar food
lunchtimes, Mon–Fri. No children.

Navigation Tavern Station Road, Mirfield
(01924 492476). Canalside near Shepley Bridge
Flood Lock. Bass, Worthington and John Smith's
real ales. Bar meals and snacks *lunchtimes*.
Canalside garden and limited moorings.

Black Bull Hotel Huddersfield Road, Mirfield
(01924 493180). North of bridge 18. Imposing
Tetley's real ale hotel. Food *lunchtimes and evenings*.

Pear Tree Inn Huddersfield Road, Battyeford
(01924 493079). Near Battyeford Lock. Wards and
Vaux real ales. Food available *lunchtimes and evenings,
7 days a week*. Children welcome. Moorings.

side gardens make this a pleasant spot. At Greenwood Flood Gates the river is briefly rejoined on a sweeping bend, before the navigation enters another artificial cut. The towpath is generally good on the canal sections, less so, or indeed non-existent, on the river sections. At Battyeford there is a short canal section which rejoins the river opposite a large sewage works. A fine display of roses suggests they are not short of fertilizer! Cooper Bridge marks the junction of the Calder & Hebble with the Huddersfield Broad Canal (see page 50), which branches off to the south below the flood gates, overlooked by the tall chimney of Bottomley & Sons. Kirklees Park lies on a hillside to the north before the navigation passes under the M62 motorway.

BOAT TRIPS
Pearly Monarch offering *Sunday* trips from Shipley Bridge Marina. Ring 01924 491872 for further details.

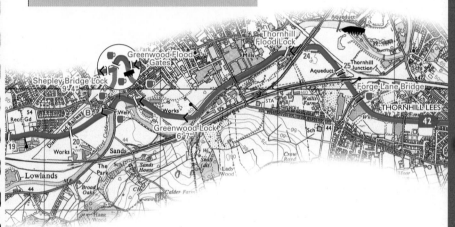

● **Thornhill**
W. Yorks. PO, tel, stores. This old stone-built mining village up on a hill above the canal offers fine views across the valley.

● **Mirfield**
W. Yorks. EC Tue. All services. A useful place to get supplies.

Kirklees Park In the grounds are the modest ruins of a priory founded in the 12thC for Cistercian nuns. Most of the stones were incorporated in the construction of Kirklees Hall during the late 16thC. It is believed that Robin Hood died whilst at the priory but before so doing he shot two arrows from the window to mark his burial place. One landed in the River Calder and floated away, the other landed in the grounds of the park. A tablet marks the spot thought to be his grave.

Boatyards

ⓑ **Ledgard Bridge Boat Company** Ledgard Bridge, Newgate, Mirfield (01924 491441/0850 249449). Gas, overnight mooring, crane, boat sales and repairs, engine repairs, boat building and alterations, chandlery, boat fitting-out. *24hr* emergency call out – ring 01924 491315 *outside working hours.*

ⓑ **Mirfield Boatyard** 10 Station Road, Mirfield (01924 492007). Below Shepley Bridge Flood Lock. 🚽 🚿 ♿ D Gas, pump-out, long-term mooring, crane, winter storage, dry dock, boat building and repairs, engine repairs, boat fitting-out, toilets and showers, laundrette, telephone. *24hr* emergency call out.

ⓑ **Shepley Bridge Marina** Huddersfield Road, Mirfield (01924 491872). 🚽 🚿 ♿ D E Pump-out, gas, narrow boat hire, day craft hire, overnight mooring, long-term mooring, winter storage, slipway, crane, boat sales, engine repairs, chandlery, books, maps and gifts, toilets, showers, dry dock, wet dock, coffee shop. *24hr* emergency call out.

Brighouse

Leaving the river the navigation enters an artificial cut on its approach to Brighouse, completely enclosed by factories. There are good moorings between the two Brighouse Locks, and the passage through the town is pleasant, with gardens, seats and willow trees. Leaving the town the canal is now more reminiscent of the narrower Midlands canals; indeed there is a pleasant wooded mooring, ideal for a picnic, at Cromwell Bottom.

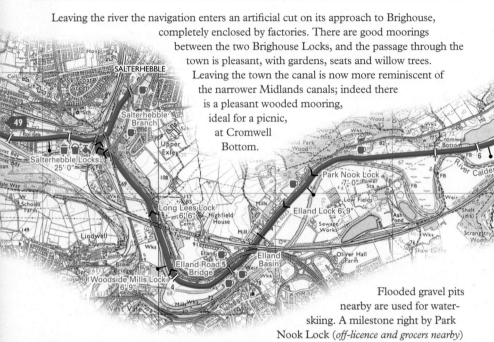

Flooded gravel pits nearby are used for waterskiing. A milestone right by Park Nook Lock (*off-licence and grocers nearby*) reveals that you are now 18 miles from Fall Ing, with just a short distance to travel to Sowerby Bridge. Elland Basin, with its tastefully restored buildings and gardens, is worth more than a fleeting glance, however, and makes a good stopping place en route. There are several pubs close by. Have a look at the fine converted warehouse with its covered dock, before pressing on to the three superbly kept and picturesque Salterhebble Locks. The bottom lock here has an electrically-powered guillotine gate operated with a British Waterways key. This was installed when the road was widened in the 1930s. The towpath passes separately through its own narrow tunnel. Immediately after this first lock the canal passes over a small aqueduct before climbing the top two. To the right is the Salterhebble Branch (where the old Salterhebble Basin has been restored), to the left the route to Sowerby Bridge. The towpath improves above Brighouse.

BOAT TRIPS

M.V. Waylon featured as *Sally H* in the TV series *Stay Lucky* available for both short and long trips for up to 12 passengers throughout the north eastern waterways. A converted working boat providing a flexible and participative, self-catering, cruising itinerary at very reasonable rates. An imaginative concept that introduces families and small parties to the waterways. For further details contact Mr Richardson at Brighouse Canal Basin on 01484 713424.

Boatyards

Ⓑ **Sagar Marine** Victoria Works, Wharfe Street, Brighouse (01484 714541). **D** Pump-out, long-term mooring, winter storage, slipway, engine repairs, boat building and repairs, boat fitting-out.

Ⓑ **Tayberg Steel Boats** Brookfoot Mills, Elland Road, Brighouse (01484 400221). **E** Winter storage, engine repairs and sales, boat building, boat repairs and alterations.

● **Brighouse**
W. Yorks. EC Tue. MD Wed, Sat. All services (but no BR station). A woollen textile producing village transformed into an important canal port with the building of the Calder & Hebble Navigation. In the 19thC silk and cotton were also spun here. Now there seems to be plenty of thriving new industry. The canal bisects the town, passing very close to the market place. A large Victorian church at the top of the hill is surrounded by trees and flowers.

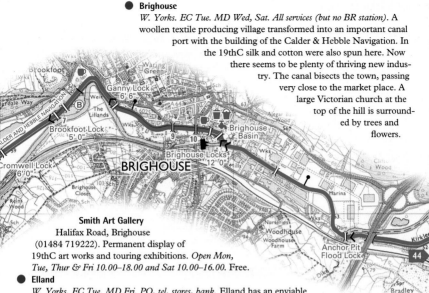

Smith Art Gallery
Halifax Road, Brighouse
(01484 719222). Permanent display of 19thC art works and touring exhibitions. *Open Mon, Tue, Thur & Fri 10.00–18.00 and Sat 10.00–16.00.* Free.

● **Elland**
W. Yorks. EC Tue. MD Fri. PO, tel, stores, bank. Elland has an enviable position on the steep south side of the Calder Valley, its narrow streets discourage through traffic, and its handsome church and terraces of stone houses give an air of tranquillity. The well-restored canal basin makes an excellent stopping point.

Pubs and Restaurants

Red Rooster 123 Elland Road, Brookfoot (01484 713737). North of Brookfoot Lock. Real ale enthusiasts' pub, with a real fire as well. Timothy Taylor, Rooster, Theakston and guest beers – always between seven and ten in total. Outside seating. Children welcome for short periods.

Prince of Wales Betnal Street, Brighouse (01484 400718). North of bridge 10. A handsome black and white half-timbered pub rebuilt in 1926 with timber from *HMS Donegal*, a wooden battleship launched in 1858. The Tudor-style interior is compromised by two TVs, a juke box and a battery of fruit machines. Webster's, Tetley's and guest real ales. *Weekend* discos and outside seating.

Rawson Arms Elland (01422 378648). Signposted half a mile below Park Nook Lock near picnic tables in the woods. Old coaching house serving Tetley's real ales with food available *lunchtimes and evenings until 20.30.* Vegetarians and children catered for. Live entertainment *Fri & Sat.* Outside seating *summer only.*

Colliers Arms 66 Park Road, Elland (01422 372704). Between Elland and Park Nook locks. Traditional canalside pub offering Sam Smith real ale. Food *every lunchtime and evenings Thur–Sat,* an open fire and waterside garden. Family room.

Barge & Barrel Elland Basin (01422 373623).

An interesting choice of real ales including Black Sheep, Old Mill, Timothy Taylor, Rooster and Hambleton in a comfortable Victorian style pub. Inexpensive, home-cooked food available *lunchtimes and evenings,* real fire. Families welcome. Quiz *Mon,* live music *Wed & Sat,* pub games and pool. *The landlord is installing toilets, showers, etc. for boaters. Ring for details.*

Royal Elland (01422 378406). South of Elland Bridge. Webster's, Courage and Tetley's real ales in an attractive stone-built pub, dating from 1780. Garden, children welcome. Quiz *Sun* and live music *Sat.* Pool.

Malt Shovels 8 Briggate, Elland (01422 373189). Next to The Royal. Sam Smith real ale. These two pubs are separated by an extravagant neo-Grecian workshop.

The Quays Salterhebble (01422 347700). A new pub and hotel at the terminus of the Salterhebble Branch. Tetley's, Theakston, Greenalls and guest real ales served in this relaxed, family-orientated establishment. A range of food available *all day, 7 days a week.* Children's and vegetarian menus. Outside seating and play area. Quiz *Thur.* B & B.

Punch Bowl Inn Salterhebble (01422 366937). By the Salterhebble Branch. Mansfield and guest real ales. Food available *lunchtimes and evenings.* Children and vegetarians catered for. Beer garden and play area.

Sowerby Bridge

The canal, now relatively narrow, clings to the side of a wooded hill, its clean water alive with small fish. A conspicuous building to the north is Wainhouse Tower, built in 1875 as a 253ft dyeworks chimney (but never used as such) and converted into a viewing tower. A superb example of stonemasonry, it is *opened on Bank Holidays* (400 steps to the top). The buildings close in as the navigation approaches the basins at Sowerby Bridge, where the Rochdale Canal once again branches off to cross the Pennines. When restored throughout its entire length a second complete Pennine crossing will be available, offering the possiblity of a dramatic northern cruising ring. The towpath throughout this section is excellent.

Boatyard

ⓑ **Shire Cruisers** The Wharf, Sowerby Bridge, Halifax (01422 832712). Facilities either here or in the basin. 🛉 🛃 **D** Gas, pump-out, narrow boat hire, overnight mooring, long-term mooring, winter storage, slipway, crane, boat sales and repairs, chandlery, books and maps, boat fitting-out, engine sales and repairs, wet dock, toilets.

● **Halifax**
W. Yorks. MD Fri, Sat, Sun. All services. Well known as the home of the Halifax Building Society, founded in 1853, which now has ultra-modern offices in Portland Place; it is worth the journey north from the canal to visit this industrial town. The splendid Piece Hall, rebuilt in 1770, is the last remaining manufacturers' hall in the country. Here weavers traded their products, the continuation of an industry that dates back to 1275 in Halifax. Now restored, the hall houses arts and craft shops, a museum, art gallery, restaurant and the **Tourist Information Centre** (01422 368725). The parish church of St John the Baptist is Perpendicular in style, battlemented and with a mass of pinnacles, parapets and gargoyles.
Calderdale Industrial Museum Next door to the Piece Hall, Halifax (01422 358087). Steam engines, a Spinning Jenny, a Flying Shuttle loom and toffee wrapping machines, all working. Re-creation of 19thC Halifax, coal mines and clay mines. *Open 10.00–17.00 Tue–Sat, 14.00–17.00 Sun. Closed Mon except B.Hols.* Small charge.
Shibden Hall Folk Museum Shibden Park, Halifax (01422 352246). A 15thC building with 17thC furniture and extensive folk exhibits. *Open Mar–Nov 10.00–17.00 Mon–Sat, 12.00–17.00 Sun. Closed Dec & Jan, and open Sun, 14.00–17.00 in Feb.* Charge.
Eureka Museum for Children Discovery Road, Halifax (01426 983191 *24 hour recorded info*).

Hands-on museum designed for children to touch, listen and smell. Three main exhibition areas: "Me and my body", "Living and working together", and "Invent, create, communicate". *Open 10.00–17.00, every day except Christmas.* Charge.
Bankfield Museum Akroyd Park, Halifax (01422 354823/352334). Magnificent 19thC mill owners residence housing a fascinating range of costumes from around the world, displayed in exotic surroundings. *Open Tue–Sat 10.00–17.00, Sun 14.00–17.00. Closed Mon except B.Hols.* Charge.
● **Sowerby Bridge**
W. Yorks. EC Wed. MD Tue, Fri. All services. Although this is an industrial town, the scale and grandeur of the surrounding landscape dominates the mill chimneys and factory roofs that are dotted about. This rare subservience to nature makes the town human and attractive. The 19thC classical church is in a good position, overlooking the newly restored deep lock and tunnel.
● **Sowerby Bridge Basin**
PO, tel, stores. This great canal centre is a classic example of the functional tradition in industrial architecture, and has thankfully survived to be given a new life in restoration, while many other such examples have disappeared. The Rochdale Canal was built to accommodate vessels up to 72ft in length, so goods had to be transhipped here into the shorter Calder & Hebble craft before they could continue their journey; hence this important centre grew in stature.

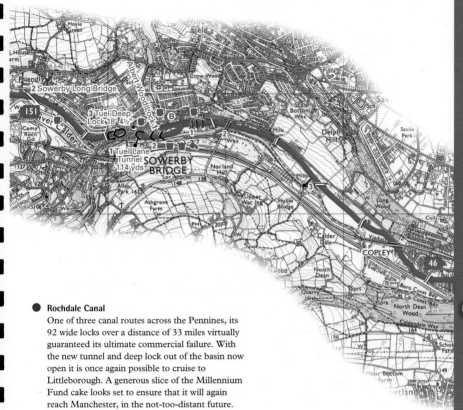

● **Rochdale Canal**
One of three canal routes across the Pennines, its 92 wide locks over a distance of 33 miles virtually guaranteed its ultimate commercial failure. With the new tunnel and deep lock out of the basin now open it is once again possible to cruise to Littleborough. A generous slice of the Millennium Fund cake looks set to ensure that it will again reach Manchester, in the not-too-distant future.

Pubs and Restaurants

🍺 **Navigation Inn** By bridge 1. Friendly 18thC canalside pub with a collection of Buckby cans. 4 rotating guest real ales and an extensive bar menu. *Open all day* with food available *lunchtimes, evenings and all day Sat & Sun.* Vegetarians and children catered for. 2 gardens.

🍺 ✕ **Moorings** No 1 Warehouse, Sowerby Bridge Basin (01422 833940). A good choice of bar food together with Timothy Taylor real ale in this attractive conversion. Wide range of foreign lagers and beers. Restaurant *open Tue–Sat evenings*, offering a predominantly Belgian menu. Patio, family room.

✕ ♀ **Java Restaurant** Wharf Street, Sowerby Bridge (01422 831654). By the basin. A restaurant specialising in Indonesian food (*D only*).

🍺 **William IV** 80/82 Wharf Street, Sowerby Bridge (01422 833584). Tetley's, Boddingtons, IV rite and 2 guest real ales served in this friendly pub close to the basin. Bar food available *lunchtimes*. Beer garden and pub games.

🍺 **Rams Head Inn** 26 Wakefield Road, Sowerby Bridge (01422 835876). *Open evenings and all day Sat & B. Hols.* The Ryburn Brewery's sole tied house, close to the plant, dispensing their full range of real ales. The pub is just as traditional as you'd expect: open fires, pub games and weekend sing alongs.

Huddersfield

Also known as Sir John Ramsden's Canal, this navigation was authorised in 1774. It leaves the Calder & Hebble at Cooper Bridge and makes a very rewarding short diversion off the main line. Stone-arched bridges and a succession of locks maintain interest, and although industry is omnipresent, there are plenty of green patches, and a vast expanse of sports fields, to bring light relief. After climbing Red Doles Lock, the last of the nine, a tight bend under three bridges brings you to the remarkable Turnbridge loco lift bridge. Dated 1865, you will need a British Waterways key to unlock it. On the offside, before Aspley Basin (which is currently the effective limit of navigation) is a useful Sainsbury's complete with extensive moorings. The new Wakefield Road Bridge has made access to the Huddersfield Narrow Canal possible (for craft of 7 ft beam) and this is well worth exploring on foot, especially to have a look at the warehouse south of the bridge. Built prior to 1778 it is probably the oldest surviving example of such a building, demonstrating an early stage in the development of the large multi-storey warehouses of the 19thC. It has now been converted into dwellings. The crane beside it dates from the early 19thC. Further along, beyond Huddersfield University, is the first restored lock on the narrow canal. The towpath on the Broad Canal is in good repair and makes an excellent, traffic-free way into Huddersfield for walker and cyclist alike.

NAVIGATIONAL NOTES

1 This waterway is a branch off the Calder and Hebble. See also the map on page 44.
2 When joining the Huddersfield Broad Canal at Cooper Bridge, take care to avoid the weir on the river just beyond the entrance lock 1.
3 Although there are mooring rings on the Huddersfield Narrow Canal south of Aspley Basin, turning here may be difficult.

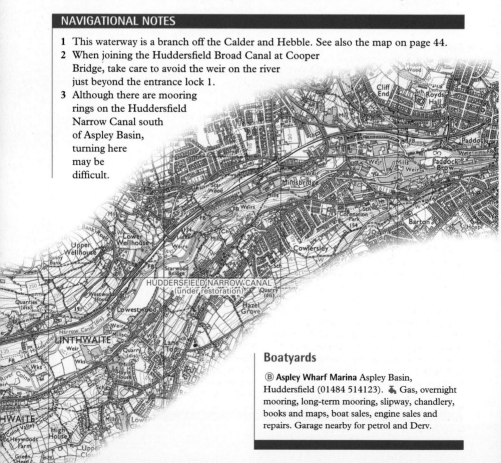

Boatyards

Ⓑ **Aspley Wharf Marina** Aspley Basin, Huddersfield (01484 514123). ⚓ Gas, overnight mooring, long-term mooring, slipway, chandlery, books and maps, boat sales, engine sales and repairs. Garage nearby for petrol and Derv.

● **Huddersfield**
W. Yorks. MD Mon. All services. Huddersfield is in the best tradition of
Victorian industrial towns: all built to a grand scale of dark local
stone, in a happy mixture of 19thC styles. The most striking
part of the town is around the railway station, built in
1847 with its powerful classical façade of Corinthian
columns, considered one of the finest examples of
railway architecture. The renowned
Huddersfield Choral Society operates from
the 19thC Town Hall.
Art Gallery Princess Alexandra Walk,
Huddersfield (01484 442845).
Above the library. Presents an
international programme
embracing all media together
with changing displays from
the permanent collection.
*Open Mon–Fri, 10.00–17.00
& Sat 10.00–16.00.* Free.
Automobilia Transport Museum
The Heritage Centre, Leeds
Road, Huddersfield (01422
844775). Recently moved
from Hebden Bridge
having outgrown its
space. Ring for
further details.

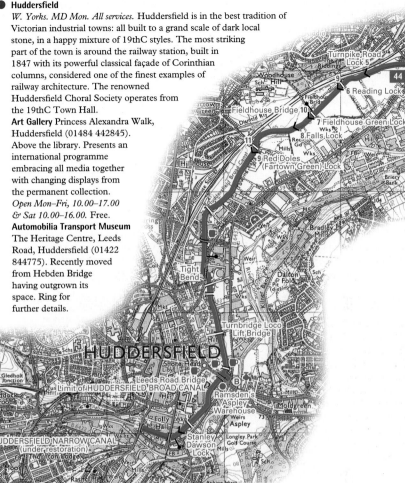

Castle Hill and Jubilee Tower Castle Hill,
Almondbury, Huddersfield (01484 530591).
A striking local landmark occupied since the
Stone Age and now topped by a Victorian
tower. Splendid views and an exhibition
tracing the hill's 4000 years of history.
Charge. Bus No 304 from Huddersfield.
Colne Valley Museum Cliffe Ash, Golcar, Nr
Huddersfield (01484 659762) The hand
weaver's working life circa 1850 depicted in a
working exhibit in period settings. Also clog
making by gas light and a range of changing
craft exhibitions. Books, gifts and light
refreshments available. *Open weekends and B.
Hols 14.00–17.00.* Small charge. Regular
buses – Nos 301, 302 & 303 – from
Huddersfield bus station.

Holmfirth Nr Huddersfield. An essential visit
for all 'Last of the Summer Wine' devotees,
easily accessible by bus from Huddersfield.
Exhibition gallery contains photographs and
memorabilia dating from the series beginning
in 1972. *Sat* craft market and galleries.
Holmfirth Tourist Information Centre 49–51
Huddersfield Road (01484 687603). Also
home to the **Holmfirth Postcard Museum**
(01484 682231) containing a collection of
Bamforths saucy seaside postcards, as well as
song sheets and silent films. *Open Mon–Sat,
10.00–16.00 & Sun 12.00–16.00.* Small
charge.

Huddersfield Narrow Canal

One of three Pennine canal crossings, and noted for the length of its summit tunnel at Standedge, fully 5698yds end to end. Authorised in 1794 and completed in 1811, this canal packs 74 locks into its 20 miles between here and Manchester. Active restoration is afoot throughout its length.

Kirklees Light Railway Park Mill Way, Clayton West, Nr Huddersfield (01484 865727). Scenic ride on a narrow-gauge railway along a disused branch line. Children's playground and miniature fairground rides. Café. *Open every day from Easter–Sep & weekends and most school holidays in winter.* Charge. Bus No 484 from Huddersfield.

Tolson Memorial Hall Ravensknowle Park, Huddersfield (01484 530591). Fine Italianate mansion housing natural history, archaeology and local history exhibits. Workshops, events and children's activities. *Open Mon–Fri 11.00–17.00; Sat & Sun 12.00–17.00.* Free. There are buses from Huddersfield.

Tourist Information Centre 3–5 Albion Road, Huddersfield (01484 430808).

Pubs and Restaurants

⬤ ✗ **Royal and Ancient** East of bridge 2. A fine pub, tastefully furnished, achieving a balance between genuine olde worlde and traditional comfort. An intimate, cosy atmosphere in the separate restaurant area – screens, scatter cushions and an inviting window settle – together with interesting wall decorations and an intriguing array of curios to captivate the eye. An elaborate, varied and exciting range of food available in both the bar and restaurant *lunchtimes and evenings except Sun evenings.* Tetley's, Timothy Taylor and Joule's Crown Ale are the real ales dispensed from a bar dominated by a dark burr-oak post, uncarved, but appearing to depict the head of a Hereford bull.

⬤ **White Horse Inn** Huddersfield (01484 423899). South of bridge 8. Handy pub by the cricket pitches. *Lunchtime bar meals.*

⬤ **Spinners Arms** Huddersfield (01484 421062). East of the canal, approaching Turnbridge. Inexpensive bar snacks *available all day, every day.* Large pub geared up around entertainment which includes a stripper *Wed,* karaoke *Fri* and a live act *Sat.*

There are plenty of pubs and restaurants in Huddersfield. These are just a selection close to Aspley Basin:

⬤ ✗ **The Aspley** Aspley Basin, Huddersfield (01484 544250). Whitbread Brewers Fayre Chain. Boddingtons, Morland, 4 guest real ales and food *available all day.* Vegetarians and children catered for. Canalside seating and moorings.

⬤ **Dr. Brown's** Huddersfield (01484 423009). South of Wakefield Road Bridge. Striking combination of dingy woodwork, exposed brickwork and flagstone floors making these earthy surroundings ideal for the consumption of Black Sheep, Tetley's and guest real ales. Interesting selection of inexpensive bar food *at lunchtime* and pizzas *in the evening.* Live music *Tue & Thur;* disco *Wed, Fri & Sat* and quiz *Mon.* Beer garden. Children welcome.

⬤ **College Arms** 33 Queensgate, Huddersfield. Close to the basin. John Smith's, Courage and Ruddles real ales in this unusual, student pub – formerly the Dog & Gun. Inexpensive bar snacks *lunchtimes and evenings (not Sun evening).* Children and vegetarians catered for. Pool.

⬤ **Yates** Queensgate, Huddersfield (01484 510974). Next to College Arms. Originally cottages, now with most of the first floor removed to give soaring ceilings; decorated with chintzy wall coverings and bright paintwork. John Smith's, Thwaites and Bass real ales together with inexpensive *lunchtime* bar snacks. Vegetarian options and children welcome only if eating.

✗ ♀ **Memsahib** 37/39 Queensgate, Huddersfield (01484 422002). Indian cuisine from a restaurant whose proprietor takes a real interest in serving authentic, regional dishes using fresh ingredients. Excellent value and *open L & D.* Take-away service – within jogging distance of the basin.

⬤ **Ship Inn** Queensgate, Huddersfield (01484 424123). Large, one-roomed student pub with a poster covered ceiling. Seven real ales always on tap including Rudgates, Worthington and Stones. Live music *Thur* and quiz *Sun.*

■ LANCASTER CANAL

MAXIMUM DIMENSIONS	MILEAGE
Preston to Tewitfield	*PRESTON to*
Length: 75'	Garstang: 16^1/$_4$
Beam: 14'	Junction with Glasson Branch: 24
Headroom: 7' 6"	Lancaster: 29^1/$_4$
Glasson Branch	Carnforth: 37^1/$_4$
Length: 70'	*CANAL TERMINUS:* 41^1/$_4$
Beam: 14'	No locks
Headroom: 8'	
	Glasson Branch: 2^3/$_4$ miles, 6 locks
MANAGER	
(01524) 32712	

Industrial developments during the late 18thC created a demand for access between Lancaster and Preston and Manchester. After a range of proposals had been mooted, a broad canal between Kendal and Westhoughton (a few miles east of Wigan) was promoted, and construction began in 1792, following a survey by John Rennie. The chosen route included several aqueducts, but only eight locks, at Tewitfield.

By 1799 the canal between Tewitfield and Preston, including the aqueduct over the Lune, and the separate section between Clayton and Chorley, was opened. The five mile gap thus created was never bridged by water. A temporary tramway was built, and this survived until 1857, since when the north end has remained separated from the national canal network.

The route north was extended to Kendal in 1819, and the short arm to Glasson Dock, falling through six locks, was opened in 1826, finally providing a direct link with the sea.

A dearth of locks, and having the towpath on one side for virtually the whole length of the canal, fostered the growth of express passenger, or 'fly', boats, which could average 10 mph on the run from Preston to Kendal.

Eventually the south end of the canal was leased in perpetuity to the Leeds & Liverpool Canal Company, and in 1885 the north end was sold to the London & North Western Railway. In 1968 the canal north of Tewitfield was finally abandoned with the building of the M6 motorway, and the route in Preston was shortened by about a mile. What remains is remarkably rural, surprisingly quiet and well worthy of exploration.

'The date of the new town (Kendal) may truly be placed here (1819) at the opening of the Lancaster Canal. This event gave an impulse to the new public spirit of the inhabitants, and formed a new era in the history of Kendal. The large warehouses and other buildings at the canal harbour were all erected at this time. The Union Building Society commenced operations about this time; and indeed on every side numerous habitations were super added to the town. In a very short time the town assumed a new and modern appearance – so very different that any person having been absent a few years, could scarcely have identified it'.

C. Nicholson, *The Annals of Kendal*, 1861

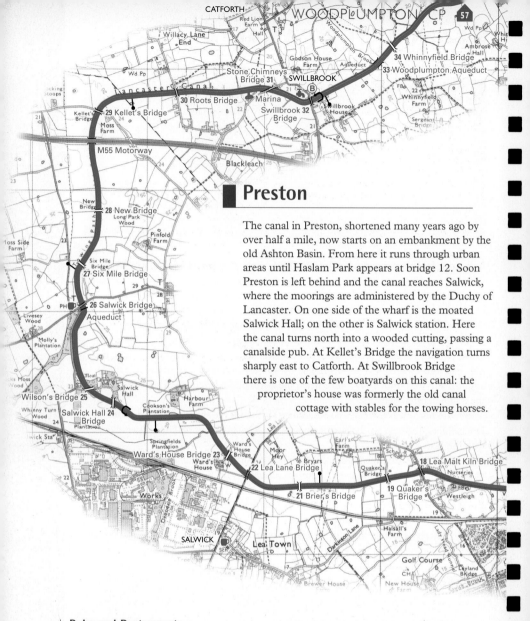

Willacy Lane End

Red Lion Farm

Godson House Farm

Aqueduct

34 Whinnyfield Bridge

33 Woodplumpton Aqueduct

Stone Chimneys Bridge **31**

SWILLBROOK

Whinnyfield Farm

30 Roots Bridge

Marina

Swillbrook **32** Bridge

Swillbrook House

Kellet's Bridge

29 Kellet's Bridge

Moss Farm

M55 Motorway

Blackleach

New Bridge

28 New Bridge

Long Park Wood

Pinfold Farm

Moss Side Farm

Six Mile Bridge

27 Six Mile Bridge

Livesey Wood

PH

26 Salwick Bridge

Aqueduct

Molly's Plantation

Salwick Hall

Harbour Farm

Wilson's Bridge **25**

Whinny Turn Wood

Salwick Hall 24 Bridge

Cookson's Plantation

Springfields Plantation

Ward's House Bridge

Ward's House Bridge **23**

Ward's House

22 Lea Lane Bridge

Moor Hey

Bryars

Quaker's Bridge

18 Lea Malt Kiln Bridge

Nurseries

Westleigh

21 Brier's Bridge

19 Quaker's Bridge

Works

SALWICK

Lea Town

Halsall's Farm

Golf Course

New House Farm

Preston

The canal in Preston, shortened many years ago by over half a mile, now starts on an embankment by the old Ashton Basin. From here it runs through urban areas until Haslam Park appears at bridge 12. Soon Preston is left behind and the canal reaches Salwick, where the moorings are administered by the Duchy of Lancaster. On one side of the wharf is the moated Salwick Hall; on the other is Salwick station. Here the canal turns north into a wooded cutting, passing a canalside pub. At Kellet's Bridge the navigation turns sharply east to Catforth. At Swillbrook Bridge there is one of the few boatyards on this canal: the proprietor's house was formerly the old canal cottage with stables for the towing horses.

Pubs and Restaurants

🍺 **Mighty Muldoons** Water Lane, Aston, Preston (01772 721567). ¼ mile south of Ashton Basin. A good basic pub, formerly named the Wheatsheaf, serving Tetley's, Theakston's and guest real ales and bar meals *lunchtimes* only, with vegetarian menu. Children welcome. Regular entertainment.

🍺 **Hand & Dagger** Treales Road, Salwick (01772 690306). Canalside at bridge 26. Once the Clifton Arms, this pub was at that time known as the Hand & Dagger, because of its signs. It was renamed when it was modernised. Greenalls real ale and food *lunchtimes & evenings, all day Sun* with vegetarian menu. Children welcome.

● **Preston**

Lancs. MD Mon, Wed, Sat. All services. A large industrial town. Henry II granted a Royal Charter in 1179, with the right to hold a Guild Merchant. Guild celebrations are held every 20 years, with the next in 2112. An outdoor market was also established and still thrives today. The teetotal movement was founded in Preston in 1834, and Joseph Livesey's Temperance Hotel (the world's first) used to stand at the corner of Church Street and North Road. There are many churches whose tall spires are a distinctive feature of the town. There is a good shopping precinct and a large modern bus station. The huge basin of Preston Dock has been developed as a marina complex, with the turbine steamer *Manxman* as the centre-piece.
Harris Museum & Art Gallery Market Square, Preston (01772 258248). This museum has a specialised collection of the Devis family of painters and exhibits illustrating 18thC and 19thC art, including ceramics, toys, stamps and costume. *Open Mon–Sat, 10.00–17.00; closed B. Hols.* Free.
Lancaster Tourist Information Centre Guildhall Arcade, Lancaster Road, Preston (01772 253731).

● **Catforth**

Lancs. PO, tel, stores in a straightforward village.

● **The Fylde**

A large flat area of north-west Lancashire (west of the canal) which is the 'market garden' of the many industrial towns in the area. There used to be a wonderful array of windmills covering the land, but virtually all of these are now gone.

● **Salwick**

Lancs. Tel, stores, station. A scattered village.

Boatyards

ⓑ **Adventure Cruisers** The Boathouse, Canal Wharf, Catforth (01772 690232). 🚽 🪣 D E Gas, narrow boat and day hire, overnight and long-term mooring, winter storage, slipway, chandlery, public telephone, books and maps, boat and engine sales and repairs, gift shop, toilet.

ⓑ **Arlen Hire Boats** Ashton Basin, Tulkuth Brow, Preston (01772 769183). 🚽 🚽 🪣 Narrow boat hire, day hire boats, long-term mooring, winter storage, slipway, toilets.

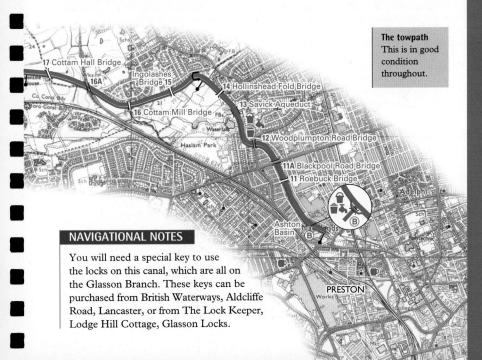

The towpath
This is in good condition throughout.

NAVIGATIONAL NOTES

You will need a special key to use the locks on this canal, which are all on the Glasson Branch. These keys can be purchased from British Waterways, Aldcliffe Road, Lancaster, or from The Lock Keeper, Lodge Hill Cottage, Glasson Locks.

Bilsborrow

Passing the marina at Moons Bridge, the canal gently meanders along its remote route towards White Horse Bridge where, a 1/4 mile walk to the east, there is a pub, garage, post office and telephone kiosk. The canal then sweeps round to enter the village of Bilsborrow on a minor embankment: the A6 joins the canal here, as does the main railway line to Scotland, and the M6. Generally these rival transport routes keep their distance and the canal is for the most part delightfully quiet, still passing through peaceful green farmland, while the foothills of the Pennines begin to converge from the east. The River Brock is crossed on an aqueduct, with a good view to the west.

● **Bilsborrow**
Lancs. PO, tel, stores, garage. A village which straggles along the A6. The church of St Hilda, built 1926–7, is set apart, up on a hill: there are three pubs very close to the canal.

Boatyards

Ⓑ **Moons Bridge Marina** Hollow Forth Lane, Woodplumpton (01772 690627 or 01257 482781). 🛇 🛇 🛠 [evenings] Gas, boat hire, winter storage, slipway, boat sales, engine repairs, chandlery, mooring.

Pubs and Restaurants

🍺 **White Horse Hotel** Barton (01995 640236) 1/4 mile east of bridge 42 . Small, comfortable pub serving home-made food *lunchtimes & evenings* and Theakston's real ale.

🍺 ✗ **Owd Nell's** Canalside at bridge 44. (01995 640010). A farmhouse-style thatched pub and restaurant complex, with all sorts of attractions. There are craft shops, a thatched terrace, a timber castle and games areas with cricket pavilion. Generous bar meals *all day, lunchtimes & evenings until 21.30, snacks until 22.30.* Boddingtons, Whitbread and many other real ales, with a choice of well furnished bars in which to drink them (some with no smoking areas). Morris dancing on summer weekends. Hotel accommodation.

🍺 **Roebuck** Garstang Road, Bilsborrow, close to the White Bull (01995 640234). Theakston's real ale and food *lunchtimes & evenings and all day Sun* with vegetarian options. Children welcome, garden with play area.

🍺 **White Bull** Garstang Road, Bilsborrow (01995 640324). Canalside at bridge 44. Friendly village local dispensing Scottish & Newcastle, Theakston's and guest real ales. Open fire. Garden.

🍺 ✗ **Green Man** Garstang Road, Brock (01995 640220). South of bridge 47. Serves Tetley's and Boddingtons real ales. English and Cantonese restaurant open *7 days a week 18.00–24.00.* Children welcome, garden with play area. Regular entertainment.

BOAT TRIPS

The Bilsborrow Lady
Old Duncombe House,
Bilsborrow Wharf,
Garstang Road (01995
640336). A comfortable
12-seater boat offering a
wide range of trips and
cruises. Bar and buffet
available. Between
bridges 44 and 45.

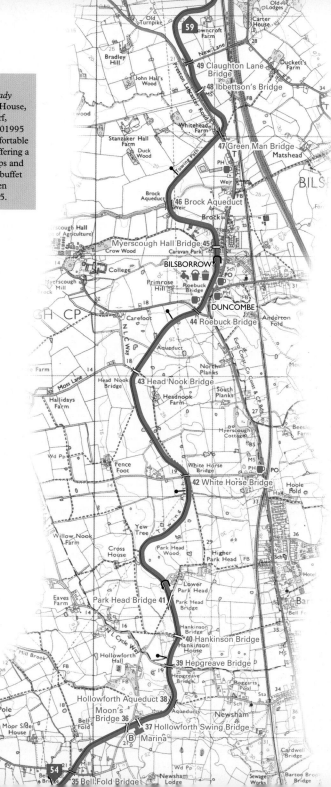

Garstang

There is a flurry of canal
interest around the Calder
Aqueduct and Catterall Basin, and
those who moor here and walk up the hills to
the east of bridge 54 will also be rewarded with
splendid views over Cockerham Sands and the Fylde. The canal
then temporarily moves away from the hills and the remains of Greenhalgh
Castle to cross the River Wyre on a fine stone aqueduct, 110ft long and 34ft
high, attributed to John Rennie. There are steps down if you wish to have a better
look at it. The attractive town of Garstang is soon reached; the area around Garstang
Basin is a popular mooring for pleasure boats. There is a restaurant and museum in the
restored wharf buildings here, with the town centre up to the north-east. The canal
then passes a new marina and continues to wind through countryside that is as green
and pleasant as ever, but which is now overlooked by the steep slopes of the Pennines.

Boatyards

ⓑ **Bridge House Marina** Crossing Lane, Nateby
(01995 603207). Between bridges 64 & 65.
🗑 🛢 ⚓ [evenings] Gas, long-term mooring,
winter storage, slipway, chandlery, boat sales,
engine repairs, toilets, showers, grocery shop,
telephone, laundry.

Pubs and Restaurants

⚓ **Kenlis Arms Hotel** Ray Lane, Barnacre (01995 603307) East of bridge 54. Once a shooting lodge, then a station hotel (until the station closed) it is now a friendly country local. Tetley's, Boddingtons and John Smith's real ales, straightforward food *lunchtimes & evenings, except Tue & Sun.* Outside seating. Family room. B & B.

⚓ **Th'Owd Tithebarn** The Wharf Cottage, Church Street (01995 604486). Canalside at bridge 62. A uniquely old-fashioned establishment where it is hard to discern where the bar ends and the museum, which the building contains, begins. Serving Mitchell's real ale and substantial bar and restaurant meals *lunchtimes & evenings* and good country wines. Children welcome. Morris dancing in the summer. Canalside terrace. *Closed Mon (except B. Hol lunch).*

⚓ ✕ **Royal Oak Hotel** Market Place, Garstang (01995 603318). A coaching inn, dating from the 1670s but with parts surviving from 1480. Robinson's real ale. Bar meals and à la carte menu *lunchtimes & evenings, 7 days a week,*

vegetarian menu. Children welcome. Outside seating. B & B.

⚓ **Eagle & Child** High Street, Garstang (01995 602139). Serves Theakston's and Morland real ale. *Lunchtime only* bar meals with vegetarian options. Children's room. Garden. A good place to rest your feet on Thursday, market day. B & B.

⚓ ✕ **Chequered Flag** Parkside Lane, Nateby (01995 602126). 200yds south of bridge 64. Marston's and John Smith's real ale and bar meals *lunchtimes & evenings,* with vegetarian menu. Indoor play area for children. Regular entertainment, with monthly special nights such as medieval banquets.

⚓ **Crown Hotel** High Street, Garstang (01995 602152). Serving Thwaites real ale and bar snacks *lunchtimes only.* Children welcome. Bowling green.

⚓ **Kings Arms** High Street, Garstang (01995 602101). Serving Boddingtons real ale and bar meals *lunchtimes (not Sun),* with vegetarian menu. Outside seating. Regular disco.

● **Claughton Hall** 1/4 mile east of the canal. This hall was originally an Elizabethan mansion built next to the village church for the Croft family, but in 1932–5 the whole house, except for one wing, was dismantled and reassembled on top of the moor north of the village. It was quite a remarkable undertaking and still stands in defiant isolation.

● **Greenhalgh Castle** Just north of the canal on a grassy knoll are the modest ruins of Greenhalgh Castle. It was built in 1490 by the Earl of Derby, who placed Richard III's crown on Henry Tudor's head after the victory at Bosworth Field. In the 17thC it was destroyed by the Roundheads during the Civil War when the Royalists made a final stand there. Ask at the adjacent farm to visit the ruins.

● **Garstang**
Lancs. PO, tel, stores, bank, garage. A friendly place, north-east of the canal, which retains the atmosphere of a small market town. Just near the canal is the 18thC church of St Thomas, surrounded by a tidy churchyard. Opposite the cobbled market place is an interesting town hall with its diminutive bell-tower. Built 1755–64 to acknowledge the town's promotion by the king to borough status, it was rebuilt in 1939. The market cross, erected in 1754, is an elegant column topped by a ball. There was at one time a dozen ale houses in the town; the present six seem quite adequate.

Garstang Tourist Information Centre Discovery Centre, Council Offices, High Street (01995 602125).

Potters Brook

Continuing northwards through quiet, modest and unspoilt pasture land, the canal passes countryside that is empty of villages but full of farms and houses dotted about the landscape. The absence of any locks certainly makes this an ideal waterway for restful cruising, while the wildlife and the generously proportioned stone-arched bridges always supply interest along the way. From Potters Brook Bridge (81) a lane across the A6 leads to a telephone and hotel beside what used to be Bay Horse Station. Just north of Potters Brook is the Ellel Grange estate with its remarkable spired church, ornamental canal bridge and the Grange itself, shrouded by tall trees; unfortunately the estate is private.

● **Ellel Grange** On the banks of the canal. A very fine Italianate villa built for William Preston, a merchant, in 1857–9. It is a large mansion with two broad towers that compete in vain with the graceful spire of the charming little church of St Mary, built in 1873 at a cost of £7000, that stands in the grounds of the house. It was also built by William Preston. Both are private.

Pubs and Restaurants

● **Bay Horse** Bay Horse, Forton (01524 791204). North east of bridge 81, across the A6. Mitchell's real ale and bar meals *lunchtimes & evenings (not Mon)* in a cosy pub which has its own rugby team. Family room. Open fire. Garden.

Stone-arched bridge, Lancaster Canal

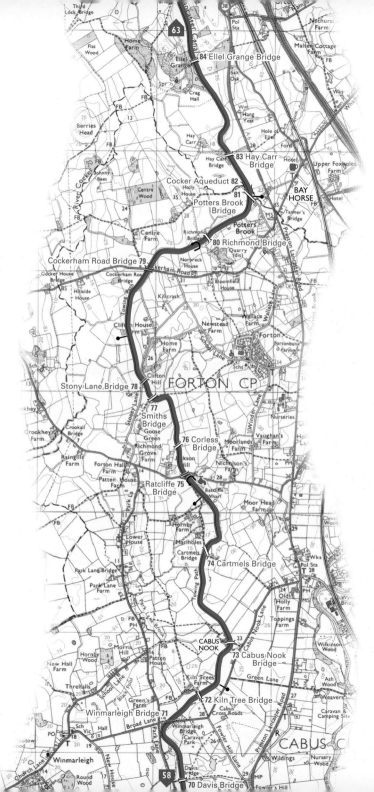

The Glasson Branch

Double Bridge marks the end of a rocky cutting and the junction with the Glasson Branch. Just around the corner on the main line is Galgate and a large boatyard and mooring site.

The Glasson Branch leads off down to the west to connect the Lancaster Canal with the Lune Estuary via Glasson Dock. The branch was finished in 1826, long after the main line of the canal was completed, and provided the canal with its only direct link with the sea. There are six wide locks whose bottom gates feature the same excellent type of sliding paddles seen on the Leeds & Liverpool Canal. The top gates are all kept padlocked for security reasons: the key is available from the British Waterways lock keeper. Gates must be locked after use, and the locks left *empty*, even when going up. The arm falls through the Conder Valley, a pleasant, quiet stretch of countryside whose proximity to the sea is betrayed by the many seagulls cruising around. After the bottom lock, the canal runs in a straight line through saltings and marshland to Glasson Basin, where there is a large boatyard, mainly for seagoing yachts, and British Waterways moorings.

The main line of the canal continues northwards through beautiful undulating green countryside, then passes through an unusually long wooded cutting, marked by Deep Cutting Bridge, and ends in the outskirts of Lancaster.

NAVIGATIONAL NOTES

1 The entrance lock from Glasson Dock up into Glasson Basin will take boats 95ft x 24ft, and 12ft draught, and operates *2hrs* before high water. Anyone wishing to use the lock (for which *24hrs* notice is required) or take up a mooring in the basin should contact the lock keeper on 01524 751566.

2 The locks on the Glasson Branch will take boats up to 72ft long, 14ft wide and 4ft draught. You will need a key to operate them, available either from the Lock Keeper, Lodge Hill Cottage, Glasson Locks or British Waterways, Aldcliffe Road, Lancaster.

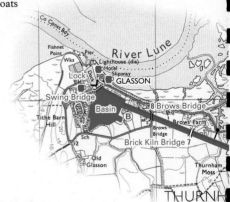

● Galgate
Lancs. PO, tel, stores, garage. An unassuming village on the A6, dominated by the main railway to Scotland. The back of the village up the hill is quiet; by the church of St John, built 1906–7, are the buildings of what is apparently the oldest surviving silk spinning mill in England, built in 1792. There is another, apparently older, built originally as a corn mill, close by. Some of the nearby cottages were built for the mill-workers.
Canalside Craft Centre Pear Tree Barn, Galgate (01524 752223). A craft shop next to the marina. Tea, coffee, light lunches and snacks. *Open Easter to mid–Oct 10.00–17.30 (17.00 in winter, and closed Mon except B. Hols).*

● Glasson
Lancs. PO, tel, stores, garage. A fascinating tiny port built in 1787 to serve Lancaster. The huge basin is now only occupied by an assortment of pleasure boats using its excellent sheltered moorings. In the tidal dock, however, there are often coasters that discharge into lorries. The old railway line into Lancaster has now been converted into a footpath and cycle-way.

Boatyards

Ⓑ **Marina Park** Canal Wharf, Galgate, Lancaster (01524 751368). 🚻 🚿 ⚓ [evenings] Ⓓ Gas, narrow boat hire, day hire craft (cruisers), long-term mooring, winter storage, slipway, dry dock, chandlery, books and maps, boat sales, toilets, showers, laundrette.

Ⓑ **Glasson Basin Yacht Co.** Boatyard, Glasson Dock, Lancaster (01524 751491). ⚓ [for customers only] Ⓓ Gas, overnight and long-term mooring, winter storage, slipway, crane (80 ton), chandlery, books and maps, boat and engine sales and repairs, telephone.

Pubs and Restaurants

🍺 **Millers Canalside Tavern** Conder Green, Thurnham Mill, on the Glasson Branch (01524 752852). Webster's real ale and food *lunchtimes & evenings*, in a heavily converted mill.

🍺 **Victoria** Glasson Dock (01524 751423). Mitchell's real ale and bar meals *lunchtimes & evenings* with vegetarian options. Children welcome. Garden. Open fire.

🍺 **Caribou Hotel** Glasson Dock (01524 751356). Dating from 1781 and quite probably the oldest building in Glasson, this large pub was originally known as the Pier Hall, and later The Grapes. It has an open fire and plenty of cosy corners. Thwaites real ale. Children welcome. B & B.

🍺 **Green Dragon** Main Road, Galgate (01524 751062). Thwaites real ale in a village pub which has its own football team. Food *lunchtimes & evenings* with a vegetarian menu. Children welcome. Outside seating. Regular live entertainment and games nights.

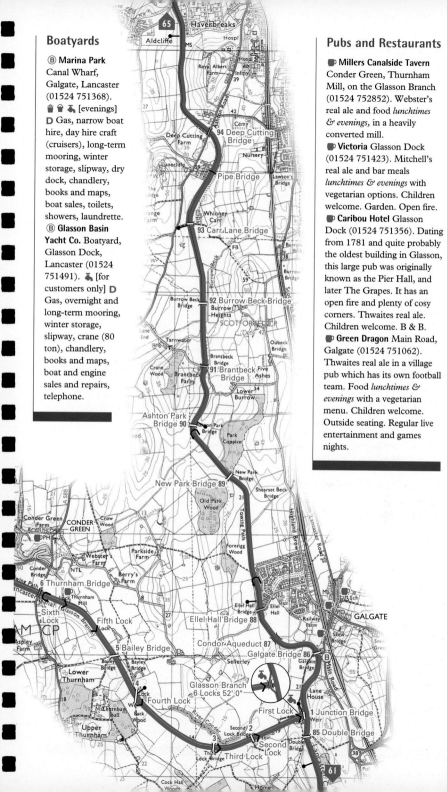

Lancaster

The canal now enters Lancaster, losing its rural identity as buildings close in. At bridge 100 the towpath returns to the west side of the canal, where it stays for the rest of the journey northwards. Leaving Lancaster the navigation crosses a new aqueduct (built in 1961) over the A683. The imposing aqueduct that carries the canal over the River Lune quickly follows. The canal rejoins the side of the valley, turning west, then north again towards the sea.

● **Lancaster**
Lancs. MD Sat. All services. Today Lancaster's quay, once a great shipping port handling more cargo than Liverpool, is a quiet backwater, with a pleasant walk.
Lancaster Castle (01524 64998). On the site of Roman fortifications; mainly 13thC and 14thC construction, except for the Norman keep, which is surmounted by a beacon tower. The Shire Hall contains an impressive display of over 600 heraldic shields. Most of the castle has reverted to its earlier function as a prison. *Open Easter–Oct 10.30–16.00 for escorted tours every half hour. Closed during the winter, and some weekdays while Assizes, Quarter Sessions or County Courts are sitting (though open all weekend).* Charge.
Cottage Museum Opposite the Castle (01524 64637). Artifacts of an artisan, c. 1820. *Open Easter–Oct 14.00–17.00.* Charge.
Priory Church of St Mary Vicarage Lane, by the castle (01524 65338). Attractive 15thC church in late Perpendicular style, with original Saxon western doorway. Church *open all year round 09.30–17.00.* Free. Refectory *open from 10.00–16.00 Easter to Oct.* Interesting book stall. Nearby are the excavated remains of a Roman bath house.
Lancaster City Museum Old Town Hall, Market Square, Lancaster (01524 64637). The history

and archaeology of Lancaster. The museum of the King's Own Royal regiment is also here. *Open Mon–Sat 10.00–17.00.* Free.
Ashton Memorial Williamson Park, Quernmore Road (01524 33318). The 'Taj Mahal' of the north. A Butterfly House and Mini Beast Enclosure are among its other delights. *Open Easter–Oct 10.00–17.00 daily; Oct–Easter 11.00–16.00 daily.* Charge varies according to number of attractions visited.
Maritime Museum Old Customs House, St George's Quay, Lancaster (01524 64637). Walk towards the river from bridge 99, turning left into Damside. *Open daily 11.00–17.00 Easter to Oct (14.00–17.00 in winter).* Charge. Café. The riverside path to the west connects with Glasson Dock about 5 miles away, making an excellent but energetic walk, or an easier bicycle ride.
Lancaster Tourist Information Centre Castle Hill (01524 32878) for details of all of Lancaster's delights, including occasional conducted walks and festivals.
● **Lune Aqueduct**
This splendid edifice carries the navigation for some 600ft across the River Lune, which is 60ft below.
● **Hest Bank**
Lancs. PO, tel, stores, bank. The seashore is only a couple of hundred yards from the navigation, and at low water miles of sandy beach are uncovered.

Pubs and Restaurants

🍺 ✕ **Waterwitch** Aldcliffe Road (01524 63828). Canalside between bridge 98 and 99. Real ales and food in the bar or restaurant. Children welcome at meal times.
🍺 **Farmers Arms Hotel** (01524 36368). Serving Thwaites real ale and bar meals *lunchtimes & evenings* with vegetarian menu. Children welcome.
🍺 **The Navigation** (01524 849484). German beers and Tetley's real ale. Meals *lunchtimes and evenings in summer, evenings in winter.* Vegetarian choices.
🍺 ✕ **White Cross** Quarry Road (01524 841048). Canalside after bridge 99. Bass and Stones real ales, bar and restaurant meals *lunchtimes &*

evenings and all day Sun, vegetarian menu. Children welcome *only at lunchtimes.*
🍺 **The Golden Lion** Moor Lane (01524 63198). Theakston's, Whitbread and Boddingtons real ale.
🍺 **Waggon & Horses** St George's Quay, Lancaster (01524 846094). Worth a look in if you are visiting the Maritime Museum. Robinson's and Hartleys real ale. Food *lunchtimes only.*
🍺 **Hest Bank** (01524 822226). Canalside at Bridge 118. Boddingtons real ale and bar food *lunchtimes & evenings, every day.* Vegetarian, braille and children's menu. Canalside garden and regular entertainment.

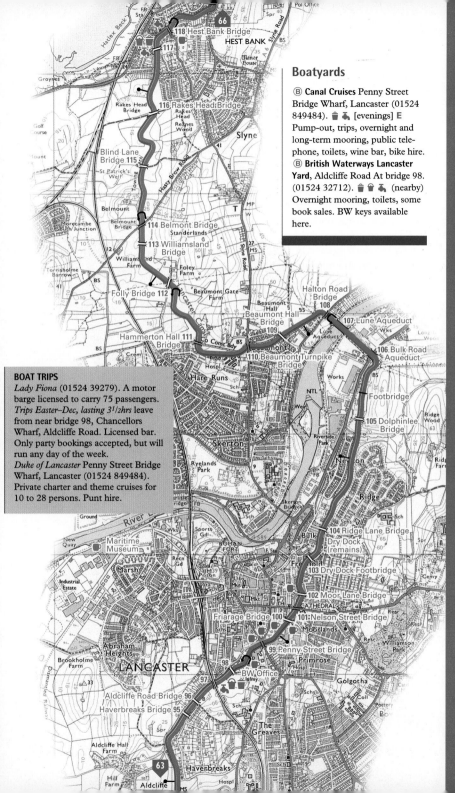

Boatyards

Ⓑ **Canal Cruises** Penny Street Bridge Wharf, Lancaster (01524 849484). 🚽 🚲 [evenings] **E** Pump-out, trips, overnight and long-term mooring, public telephone, toilets, wine bar, bike hire.

Ⓑ **British Waterways Lancaster Yard**, Aldcliffe Road At bridge 98. (01524 32712). 🚽 🚰 🚲 (nearby) Overnight mooring, toilets, some book sales. BW keys available here.

BOAT TRIPS

Lady Fiona (01524 39279). A motor barge licensed to carry 75 passengers. *Trips Easter–Dec, lasting 3¹/₂hrs* leave from near bridge 98, Chancellors Wharf, Aldcliffe Road. Licensed bar. Only party bookings accepted, but will run any day of the week.
Duke of Lancaster Penny Street Bridge Wharf, Lancaster (01524 849484). Private charter and theme cruises for 10 to 28 persons. Punt hire.

Carnforth

The canal now passes Hest Bank and Bolton-le-Sands, with the sea never far away to the west and the A6 beside and below as the waterway comes into Carnforth. The canal then sneaks inconspicuously through the town, mostly in a cutting. After passing under the motorway spur road, the canal finds itself diverted along a new channel for several hundred yards before going under the main line of the M6: this diversion was presumably cheaper to build than a long, finely angled skew bridge over the navigation. Beyond the motorway lies peaceful green countryside backed, unmistakably, by the foothills of the Lake District. At Capernwray the canal crosses the River Keer on a minor aqueduct; the nearby railway, which goes to Leeds, crosses the Keer on an impressive viaduct.

Boatyards

Ⓑ **Nu-Way Acorn** Lundsfield, Carnforth (01524 734457). 🏠 🛁 [evenings] Ⓔ Pump-out, gas, narrow boat hire, day hire craft, overnight mooring, long-term mooring, winter storage, slipway, boat sales, engine repairs, toilets, showers.

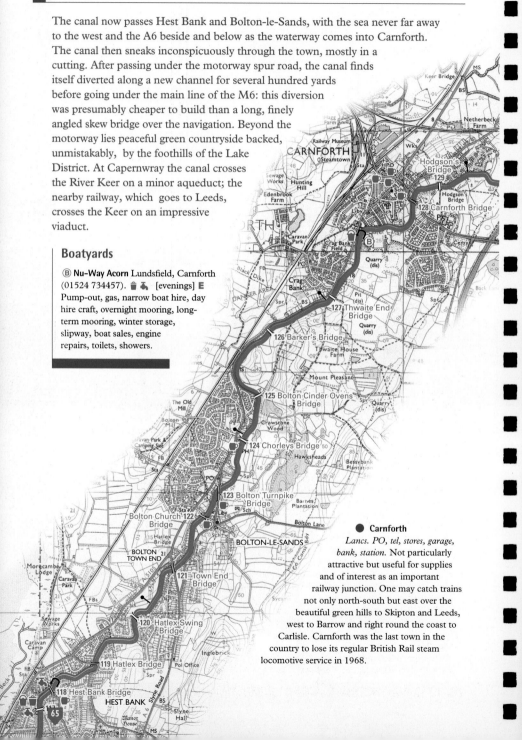

● Carnforth
Lancs. PO, tel, stores, garage, bank, station. Not particularly attractive but useful for supplies and of interest as an important railway junction. One may catch trains not only north-south but east over the beautiful green hills to Skipton and Leeds, west to Barrow and right round the coast to Carlisle. Carnforth was the last town in the country to lose its regular British Rail steam locomotive service in 1968.

Steamtown Railway Centre Warton Road, Carnforth (01524 732100). A fine collection of railway relics housed in what was one of the country's last steam depots. Admire the collection of locomotives large and small, explore the rolling stock and wallow in the nostalgia of smoky days gone by. From *mid–June to mid–Sept* you are most likely to see steam in action, even if it is only their miniature railway, but the timetable reveals all. *Open Easter–Oct 10.00–17.00 (16.00 in winter). Buffet. Children under 16 years old must be accompanied by an adult.* Charge.

Pubs and Restaurants

Hest Bank (01524 822226). Canalside at Bridge 118. You can still see the window for the guiding light, which once showed the way across the sands. Now this old coaching inn, which dates from 1554, is justly popular and you can share the shelter it once offered to abbots and monks, soldiers and highwaymen, The Duke of Devonshire and Prince Frederick of Prussia. Boddingtons real ale and bar food *lunchtimes & evenings, every day.* Vegetarian, braille and children's menu. Canalside garden and regular entertainment. The Cellar Bar is recommended.

Blue Anchor Main Road, Bolton-le-Sands (01524 823241). Serving Mitchell's real ale and bar and restaurant food *lunchtimes & evenings and all day Sun,* with a vegetarian menu. Children welcome. Garden. Regular quiz nights and live entertainment. B & B.

Packet Boat Hotel Main Road, Bolton-le-Sands (01524 822289). Thwaites real ale and food *lunchtimes & evenings.* Children welcome. Outside seating.

Royal Hotel Bolton-le-Sands (01524 732057). Mitchell's real ales. Food *lunchtimes*

& evenings and all day Sun. A large and very comfortable pub where the original layout remains, although the total space has been made one area. You can still find yourself a cosy corner, with books and a fire in winter. Children welcome. Garden.

Shovel North Road, Carnforth (01524 733402). West of bridge 128. Boddingtons real ale. Children welcome. Outside seating. Regular quiz nights.

Carnforth Hotel Lancaster Road, Carnforth (01524 732902). Offering Vaux and Marston's real ale and bar meals *lunchtimes & evenings,* with a vegetarian menu. Children welcome. Outside seating. Regular disco and live entertainment. B & B.

Queens Hotel Market Street, Carnforth (01524 732978).

✕ Station Hotel Market Street, Carnforth (01524 732033). Bang in the centre of town, this handsome establishment offers Mitchell's real ale, bar and restaurant meals *lunchtimes & evenings, except Sun,* with a vegetarian menu. Children welcome at meal times. B & B.

Borwick

Beyond Keer Aqueduct and the railway viaduct is the Capernwray Arm, a short branch to a worked-out quarry, and now offering some sheltered moorings. The canal then winds around the hillside to end abruptly just beyond Borwick and right beside the M6. The abandoned Tewitfield locks begin just across the road from the present terminus. It is possible to walk the 15 miles or so from Tewitfield to the original terminus at Kendal (and get a bus back). Boats can safely be left at the moorings here.

● **Borwick**
Lancs. Tel. A small, old and attractive village, spread around a green. Overlooking the canal is Borwick Hall, a large and sombre Elizabethan manor house, built around a high 15thC tower and with extensive gardens.

● **Warton**
Lancs. PO, tel, stores. About 2 miles west of Borwick. Ancestors of George Washington lived in this village and their family crest containing the famed Stars and Stripes is to be seen on the 15thC tower of the church of St Oswald.

Pubs and Restaurants

🍺 ✕ **Longlands Hotel** Tewitfield (01524 781256). 100yds north east of the canal terminus. This spacious pub serves Theakston's and Worthington real ale and bar and restaurant meals (with extensive vegetarian menu) *lunchtimes & evenings* in a friendly atmosphere. Children are welcome, and there is a garden with a play area. Regular entertainment. B & B.

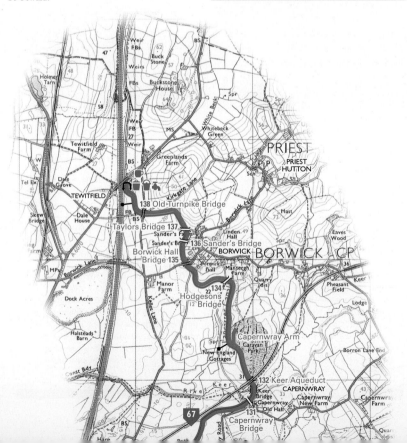

LEEDS & LIVERPOOL CANAL

MAXIMUM DIMENSIONS

Liverpool to Wigan, and Leigh Branch
Length: 72'
Beam: 14' 3"
Headroom: 8' 6"

Wigan to Leeds
Length: 60'
Beam: 14' 3"
Headroom: 8'

Rufford Branch
Length: 62'
Beam: 14'
Headroom: 8'

MANAGER

Liverpool to Greenberfield Bridge 156: (01942) 242239

Greenberfield Bridge 156 to Leeds: (01274) 611303

MILEAGE

LIVERPOOL. Canal terminus to Burscough, junction with Rufford Branch: 24$\frac{1}{2}$

Wigan, junction with Leigh Branch: 35
Johnson's Hill Locks: 47$\frac{1}{4}$
Blackburn, Top Lock: 56
Burnley: 72$\frac{1}{2}$
Skipton: 98
Bingley Five Rise: 110$\frac{3}{4}$
Apperley Bridge: 118
LEEDS, River Lock: 127
Locks: 91
Leigh Branch: 7$\frac{1}{4}$ miles, 2 locks
Rufford Branch: 7$\frac{1}{4}$ miles, 8 locks

BW produce an excellent navigation guide for this canal (obtainable, free, from lock keepers and the managers offices listed above) to assist boaters in the safe operation of the many swing bridges and staircase locks.

With a length of 127 miles excluding branches, the Leeds & Liverpool Canal is the longest single canal in Britain built by a single company. The canal has its beginnings in the River Douglas, a little river made navigable by 1740 from Wigan to Parbold, Tarleton and the Ribble estuary. Several ambitious trans-Pennine canal schemes had been mooted; one for a canal from Liverpool to Leeds, to connect with the head of the Aire & Calder Navigation. The Leeds & Liverpool Canal was authorised in 1770, and construction began at once, with John Longbotham as engineer. The first (lock-free) section from Bingley to Skipton was opened within 3 years; by 1777 two long sections were open from the Aire & Calder at Leeds to Gargrave (incorporating many new staircase locks) and from Wigan to Liverpool. The L & L bought out the River Douglas navigation at an early stage to gain control of its valuable water supply. It was replaced by a proper canal branch to Rufford and Tarleton, where it joined the (tidal) River Douglas. In 1790 work began again, with Robert Whitworth as the company's engineer; but after 1792 and the outbreak of war with France investment in canals declined steadily. The whole of the main line from Leeds to Liverpool was finished by 1816 actually *sharing* the channel of the Lancaster Canal for 10 miles from Wigan Top Lock to Johnson's Hill Bottom Lock. The Lancaster used to branch off up what became the Walton Summit Branch. In 1820 a branch was opened to join the Bridgewater Canal at Leigh. A short branch (the Springs Branch) was also made to rock quarries at Skipton and an important 3-mile-long canal from Shipley to Bradford. The cut down into the Liverpool Docks was made in 1846. The prosperity of the company after 1820 was not, at first, greatly affected by the advent of railways. The scale of the navigation (the locks were built as broad locks 62ft by 14ft, allowing big payloads to be carried along the canal) contributed to the high dividends paid to shareholders for several years. Water supply was, however, a problem and in spite of the building of copious reservoirs, the canal had to be closed for months on end during dry summers driving carriers' custom away to the railways. Use of the navigation for freight has declined throughout this century; the hard winter of 1962/63 finished off many traders. Today this canal offers the boater, walker and cyclist alike an exhilarating link between two superb cities.

Liverpool

The first 3/4 of a mile of this canal has been filled in, so the navigation now begins just north of bridge 'B'. It runs north from the city centre for about 6 miles, parallel and close to Liverpool Docks, before turning east to Aintree, Wigan and the Pennines. Liverpool, while at one time not an attractive place from the canal, is slowly changing and although some factories still have their backs to the canal, considerable effort has been made to improve the access to the towpath which is alive with walkers, fishermen and cyclists. The water, however, is surprisingly clear. The newly constructed Eldonian Village forms an attractive backdrop to the moorings in the terminus basin.

NAVIGATIONAL NOTES

1 Just north of the terminus is the Stanley Dock Branch. This useful connection from the canal down into Liverpool Docks and the River Mersey is nowadays the main *raison d'être* of the west end of the Leeds & Liverpool Canal. There are four locks on the branch: they can be opened only by the resident lock keeper *during working hours Mon–Fri*. Boaters wishing to use these locks should give *24hrs notice* to the BW Wigan office (01942 242239). Immediately below the locks is Stanley Dock: this belongs to the Mersey Docks & Harbour Company, whose permission should be sought before one enters the dock. (Ring 0151 949 6000). The MD & HC is unlikely to refuse such a request, but does not like pleasure boats to tie up in the dock. Navigators are encouraged to move straight on to the big lock down into the tidal River Mersey. The lock is operated *24hrs a day*.
2 Those navigating the Leeds & Liverpool will need, as well as a windlass, a British Waterways handcuff key and a sanitary station key.
3 Mooring at unrecognised sites in the city centre is not recommended.
4 If you wish to navigate the remainder length (Liverpool to Aintree) and require assistance or details of safe mooring locations please contact BW on 01942 242239.

● **Liverpool**
Merseyside. All services. In the first century AD it was 'lifrugpool', a settlement next to a muddy creek; now it is one of Britain's largest ports with a population of over 1/2 million. Famous worldwide as the place where the Beatles began their march to fame, and equally well known for the exploits of Liverpool Football Club. There is much to be seen in this ancient port. The Anglican Cathedral, begun in 1904 and finished in 1978, is the largest in the world; the Roman Catholic Cathedral has stained glass by John Piper and Patrick Reyntiens. The superb new Albert Dock development and Liverpool Tate Art Gallery are attracting increasing numbers of tourists. On the pierhead is a memorial to the engineers lost on the *Titanic*, which sank in 1912.
Tourist Information Centres Unit 47, Clayton Square Shopping Centre (0151 709 3631) and Atlantic Pavilion, Albert Dock (0151 708 8854).
Beatles Story Britannia Vaults, Albert Dock, Liverpool (0151 709 1963). *Open 10.00–18.00, last admission 17.00. Closed Xmas Day & Box. Day.* Charge.

City Museum and Natural History Centre William Brown Street, Liverpool (0151 207 0001). *Open Mon–Sat 10.00–17.00, Sun 12.00–17.00. Closed New Year's Day, G. Fri, Xmas Eve, Xmas Day & Box. Day.* Free. (Charge for planetarium).
Conservation Centre Queen Square, Liverpool (0115 478 4999). Housed in an impressively restored, listed Victorian warehouse (the former Midland Railway Goods Offices) this interactive exhibition provides a rare insight into work that normally goes on behind the scenes. Surrounded by classical sculpture, the Café Eros makes a good place to meet and eat. *Open daily 10.00-17.00. Closed Xmas Eve-Box. Day & New Year's Day.* Charge. Full disabled access.
HM Customs & Excise National Museum Albert Dock, Liverpool (0151 478 4499). *Open daily 10.30–17.30, last admission 16.30. Closed as per City Museum.* Charge.
HMS Plymouth and HMS Onyx East Float, Dock Road, Birkenhead, Merseyside (0151 650 1573). Take the Mersey Ferry (see below) to Seacombe and then bus 1C (last return ferry 18.55). *Open 10.00–17.00 except Xmas Day & Box. Day.* Charge.

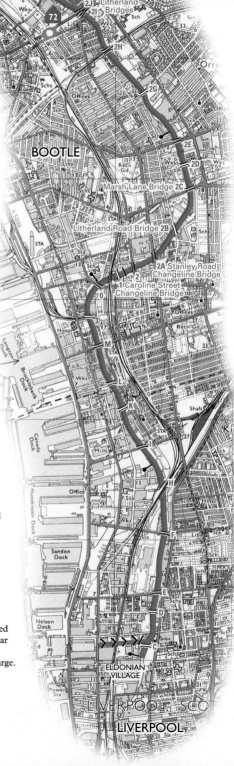

Lady Lever Art Gallery Port Sunlight Village, Bebington, Wirral (0151 645 3623). Close to Bebington railway station. Gallery shop and restaurant. *Open as per City Museum.* Free.

Liverpool Life Museum Albert Dock, Liverpool (0151 207 0001). *Open as per HM Customs & Excise Museum.* Charge.

Mersey Ferries The Pier Head Centre, George's Parade, Pier Head, Liverpool (0151 630 1030). Regular service (last ferry 19.15) across the Mersey operating *10.00–15.00 Mon–Fri and 10.00–18.00 Sat, Sun & B. Hols sailing on the hour* from Pier Head. Ticket includes stop off at Seacombe or Woodside.

Merseyside Maritime Museum Albert Dock, Liverpool (0151 207 0001). *Open as per HM Customs & Excise National Museum.* Charge. **Note:** The three members of the National Museums & Galleries on Merseyside, based on Albert Dock, share a joint ticket offering unlimited access and valid for one year.

Seacombe Aquarium Mersey Ferries Ltd, Victoria Place, Wallasey, Wirral (0151 630 1030). Take the Mersey Ferry to Seacombe (last return ferry 18.55). *Open 10.00–16.00 every day except Xmas Day, Box. Day & New Year's Day. Extended summer evening opening.* Charge.

Sudley Mossley Hill Road, Liverpool (0151 207 0001). Take the train to either Airburth or Mossley Hill stations. Victorian interior decoration and crafts-manship. *Open as per City Museum.* Free. Victorian tearooms *open Sat & B. Hols 10.00–16.30, Sun 12.00–16.30.*

Tate Gallery Albert Dock, Liverpool (0151 709 3223). *Open 10.00–18.00 Tue–Sun & B. Hol Mons. Closed Xmas Eve, Xmas Day & Box. Day.* Free to see collection; charge for touring exhibitions.

Walker Art Gallery William Brown Street, Liverpool (0151 207 0001). *Open as per City Museum.* Free.

Western Approaches 1 Rumford Street, Liverpool (0151 227 2008). Re-creation of the underground centre that orchestrated the Battle of the Atlantic during World War II. *Open daily (except Fri & Sun) 10.30–16.30. Closed Xmas Day & Box. Day.* Charge.

Pubs and Restaurants

There are many to be found here.

Maghull

North of Litherland the canal turns east to Aintree. Soon the first of many swing bridges is encountered; for the first few miles these bridges have to be padlocked to combat vandalism. All navigators should ensure that they have the requisite key before reaching these bridges (obtainable from the British Waterways offices at Wigan and Apperley Bridge). Aintree marks the limit of Liverpool's outskirts and here is of course the Aintree Race Course. At the east end of the racecourse is another swing bridge; this carries a main road and traffic lights are installed, but boat crews operate the bridge themselves. The canal turns north again and emerges into open countryside, although Maghull soon interrupts this with a series of swing bridges.

Pubs and Restaurants

Old Roan Netherton (0151 526 8422). Near Old Roan Bridge 7D. Boddingtons and Cains real ales are served in this most unusual establishment. An original canal pub with stables, it is now, internally, a most curious mixture of architectural styles. A vast array of old doors, haphazardly fixed to walls, vie with almost 100 different wallpapers and a variety of stucco finishes. Multiple TV screens juxtapose flashing neon signs reflecting off randomly exposed brickwork. A real magpie's nest with something for everyone. Sensibly priced bar food served *12.00–16.00 every day*. Disco *Wed*.

Horse & Jockey Aintree (0151 546 9406). Near bridge 9C. Bar food *lunchtimes, not Sat*. Live music *Fri–Sun nights*.

X Bootle Arms Rock Lane, Melling (0151 526 2886). Burtonwood and guest real ales. Food served *L & D* in large restaurant, *7 days a week*. Children's play area.

Hare & Hounds Maghull (0151 526 1168).

Near bridge 14. Tetley's real ale (including Imperial) and guest. Snacks *lunchtime*. Vegetarians and children catered for. Beer garden. Entertainment evenings and folk club *Tue* night.

Coach & Horses Maghull (0151 526 1093). On A567 east of the canal between bridges 15 & 16. Snacks and bar meals (*lunchtimes and evenings until 20.00, not Sun evening*). Cains, Stones and Greenalls real ales. Garden and children's play area. Quiz night *Wed*, Irish folk *Thur* night.

Running Horses Maghull (0151 526 3989). Canalside, at bridge 16. Tetley and Walkers real ales. Bar meals *lunchtimes and evenings (not Sun evening)*. Children and vegetarians catered for. Quiz *Tue*.

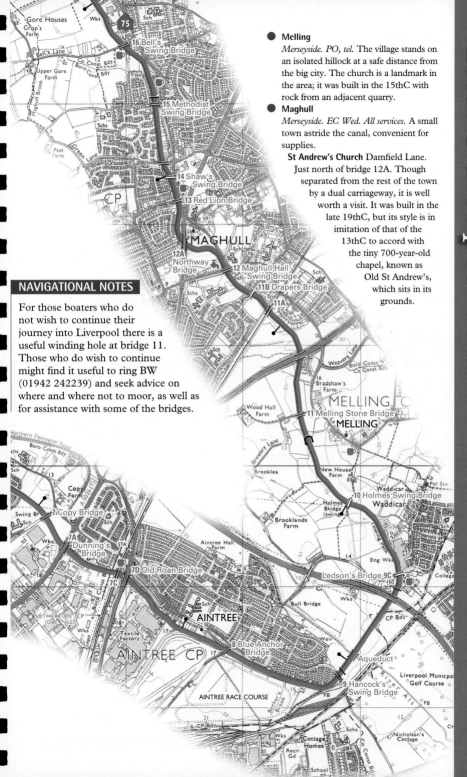

● **Melling**

Merseyside. PO, tel. The village stands on an isolated hillock at a safe distance from the big city. The church is a landmark in the area; it was built in the 15thC with rock from an adjacent quarry.

● **Maghull**

Merseyside. EC Wed. All services. A small town astride the canal, convenient for supplies.

St Andrew's Church Damfield Lane. Just north of bridge 12A. Though separated from the rest of the town by a dual carriageway, it is well worth a visit. It was built in the late 19thC, but its style is in imitation of that of the 13thC to accord with the tiny 700-year-old chapel, known as Old St Andrew's, which sits in its grounds.

NAVIGATIONAL NOTES

For those boaters who do not wish to continue their journey into Liverpool there is a useful winding hole at bridge 11. Those who do wish to continue might find it useful to ring BW (01942 242239) and seek advice on where and where not to moor, as well as for assistance with some of the bridges.

Haskayne

The canal now enters continuous open countryside, which soon establishes itself as extremely flat and intensively cultivated lowlands: indeed it is more akin to Cambridgeshire or Lincolnshire than to the rest of Lancashire. However, it is pleasant enough and the canal forms one of its more important features – a view which is borne out by the large number of people usually to be seen walking and boating upon it, as well as the hundreds of anglers enjoying their sport in this well-stocked length of canal. As if in compensation for the unexciting landscape, the traveller is offered a truly astonishing number (and variety) of pubs on or near the canal, all the way from Lydiate to Wigan. The digging of the canal is reputed to have commenced in the low cutting between bridges 24 and 25 which clearly provided an excellent source of stone for local bridges.

● **Haskayne**
Lancs. tel. There are just two pretty houses here: the old post office and a thatched cottage opposite. No sign of a church.

FERTILE RELIEF

This was once an area of low lying marshland, much of it below sea level and, consequently, thinly populated. The original course of the River Douglas ran close by, joining the sea near Southport. At some point its course was blocked – possibly by giant sand dunes thrown up by a great storm – and it found a new, northern mouth in the Ribble estuary, leaving behind the area known today as Martin Mere. This once extended to 15 square miles but in 1787 Thomas Eccleston of Scarisbrick Hall, with the help of John Gilbert, set about draining it for agricultural use (it was Gilbert who, as agent to the Duke of Bridgewater, enlisted James Brindley's help in constructing Britain's first major canal). Once drained the mere required vast quantities of manure to raise its fertility for crop production. 'Night soil' was shipped in along the canal from the large conurbations of Liverpool and Wigan and off-loaded at a series of small wharfs, some still visible today. Part of the mere remains undrained, a haven for migrating geese.

Pubs and Restaurants

🍺 **Scotch Piper** Lydiate (0151 526 0503). 500yds west of canal, access from bridge 19, left at A567 junction. A beautifully preserved award-winning pub with no bar, serving Burtonwood real ale straight from the barrel. Unchanged for fifty years, conversation and the chance to unwind in friendly surroundings, are the very real attractions of this traditional establishment.

🍺 ✕ **Scarisbrick Arms** Downholland (0151 526 1120). Canalside, at Downholland Bridge. An original estate-owned pub dating from 1899, now smartly adorned by a host of floral tubs and hanging baskets. Wide range of food from bar snacks to full à la carte restaurant menu served *L & D, 7 days a week and all day Sun.* Greenalls real ales. Children welcome. Patio.

🍺 **King's Arms** Haskayne (01704 840245). 100yds north of bridge 21A. Tetley's real ale and

a guest real ale served in this traditional, old fashioned village local. Snacks available *lunchtimes.* Beer garden, children welcome.

🍺 **Ship** Haskayne (01704 840572). Canalside, at Ship Bridge. A well-known canal pub with a garden and children's play area serving Tetley's (including Imperial) real ale. Excellent food available *7 days a week lunchtimes and evenings* served in a homely, dark-beamed bar tastefully decorated with horse brasses. Reputed to be the first pub on the canal which was started in the adjacent cutting. Quiz *Tue.*

🍺 ✕ **Saracen's Head** Halsall (01704 840204). Canalside, at Halsall Warehouse Bridge. Tetley's, Marston's and guest real ales together with a wide range of food served *L & D and all day Sun.* Children welcome and wide choice of vegetarian food. Regular barbecues *all year.* Pool and disco *Sat.* Full disabled facilities.

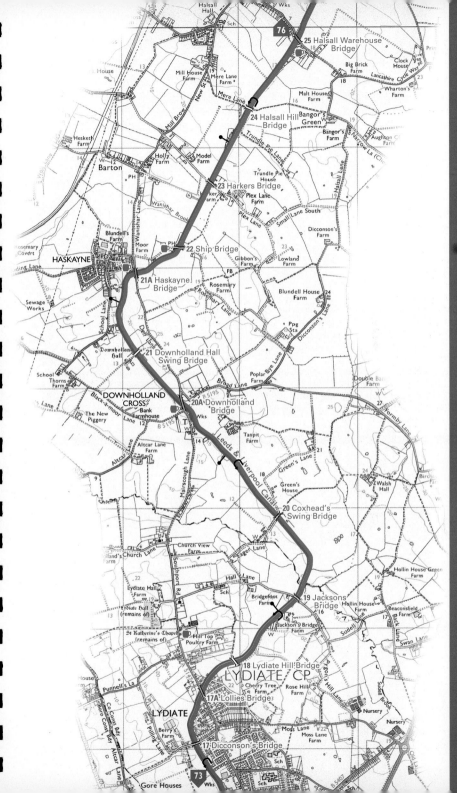

Burscough

One moves now past a massive caravan site on one side and attractive woods containing the private Scarisbrick Hall on the other; then out again into the open flatlands. An attractively produced information board, at the north end of bridge 27A, offers a fascinating insight into the history of the parish and the past habitation of the hall. The Southport–Manchester line converges from the north west; it runs near the canal all the way into Wigan, and has some wonderfully remote stations. A flurry of swing bridges bring the canal into Burscough: just beyond is the junction with the Rufford Branch.

● **Halsall**
Lancs. PO, tel, garage. 1/2 mile west of canal. There is a handsome tall 14th-15thC church here (St Cuthbert's), with a fine spire. The choir vestry, erected in 1592, was formerly a grammar school. There is an interesting pair of pulpits/lecterns. One of them is generously illuminated by a solitary overhead window; the other, more sheltered, gives the occupant the unfortunate air of being behind bars . . .

● **Burscough**
Lancs. PO, tel, stores, take-aways, garage, bank, station. Formerly a canal village and a staging post on the one-time Wigan–Liverpool 'packet boat' run, this place attaches more significance nowadays to the benefits of road and rail transport. It still boasts two stations (one is on the Preston–Liverpool line) and suffers from heavy through traffic. A very convenient place for taking on provisions.

Boatyards

Ⓑ **Red Lion Caravan Centre** Scarisbrick Bridge, Southport Road, Ormskirk (01704 840032). ♿ D E gas, groceries, large selection of spares and parts for caravans, many of which are 'boat compatible'.

Ⓑ **Lathom Marina** The Workshop, Crabtree Lane, Burscough (01704 894782). D winter storage, slipway, chandlery, boat and engine sales and repairs, salvage, canopy manufacture and repairs.

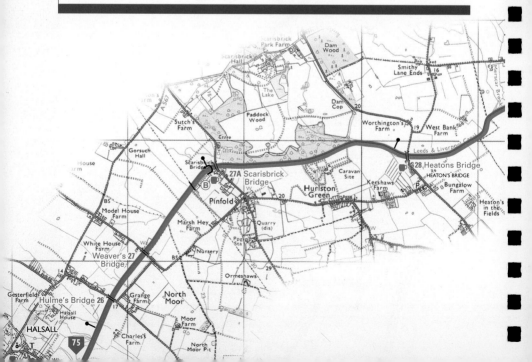

Pubs and Restaurants

🍺 ✕ **Red Lion** Scarisbrick (01704 840317). Near Scarisbrick Bridge No 27A. Newly refurbished in brewery chintz this pub serves Tetley's real ales and offers an extensive menu, including carvery, *lunchtimes and evenings (available from 17.00)*. Vegetarians and children catered for. Outdoor patio and play area.

🍺 **Heatons Bridge** Heatons Bridge (01704 840549). Friendly unspoilt canalside pub, at bridge 28. Tetley's (Imperial) and Walkers real ales together with inexpensive, traditional pub food served *lunchtimes, evenings and all day Sun*. This pub has been in the same family for over 180 years and their philosophic approach to their patrons is depicted by a plaque which reads: "All our visitors bring happiness – some by coming, some by going". Clairvoyant *Wed* nights. Garden and moorings.

🍺 ✕ **Martin Inn** near Burscough (01704 892302). 200yds north of bridge 29. An inn of coincidences: the present incumbent is the third landlord to be named John Mawdsley in exactly 100 years with only a distant relationship traced between Nos 2 & 3. Excellent Bass, Tetley's, Walkers, Boddingtons and guest real ales dispensed in a traditional, oak-beamed bar. A wide range of bar food and restaurant meals available *lunchtimes and evenings*. Children and vegetarians catered for. B & B.

🍺 ✕ **Farmers Arms** near Burscough (01704 892168). Canalside, by bridge 31. A bright, friendly pub of great character with an open fire, serving Tetley's real ales. Full à la carte menu together with a wide and interesting range of bar food *L & D 7 days* served in nicely furnished surroundings. Vegetarians and children catered for. Quiz night *Sun*. Good moorings.

🍺 **Lathom Slipway** Burscough (01704 893312). Canalside at bridge 32. Thwaites and guest real ales and an extensive range of food *lunchtimes and evening and all day Sat & Sun*. Children's menu and play area. Quiz night *Thur*. Good moorings.

🍺 **Admiral Lord Nelson** Burscough (01704 579888). Canalside bridge 32A. Boddingtons real ale.

🍺 **Royal Coaching House** Liverpool Road, Burscough (01704 893231). Boddingtons and Higsons real ales in a pub two minutes' walk from the canal. Wide range of interesting snacks and bar food *lunchtimes 7 days a week*. Children's menu. Quiz *Mon* and live music *Sat*.

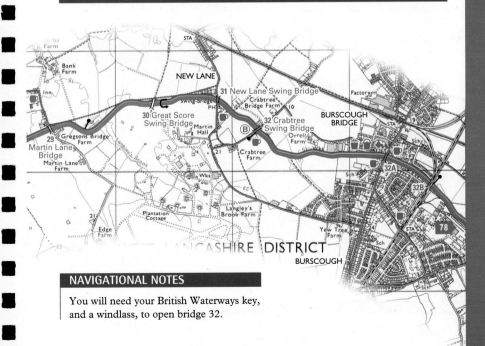

NAVIGATIONAL NOTES

You will need your British Waterways key, and a windlass, to open bridge 32.

Parbold and Rufford

The Rufford Branch leaves the Leeds & Liverpool main line just east of Burscough, through an imposing arched bridge dated 1816. A canal settlement, now a conservation area, surrounds the top lock and the roomy dry dock here (also showers and the usual facilities). The locks come thick and fast to begin with, as the canal falls through the fertile and gently sloping farmland towards the distant Ribble estuary. The country is generally quiet, flat and unspectacular. At times the busy A59 intrudes noisily. East of the junction with the Rufford Branch, the canal meanders through the flat countryside to the village of Parbold with its ancient sail-less windmill. Here the canal crosses the River Douglas and then joins the Douglas Valley, a pretty, narrow wooded valley which the canal shares with the railway. Appley Lock is reached: there are two locks alongside, now restored, and you can choose to use either these or the very deep main lock. The shallower locks were once used as a navigable sidepond for boats passing in opposite directions.

As with all subsequent locks, the gates should be closed and the paddles lowered and padlocked after use to combat vandalism and wastage of water.

NAVIGATIONAL NOTES

1 If you wish to make the diversion off the main line to visit Tarleton, please note that craft over 60ft will have difficulty turning at James Mayor's boatyard.
2 You will need your British Waterways key to open bridges 33 and 36.

● **Parbold**

Lancs. PO, tel, stores, butcher, take-away, garage, station. Parbold is prettiest near the canal bridge, where the brick tower of the old windmill is complemented by an equally attractive pub. Unfortunately the rest of the village is being engulfed by acres of new housing. Local landmarks are the tall spires of Parbold's two churches, and Ashurst's Beacon high on a hill to the south. The latter was built in 1798 by Sir William Ashurst in anticipation of an invasion by the French. (The beacon was intended as a local warning sign.)

● **Douglas Navigation**

The little River Douglas, or Asland, was made navigable in the first half of the 17thC, well before the great spate of canal construction. It provided the Wigan coalfield with a useful outlet to the tidal River Ribble, from which the cargoes could be shipped over to Preston or along the coast. When the Leeds & Liverpool Canal was built, the old river navigation became superfluous. The new company constructed their own branch to the Ribble estuary (the Rufford Branch). Between Parbold and Gathurst it is possible to find many traces of the old navigation, including several locks.

Pubs and Restaurants

🍺 **Ship Lathom** (01704 893117). Near second lock down, on Rufford Branch. An old canal pub formerly known as the 'Blood Tub' – black puddings were once made here, and a bucket of pig's blood could be exchanged for a pint of beer. Rightly described by CAMRA as 'the gem of the area' this establishment serves Moorhouse's and a range of Theakston real ales. There are also 5 changing guest beers. Busy, welcoming, comfortable with excellent bar food *lunchtimes only.*

🍺 **Ring O'Bells** Lathom (01704 893157). Canalside at bridge 34. Tastefully modernised country pub serving an interesting variety of bar meals (*lunchtimes, evenings and all day Sat & Sun*) along with Higsons, Boddingtons, Cains and guest real ales. Canalside tables, indoor and outdoor children's play areas. Quiz *Wed.*

🍺 **Railway Tavern** Hoscar Station (01704 892369). North east of bridge 35. Small country pub serving Tetley's and Jennings real ales and excellent food *lunchtimes and evenings (except Mon)*. Children's menu, beer garden, Quiz *Thur.* Pub games.

✕ **Rocking Horse Tearoom** Parbold (01257 462090). Canalside, bridge 37. *Open Tue–Sat*

10.00–17.00 & Sun 13.00–17.00. Traditional chintzy tearoom serving coffee, lunch and tea.

🍺 **Windmill** Parbold (01257 464130). Beside bridge 37. Old village local dispensing Greenalls, Theakston and Tetley's real ales, and an imaginative selection of meals *lunchtimes, evenings and all day Sun.* Outside seating and *Tue* quiz.

🍺✕ **Stocks Tavern** Alder Lane, Parbold (01257 462902). South of bridge 37. Fine traditional country pub, dating from 1810 and serving excellent meals *lunchtimes, evenings and all day Sun.* Tetley's and guest real ale. Children and vegetarians catered for.

✕♀ **Wayfarer Restaurant** 1 Alder Lane, Parbold (01257 462542). South of bridge 37. Dating back to before 1668 this cosy restaurant is *open Tue–Sun evenings and for Sunday lunches.* Full à la carte menu and live music *Thur & Fri.* Log fires in winter. B & B.

🍺 **Railway** Parbold (01257 462917). North of bridge 37. Typical village local. Burtonwood real ale and inexpensive meals and snacks *lunchtimes (and evenings by request)*. Children welcome and outside seating.

🍺✕ **Railway** Appley Bridge (01257 252112). Canalside beside bridge 42. Tetley's and guest real ale served together with food *lunchtimes, evenings and all day Sun* from predictable brewery menu. Vegetarians and children catered for. Canalside seating area.

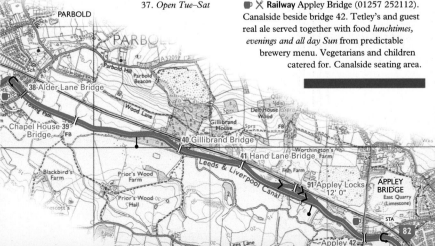

Tarleton

A line of trees and the spire of Rufford church are followed by the beautiful Rufford Old Hall, on the west bank. Then the waterway leads back out into open, flat and fairly featureless countryside, with the River Douglas never far away but initially out of sight. Beside bridge 10 there is an attractively landscaped picnic area. At Sollom there used to be a lock, but now it is no more. This is where the canal turns into the old course of the River Douglas, and it twists and turns as though to prove it. The towpath has been ploughed up from here onwards. The 'new' course of the Douglas (which was once navigable from the sea right up to Wigan) comes alongside the canal at the busy road bridge near Bank Hall, a house hidden by trees. From here it is only a short distance to the final swing bridge and Tarleton Lock, where the canal connects with the tidal River Douglas – which in turn flows into the River Ribble near Preston.

NAVIGATIONAL NOTES

1 Vessels wishing to enter or leave the Rufford Branch via Tarleton Lock can only do so at high water. The Douglas is then a relatively easy navigation, and since the removal of the old railway swing bridge a mile downstream, there has remained only one limitation on headroom from Tarleton to the open sea. This is a pipe bridge not far north of Tarleton Lock: the clearance at normal high water is about 20ft. The lock is operated by the boatyard which can be contacted for advice regarding tide times, etc . . .

2 Navigators entering the Rufford Branch canal from the sea should remember that they will need a padlock key – as well as a windlass – to open the locks up the branch. Both available from James Mayor's boatyard.

● **Rufford**
Lancs. PO, tel, stores, garage, station. Main road village noted for its Hall. The church is a small Italianate Victorian building containing many monuments to the Heskeths who owned Rufford Hall for several centuries; obviously a prolific family, judging by one large sculpture depicting a brood of 11 children, dated c1458. The family now resides in Northamptonshire.

Rufford Old Hall *NT property.* (01704 821254). On the west bank of the canal. A medieval timber-framed mansion with Jacobean extensions given to the National Trust in 1936. The interior is magnificently decorated and furnished in period style, especially the great hall with its hammerbeam roof and 15thC intricately carved movable screen – one of the few still intact in England. The Hall also houses a folk museum and an exhibition. Gardens and tearoom. *Open 13.00–17.00 Apr–Oct (closed Thur & Fri).* Charge. Note: although the Hall is beside the waterway, it is not possible to enter the grounds direct from the canal. Navigators should therefore tie up near bridge 8, then walk up to the village and turn left at the main road. The entrance is a few hundred yards along the wall on the left.

● **Tarleton**
Lancs. PO, tel, stores, garage, bank. A large village luckily avoided by the A59 road. There are some useful shops, and a good take-away pizzeria opposite the Cock & Bottle.

Boatyards

Ⓑ **James Mayor** The Boatyard, Tarleton, Preston (01772 812250). 🛁 ⚓ D E gas, overnight mooring, long-term mooring, winter storage, chandlery, five slipways up to 90ft, 3-ton crane, boats and engine sales, engine repairs, telephone, showers, toilets.

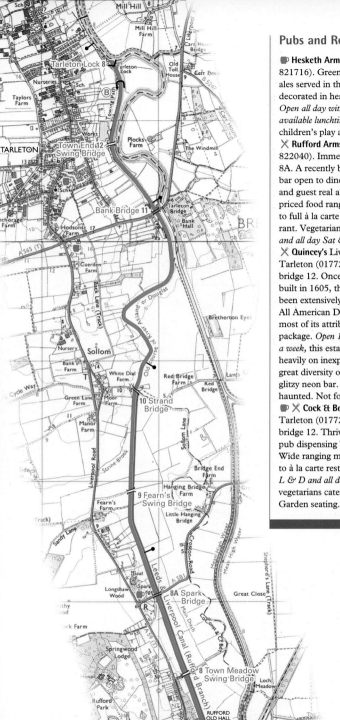

Pubs and Restaurants

Hesketh Arms Rufford (01704 821716). Greenalls and guest real ales served in this large village pub decorated in heavy brewery chintz. *Open all day with inexpensive food available lunchtimes.* Beer garden and children's play area. Quiz *Mon.*

Rufford Arms Rufford (01704 822040). Immediately west of bridge 8A. A recently built restaurant with a bar open to diners serving Burton and guest real ales. Reasonably priced food ranging from bar snacks to full à la carte meals in the restaurant. Vegetarian menu. *Open L & D and all day Sat & Sun.* B & B.

Quincey's Liverpool Road, Tarleton (01772 814528). West of bridge 12. Once the Ram's Head, built in 1605, this 'theme bar' has been extensively re-modelled on the All American Diner, incorporating most of its attributes in just one package. *Open 11.00–23.00, 7 days a week,* this establishment majors heavily on inexpensive food and a great diversity of cocktails served in a glitzy neon bar. Reputed to be haunted. Not for the faint-hearted!

Cock & Bottle Church Road, Tarleton (01772 812258). West of bridge 12. Thriving village-centre pub dispensing Thwaites real ale. Wide ranging menu from bar snacks to à la carte restaurant meals served *L & D and all day Sun.* Children and vegetarians catered for. Pool tables. Garden seating.

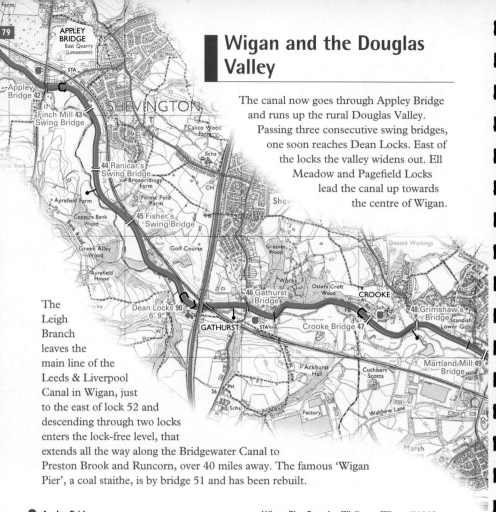

Wigan and the Douglas Valley

The canal now goes through Appley Bridge and runs up the rural Douglas Valley. Passing three consecutive swing bridges, one soon reaches Dean Locks. East of the locks the valley widens out. Ell Meadow and Pagefield Locks lead the canal up towards the centre of Wigan.

The Leigh Branch leaves the main line of the Leeds & Liverpool Canal in Wigan, just to the east of lock 52 and descending through two locks enters the lock-free level, that extends all the way along the Bridgewater Canal to Preston Brook and Runcorn, over 40 miles away. The famous 'Wigan Pier', a coal staithe, is by bridge 51 and has been rebuilt.

● **Appley Bridge**
Lancs. PO, tel, stores, station. Canalside hamlet.

● **Wigan**
Gt Manchester. MD Fri. All services. A large, heavily industrialised town whose skyline is now a mixture of industrial chimneys and towering concrete blocks of offices and flats. There is a new covered market hall in the traditional mould, and an Olympic-size swimming pool.
All Saints Church A very large and impressive parish church surrounded by beautiful rose gardens. There are several fine stained-glass windows, including a charming William Morris example depicting St Christopher.
History Shop Rodney Street, Wigan (01942 828128). Heritage Service project offering a display depicting the impact of coal on the area, exhibitions, genealogical research centre, shop and meeting room. *Open Mon 10.00–19.00; Tue–Fri 10.00–17.00 & Sat 10.00–13.00.*

Wigan Pier Complex Wallgate, Wigan (01942 322031). *All the attractions below are part of this complex and are open 10.00–17.00 Mon–Thur & 11.00–17.00 Sat & Sun. Closed Fri except G. Fri. Charge.*
The Way We Were A stunning exhibition/museum /theatre illustrating the lives of local people around the turn of the century.
Trencherfield Mill Probably the largest working mill engine in Europe, installed when the mill was built in 1907. Steamed *daily on the half hour.*
Waterbus Operates daily to transport visitors around the Wigan Pier Complex.
Pantry at the Pier Café, shops, restaurant, walks.
Waterways Gardens By Seven Stars Bridge. Boats, stonemason's blocks and a lock-keeper's garden.
Tourist Information Centre Trencherfield Mill (01942 825677).

Pubs and Restaurants

🍺 ✕ **Navigation** Gathurst (01257 252856). Canalside, at bridge 46. Tetley's and guest real ales. Food served *lunchtimes and evenings, and all day Sat & Sun.* Children's play area and canalside seating. Quiz *Thur.* Moorings.

🍺 ✕ **Crooke Hall Inn** Crooke, Wigan (01942 247524). Near bridge 47. Garden, mooring. Greenalls, Tetley's and guest real ales. Inexpensive food *lunchtimes and evenings except Tue.*

🍺 **Seven Stars Hotel** Wallgate, Wigan (01942 243126). Canalside. Thwaites real ale and food *lunchtimes Mon–Fri.* Children welcome, outside seating. Live music *Fri & Sat.*

🍺 **Royal Oak** Standish Lower Ground, Wigan (01942 512332). Burtonwood real ale and a wide variety of food *lunchtimes and evenings, 7 days a week.* Children welcome. Quiz *Tue* and live artists *Sat.*

🍺 **Swan & Railway** Wallgate, Wigan (01942 495032). Banks's real ales; food *lunchtimes Mon–Fri.* B & B.

🍺 **Orwell** Wigan (01942 323034). Large pub and restaurant in a warehouse opposite bridge 51. Tetley's, Samuel Smith's, Yates', house and guest real ales; bar meals (*12.00–14.00*). No smoking eating area and full disabled access. Tea and coffee. *Open 11.00–23.00 Mon–Sat & 11.00–17.00 Sun.*

NAVIGATIONAL NOTES

1 You will need your British Waterways key to open bridge 43.
2 The locks (Nos 85–1) between Wigan and Leeds are 60ft long and cannot accommodate a full-length narrow boat.
3 You will require a British Waterways handcuff key.

Boatyards

British Waterways Waterway Office at Wigan Bottom Lock (01942 242239). 🚽 ♿ Dry dock, keys, books and maps.

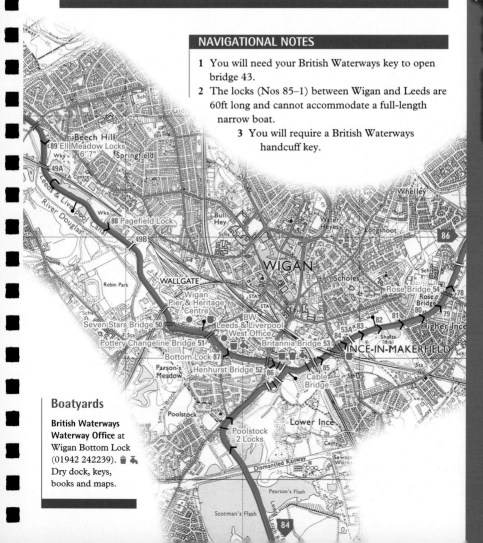

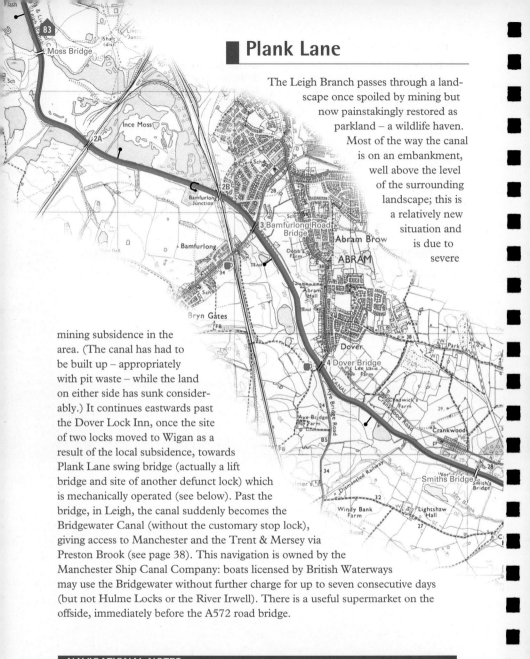

Plank Lane

The Leigh Branch passes through a landscape once spoiled by mining but now painstakingly restored as parkland – a wildlife haven. Most of the way the canal is on an embankment, well above the level of the surrounding landscape; this is a relatively new situation and is due to severe mining subsidence in the area. (The canal has had to be built up – appropriately with pit waste – while the land on either side has sunk considerably.) It continues eastwards past the Dover Lock Inn, once the site of two locks moved to Wigan as a result of the local subsidence, towards Plank Lane swing bridge (actually a lift bridge and site of another defunct lock) which is mechanically operated (see below). Past the bridge, in Leigh, the canal suddenly becomes the Bridgewater Canal (without the customary stop lock), giving access to Manchester and the Trent & Mersey via Preston Brook (see page 38). This navigation is owned by the Manchester Ship Canal Company: boats licensed by British Waterways may use the Bridgewater without further charge for up to seven consecutive days (but not Hulme Locks or the River Irwell). There is a useful supermarket on the offside, immediately before the A572 road bridge.

NAVIGATIONAL NOTES

Plank Lane swing bridge is *open summer: 08.00–18.00; Jun, Jul, Aug 08.00–20.00; winter: weekdays 08.00–16.30, weekends 10.00–14.00. Closed for lunch daily 12.00–12.45.* The bridge is operated by a bridge keeper. Contact British Waterways by ringing 01942 242239 to confirm times.

Pubs and Restaurants

🍺 **Bamfurlong Hotel** Lily Lane. 200yds south west of bridge no 3 on the Leigh Branch. Tetley's real ale. Pool. Fish and chips next door.

🍺 **Dover Lock Inn** Warrington Road, Abram (01942 866300). Canalside at Dover Bridge on the Leigh Branch. Greenalls real ale, food *L & D, 7 days a week* and children's play area in a modernised pub. There is a strong Italian influence on the excellent à la carte food served in the restaurant and bar. Garden seating.

🍺 **Nevison** Plank Lane, Leigh (01942 671394). 400yds from the swing bridge. A comfortable pub serving Tetley's and Walkers real ales. Snacks *on request*. Large beer garden,

children welcome. *Note: Winter afternoon drinkers take note of bridge operating times and moor appropriately!*

🍺 **Eagle & Hawk** Chapel Street, Leigh. Tetley's real ale and bar food *every lunchtime*. Children and vegetarians catered for. Outside seating area.

🍺 **Musketeer** Lord Street, Leigh (01942 701143). *Open all day* and serving bar meals *until 20.00.* Boddingtons and guest real ales.

🍺 **Red Brick Inn** Twist Lane, Leigh (01942 671698). A boater-friendly pub offering Hydes' and Tetley's real ales. Food available *lunchtimes and evenings until 20.00.* Children and vegetarians catered for. Outside seating. Quiz *Thur.* B & B.

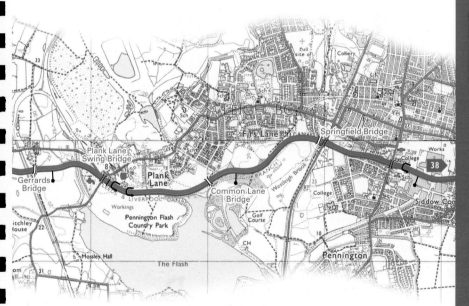

● **Leigh**
Gt Manchester. EC Wed. All services. Once the archetypal mill town, most of the tall buildings and chimneys have now been demolished. In the market place you can see the fine Edwardian baroque Town Hall, built 1904–7, facing the battlemented church of St Mary. This church was originally built in 1516 but was extensively rebuilt in the late 19thC and is the burial place of Thomas Tyldesley, killed at the battle of Wigan Lane.

Pennington Flash Country Park St Helen's Road, Leigh (01942 605253). 1100 acre park centred on the flash or lake. Walks, birdwatching, sailing, fishing, golf, picnic areas and information centre. *Open daily.*

Three Sisters Recreation Area Bryn Road, Ashton-in-Makerfield (01942 720453). Site of the 'Wigan Alps': 3 colliery spoil tips now landscaped to provide an international karting circuit (01942 270230), racing circuit, boating lake, picnic area and visitor centre. Ring for details.

Turnpike Gallery Turnpike Centre, Leigh (01942 679407). Home to major touring arts exhibitions.

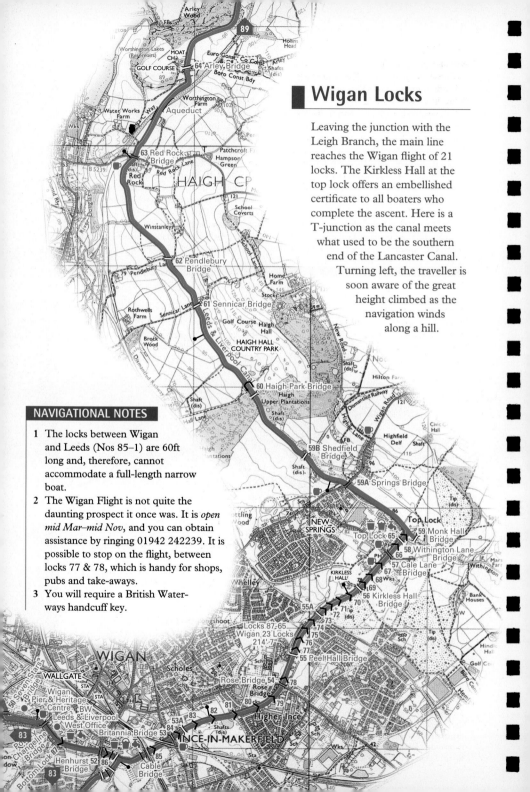

Wigan Locks

Leaving the junction with the Leigh Branch, the main line reaches the Wigan flight of 21 locks. The Kirkless Hall at the top lock offers an embellished certificate to all boaters who complete the ascent. Here is a T-junction as the canal meets what used to be the southern end of the Lancaster Canal. Turning left, the traveller is soon aware of the great height climbed as the navigation winds along a hill.

NAVIGATIONAL NOTES

1 The locks between Wigan and Leeds (Nos 85–1) are 60ft long and, therefore, cannot accommodate a full-length narrow boat.

2 The Wigan Flight is not quite the daunting prospect it once was. It is *open mid Mar–mid Nov*, and you can obtain assistance by ringing 01942 242239. It is possible to stop on the flight, between locks 77 & 78, which is handy for shops, pubs and take-aways.

3 You will require a British Waterways handcuff key.

● **New Springs**

Gt Manchester. A suburb of Wigan. Once an industrial hub with collieries and iron works lining the canal as it struggled up the 21 locks to the summit. The acres of partially land-scaped waste ground today belie the past activity of Rose Bridge Colliery (near bridge 54) and Ince Hall Coal and Cannel Company higher up. (Cannel is a dull coal that burns with a smoky, luminous flame.) Hardest of all to imagine is the massive operation of Wigan Coal and Iron Co. who, at the turn of the century, employed 10,000 people at their works beside the top 9 locks of the flight. Then one of the largest ironworks in the country, it mined 2 million tons of coal to produce 125,000 tons of iron annually. The skyline here was dominated by 10 blast furnaces, 675 coking ovens and a 339 feet high chimney. It must have been a splendid sight on the night skyline, viewed from the streets of Wigan.

Haigh Hall Wigan (01942 832895). On east bank of the canal. The pre-Tudor mansion was rebuilt by its owner, the 23rd Earl of Crawford, between 1830 and 1849. The reconstruction was designed and directed by the Earl, and all the stone, timber and iron used on the job came from the estate. The Hall is now owned by Wigan Corporation, who allow the citizens to use it for private wedding receptions, etc. There is little to see in the house and it is not normally open to the public. The park and grounds around the hall are *open daily all year, except Xmas Day, Boxing Day & New Year's day* and contain much that caters for the family: there are children's amusements, gardens and woodlands, a nature trail and selection of waymarked walks, miniature rail-way, a model village, crazy golf course, shop and cafeteria. Entry to the park is free but there is a charge for the amusements which are *open May–Sep.* Audio trail for the blind and partially sighted using a braille map and tape player.

Stables Centre Haigh Country Park, Wigan (01942 832895). Daily art and craft workshops for groups and individuals. 'Hands On' creativity – painting, batik, stencilling, clay, canal art – for adults and children. *Available Mon–Fri 10.30–12.00 & 13.30–15.00. Weekends by arrangement.* Charge.

Pubs and Restaurants

 Shepherds Arms Wigan (01942 243925). Canalside at bridge 53. *For rest and recupera-tion, there are shops and other pubs near bridge 53 together with a wholesale pie shop (minimum quantity one dozen) – sufficient to sustain the crew to the top of the flight!*

 Commercial Inn New Springs, Wigan (01942 238856). Canalside, at bridge 57. A sturdy pub dispensing Tetley's real ales and bar snacks *on request.* Outside seating and karaoke *Sun.* Payphone.

 Kirkless Hall New Springs, Wigan (01942 242821). Canalside, near Wigan Top Lock. Distinctive black and white building housing spacious and comfortable bars. Burtonwood and Forshaw's real ales and excellent bar meals *lunchtimes and evenings.* Vegetarians and children catered for. Canalside patio. Bingo *Thur* and live entertainment *Sat.*

 Crown Hotel New Spring, Wigan (01942 242539). West of bridge 59A. Burtonwood real ale, meals *lunchtimes,* garden. Entertainment *Thur–Sun evenings.*

 Colliers Arms New Springs, Wigan (01942 831171). Above bridge 59A. Small, friendly local for the nostalgic beer drinker. Burtonwood real ale in a charming old listed pub overlooking the canal.

 Crawford Arms Red Rock Lane, Haigh (01257 421313). *Open all day from 12.00,* serving inexpensive bar food *every day until 20.00.* Temporary jail to a 17thC murderer, this pub now dispenses Greenhalls real ale rather than justice. Children and vegetarians catered for, outside seating. Music quiz *Tue,* general knowledge quiz *Thur* and live Irish music *Fri. 48 hr* mooring outside.

Adlington

The canal continues to run as a 9-mile lock-free pound – known as the 'Lancaster Pool' – along the side of the valley from which the industries surrounding Wigan can be viewed in the distance. It enjoys a pleasant and quiet isolation in this lightly wooded area. Already the navigation is well over 300ft above the sea, and the bleak hills up to the east give a hint of the Pennines that are soon to be crossed. The conspicuous tower east of Adlington stands on a hill that is over 1500ft high. Wandering northwards, beyond the village, the waterway remains hemmed in for much of the way by woodland and is undisturbed by the railway and main roads that for a while follow it closely. Soon the greenery gives way to views of Chorley's rows of rooftops across the valley. The canal crosses this valley, but shuns the town. There is a slipway just to the north of Cowling Bridge 75A, on the towpath side.

Pubs and Restaurants

🍺 **Shepherd's Arms** Eaves Lane, Chorley (01257 275659). Near bridge 66. A pub renowned for its mild, serving Matthew Brown, Theakston and Younger real ales. Recently renovated, substantial local with a betting shop behind.

🍺 ✗ **Waggon & Horses** Chorley (01257 480767). East of bridge 68. Good value, home-cooked food available *all day, 7 days a week (except 14.00–17.00 Sat),* served until 20.00 (19.30 Sat). Dating from 1818, this busy pub dispenses Boddingtons, Castle Eden, Flowers, and Whitbread real ale and offers live entertainment *on Sat* and a Quiz *on Tue.* Children and vegetarians catered for. Outside seating.

🍺 **White Bear** Market Street, Chorley (01257 482357) East of bridge 69. An old roadside pub serving Theakston, McEwan and guest real ales. Inexpensive bar food available *lunchtimes and evenings 7 days a week except Mon evening.* Children and vegetarians catered for. Garden and play area. B & B.

🍺 **Cardwell Arms** Chorley Road, Adlington (01257 482357). East of bridge 71. Vaux, Ward and guest real ales in a boisterous (*at weekends*) pub. Garden and outside play area. Food available *weekends all day until 19.00. Sun* disco and jackpot.

🍺 ✗ **White Horse** Heath Charnock (01257 481766). East of bridge 71, top of Rawlinson Lane. Smart, welcoming pub serving Flowers, Boddingtons and guest real ales. Reasonably priced food *lunchtimes and Fri evening and all day Sat and Sun (no food after 19.00 Sun).* Children and vegetarians catered for. Patio, pool and pub games. Quiz *Tue.*

🍺 **Hop Pocket** Carr Lane, Chorley (01257 275597). West of bridge 75. Thwaites real ale in a modern estate pub offering entertainment or a quiz *every night except Wed.* Bar food *available every lunchtime except Sat.* Children welcome. Garden and outside seating area.

Boatyards

Ⓑ **White Bear Marina** Park Road, Adlington, Chorley (01257 481054). 🚽 ⛽ 🛥 D E Pump-out, slipway, gas, narrow boat hire, overnight mooring, long-term mooring, winter storage, boat building and fit out, boat and engine sales and repairs, showers, toilets, chandlery (mail order), books, gifts and maps, cafe, telephone.

Ⓑ **L & L Cruisers** Rawlinson Lane, Heath Charnock, Chorley (01257 480825). 🛥 D Pump-out, gas, narrow boat hire, day hire craft, overnight mooring, slipway, chandlery, books and maps, boat building, engine sales and repairs, gift shop, ice-cream, toilets.

● **Adlington**
Gt Manchester. PO, tel, stores, garage, station. A small industrialised town very useful for pubs and supplies – the local licensed store east of bridge 69 is *open late most evenings* and there is a park nearby.

● **Chorley**
Lancs. EC Wed. MD Mon, Tue, Thur, Fri, Sat. All services. On the west bank of the canal, a busy town based on the manufacture of textiles and spare parts for commercial and public service vehicles. (Leyland, where the vehicles are built, is just a few miles away to the north west.) Chorley has avoided too much industrial grimness by maintaining its market-town traditions and by extensive new housing development. Today there are two major markets: the 'Flat-Iron' Market, dating from 1498, *held on Tue* and the Covered Market *held on Tue, Thur, Fri and Sat.* A collectors market is also *held on Mon.* Sir Henry Tate, the founder of the Tate Gallery in London, was born in Chorley in 1819 and began his career here as a grocer's assistant.

St Laurence's Church Church Brow. Surrounded by trees in the centre of the town, parts of the church date back to the 14thC. The bones that are enshrined in a recess in the chancel are believed to have belonged to St Laurence and to have been brought back from Normandy.

Astley Hall Astley Park, Chorley (01257 262166). At the north-west end of the town just over a mile from Botany Bridge 78A. Set in 105 acres of wooded parkland beside an ornamental lake, the appearance of this Elizabethan mansion is very striking, for in the 17thC the existing timber framing was replaced by a new facade that is lacking in symmetry. The interior – more home than museum piece – is very fine with splendid restoration ceilings, furnishings, tapestries and pottery. *Open daily Apr–Oct 12.00–17.00, closed Mon except B. Hols; Nov–Mar 12.00–16.00, Fri, Sat & Sun.* Charge.

Tourist Information Centre
Charnock Richard Motorway Services, Chorley (01257 793773).

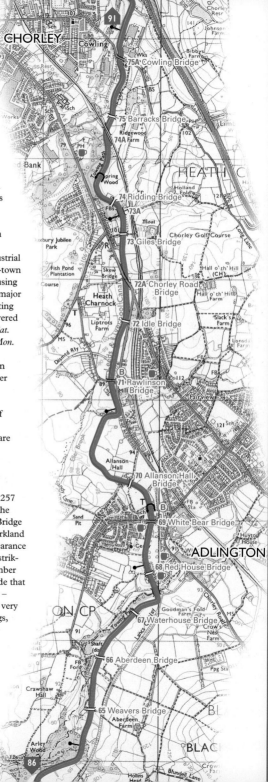

Withnell Fold

The canal side-steps the town to the east passing instead some large and resplendent outlying textile mills. The M61 motorway zooms up from Manchester around the mills and over the navigation before disappearing in the direction of Preston in a flurry of flyovers, slip roads, noise and roundabouts. There is a slipway just to the north of the M61 bridge, on the off-side. Now the boater enters a most delightful stretch of waterway. The junction with the old Walton Summit Branch features a canal cottage and the bottom lock in the Johnson's Hill flight. A short but energetic spell of windlass-wielding is required here, for the seven locks are very close together. It is rewarding work, for the steep countryside yields good views, and the locks are tidily maintained and painted. Near the middle lock is an old toll house and a telephone, while at the top lock there is a pub and, usually, a medley of boats (there is a boat club here). The canal now changes course to north east and flows along a beautifully secluded and often wooded valley at a height of over 350ft above sea level. Even the old paper mills at Withnell Fold, which once brought a glimpse of industry, have been converted into small, discreet, industrial units. There is an excellent nature reserve developed in the old filter beds and sludge lagoons opposite which, derelict for many years, gradually infilled with silt and reedswamp to provide natural plant and animal habitats.

Pubs and Restaurants

🍺 **Malt 'n' Hops** Friday Street, Chorley (01257 260967). Near the railway station. Webster's, Wilson's and Boddingtons real ales together with up to 5 guests dispensed in the congenial surroundings of this displaced antique dealer's!

🍺 **White Bull** Market Street, Chorley (01257 275300). Matthew Brown, Theakston and guest real ales served in attractively panelled, town pub. *Open all day*, food available *lunchtimes*. Pub games.

🍺 ✕ **Railway** Canalside at bridge 78A. (01257 279410). Modernised pub and restaurant (à la carte and bar meals *available all day, 7 days a week)* serving Boddingtons and Castle Eden real ales. The railway line has long since disappeared – the viaduct was blown up to make room for the motorway.

✕ 🍺 **Red Cat** Blackburn Road, Whittle (01257 263966). Wide ranging, inexpensive Italian menu served *lunchtimes, evenings and all day Sun* in pleasant surroundings in this listed building. Children's menu and play area. Patio, and live music *Thur*.

🍺 **Top Lock** Heapey (01257 263376). Canalside at Johnson's Hill Top Lock. Bar food available *lunchtimes and evenings except Sun evening*. Moor below the top lock – there is no room above.

🍺 ✕ **Dressers Arms** Briers Brow, Wheelton (01254 830041). 3/4 mile east of bridge 82. A superb pub with an excellent Cantonese restaurant upstairs (*open 18.00–00.00 except Mon)* and a fine choice of value for money, home-made food at the bar, *lunchtimes, evenings and all day Sun*. Timothy Taylors, Boddingtons, Marston's, Flowers, and 2 guest real ales, together with their own Dressers Special, are dispensed in the unpretentious, traditional bar: the amalgamation of the original tiny beer house and neighbouring cottages. Garden seating.

🍺 **Golden Lion** Blackburn Road, Higher Wheelton (01254 830855). A pleasant walk up the footpath south of bridge 86. Thwaites real ales in a small, welcoming main road pub. Extensive bar menu served *lunchtimes, evenings and all day Fri–Sun*. Patio seating back and front. Quiz *Thur*.

Boatyards

ⓑ **Top Lock Narrowboat Hire** Wheelton Top Lock, Wheelton (01704 213909). Single narrow boat for private hire.

ⓑ **Top Lock Narrowboats** Wheelton Top Lock, Wheelton (01257 241871). Fitting out service, storage, slipway, crane, boat sales, chandlery.

ⓑ **Wheelton Marine Services** Wheelton Top Lock, Wheelton (0973 753913/01772 311983). E Pump-out, long term mooring, slipway, winter storage, boat sales and repairs, engine repairs, *24hr* emergency breakdown service.

BOAT TRIPS
Royal Sovereign is a charter and trip boat operating from Botany Bay, Chorley (north of bridge 78A). Ring 01257 273269 for further details.

● **Wheelton**
Lancs. PO, tel, stores, laundrette, garage. The village is best accessed by walking east from bridge 82. Fish and chip shop *closed Sun, Mon & Thur.*

● **Walton Summit Branch**
The short branch used to be part of the Lancaster Canal, originally projected to run south from Preston to the Bridgewater Canal. The Lancaster Canal Company, after arranging with the Leeds & Liverpool Company to share a common course between Johnson's Hill Locks and Wigan Top Lock, was daunted by the prospect of constructing an expensive aqueduct over the River Ribble in Preston. A 'temporary' tramroad was built to connect the two lengths of canal between Preston and Walton Summit. The tramway, which opened in 1803, featured a short tunnel and a light trestle bridge over the Ribble. The tramroad was never replaced by a canal; indeed the whole line was closed by 1880. Most of the canal branch has recently been severed by the building of a motorway, although plenty of it still remains in an unnavigable state.
Botany Bay Villages, Botany Bay, Chorley (01257 273269). Canalside near bridge 78A. Themed shopping centre in a converted mill together with a collection of old fire engines and firefighting equipment. Charge.

● **Withnell Fold**
Lancs. A remarkable, small estate village, built to house workers at the canalside paper mills which are now demolished. Grouped around three sides of a spacious square, the terraced cottages present an intimately united front which is almost unnerving to the casual visitor – especially as on the fourth side of the square is an old set of wooden stocks.

Blackburn

Passing under the new M65 extension the canal curls round a steep and thickly wooded valley, crossing it on a high embankment before entering the outskirts of Blackburn. Close to bridge 95 the delightfully named suburb of Cherry Tree provides an excellent range of shops and take-aways. There is also a useful shop at bridge 94. It seems to take a long time to get through this large town, as there is a flight of six locks here, raising the canal's level to a height of over 400ft above sea level. The lock keeper maintains a tidy flight – indeed most of the passage through the city is now pleasant – there is little rubbish or graffiti, and the views are excellent. A good towpath exists throughout.

● **Blackburn**
Lancs. MD Wed, Fri, Sat. All services. Few of the Pennine towns which sprang up with the Industrial Revolution can be described as beautiful. In an attempt to rectify this, Blackburn has taken drastic steps in recent years to construct a new city centre. Nevertheless the most impressive features of the town are still the old cotton mills.
Blackburn Cathedral (01254 51491). Dating from 1820–6, the parish church was raised to cathedral status in 1926. Extensive renovations have been made inside. Very striking 13ft sculpture of 'Christ the Worker' in aluminium and black iron by John Hayward. Large churchyard.
Eanam Wharf Visitor Centre Eanam Wharf, Blackburn (01254 56557). Original canal depot now portraying a history of the navigation. Gift shop. Disabled access. *Open Mon–Fri 10.00–16.00 & Easter–Sep B. Hols and selected weekends.* Free.

King George's Hall Northgate, Blackburn (01254 582582). Entertainment complex promoting a wide-ranging programme of music and theatre. Charge.
Museum & Art Gallery Library Street, Blackburn (01254 667130). Exhibits include natural history, pottery, early manuscripts and a large collection of English, Greek and Roman coins. In the art gallery are over 1200 beautiful Japanese prints, as well as English watercolours of the 18thC–20thC. Also incorporated is the Lewis Textile Museum: a series of period rooms demonstrating the development of the textile industry from the 18thC by means of full-size working models, including Hargreaves' 'Spinning Jenny'. *Open Tue–Fri 12.00–16.45 & Sat 09.45–16.45; closed B. Hols.* Free.
Waves Waterfun Centre Blackburn (01254 51111). The city's own tropical paradise. Cafeteria. Full disabled access. Technical tours. Charge.

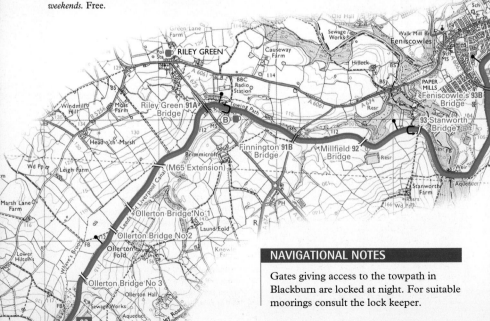

NAVIGATIONAL NOTES

Gates giving access to the towpath in Blackburn are locked at night. For suitable moorings consult the lock keeper.

Witton park (01254 55423). Nearly 500 acres of magnificent parkland, including the beautiful landmark, Billinge Hill. Tree and nature trails; wayfaring course; picnic sites and children's play area. Park *always open*. **The Visitor Centre** is *open Mon–Sat 13.00–17.00, Sun & B. Hol Mon 11.00–17.00 Apr–Sep; Thur–Sat 13.00–17.00, Sun 11.00–17.00 Oct–Mar.* Restored stables and coach house, displays of old tools, carriages and horse-drawn farm machinery. The centre has a natural history room and a British small mammal collection. Free.

Tourist Information Centre King George's Hall, Northgate, Blackburn (01254 53277). **Hoghton Tower** Hoghton, Nr Blackburn (01254 852986). Past the Royal Oak at bridge 91A. So enjoyable was a joint of beef that James I knighted the remains 'Sir Loin'. More recently this 16thC fortified hilltop mansion is visited for its dungeons, antique dolls, historic documents and picturesque gardens, as well as for the magnificent banqueting hall. *Open Sun & B. Hols, Easter– Oct. Also Tue–Thur in Jul & Aug.* Charge.

Boatyards

ⓑ **North West Narrowboats** Finningtons Marina, Bolton Road, Riley Green, Hoghton, Nr. Preston (01254 207044). 🚽 ⚓ Gas, overnight and long term mooring, slipway, boat building and fitting out, 'Boatman' solid fuel stoves manufactured on site, boat sales, telephone, toilets, showers, laundry, books, maps, gifts.

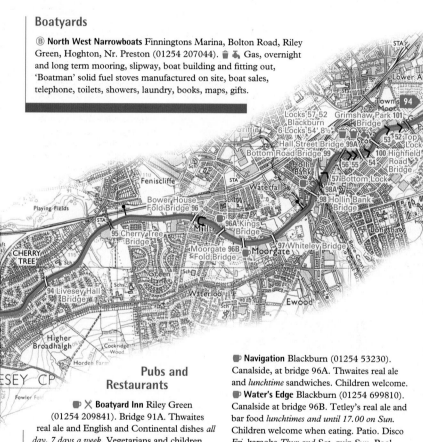

Pubs and Restaurants

🍺 ✕ **Boatyard Inn** Riley Green (01254 209841). Bridge 91A. Thwaites real ale and English and Continental dishes *all day, 7 days a week*. Vegetarians and children catered for. Terraces, games room, quiz *Sun*. Overnight mooring for customers.

🍺 **Royal Oak** Preston Old Road, Riley Green (01254 201445). North of bridge 91A. Oak-beamed pub (dating from 1620) serving Thwaites real ale. Meals and snacks with vegetarian options *lunchtimes and evenings 7 days a week*. Three open fires, no electronic games. Children welcome. Outside seating.

🍺 **Navigation** Blackburn (01254 53230). Canalside, at bridge 96A. Thwaites real ale and *lunchtime* sandwiches. Children welcome.

🍺 **Water's Edge** Blackburn (01254 699810). Canalside at bridge 96B. Tetley's real ale and bar food *lunchtimes and until 17.00 on Sun*. Children welcome when eating. Patio. Disco *Fri*, karaoke *Thur and Sat*, quiz *Sun*. Pool.

🍺 **Moorings** Blackburn (01254 664472). By bridge 99. Food served *all day*. Eight real ales. Children welcome *until 20.00*. Patio.

✕ 🍺 **Blakeys Café Bar** King George's Hall, Northgate, Blackburn (01254 667021). Café serving coffee *from 09.00–16.30* and meals and snacks *from 09.00–15.30*. Boddingtons and guest real ales available *until 16.30 during the week and evenings Thur–Sat*.

Rishton

Of particular interest to those on the canal are the fine canopied wharves of the Depot at Eanam Wharf, now converted into a business centre with a pub and visitor centre incorporated. The canal leaves Blackburn and embarks upon a course of twists and turns that emphasise the hilliness of the countryside. The scenery varies all the time between heavy industrial development (and its effects) and – just around a corner – green fields, farms and distant views of wild moorlands. The Calder Valley motorway (M65) follows the line of the canal to Burnley. Of interest is the fine wharf building with a large central arch at Simpson's Bridge, now in a serious state of dereliction. Beyond Church, the first of four swing bridges appears (no. 113 requires a handcuff key and a windlass): they are the only ones between Wigan and Gargrave.

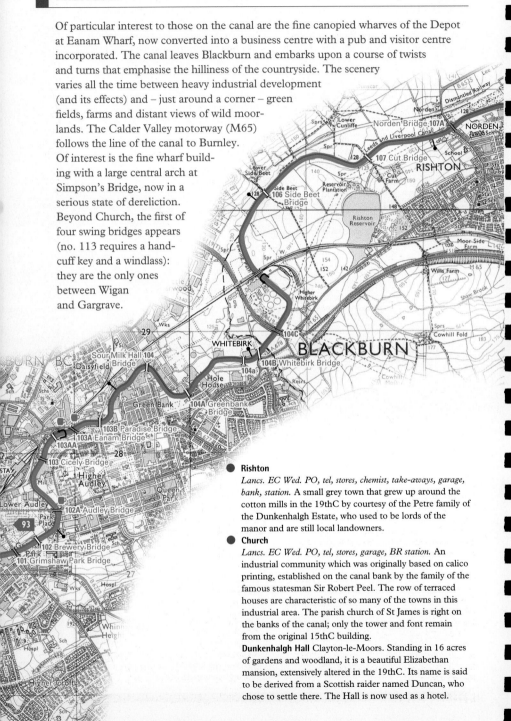

● **Rishton**
Lancs. EC Wed. PO, tel, stores, chemist, take-aways, garage, bank, station. A small grey town that grew up around the cotton mills in the 19thC by courtesy of the Petre family of the Dunkenhalgh Estate, who used to be lords of the manor and are still local landowners.

● **Church**
Lancs. EC Wed. PO, tel, stores, garage, BR station. An industrial community which was originally based on calico printing, established on the canal bank by the family of the famous statesman Sir Robert Peel. The row of terraced houses are characteristic of so many of the towns in this industrial area. The parish church of St James is right on the banks of the canal; only the tower and font remain from the original 15thC building.

Dunkenhalgh Hall Clayton-le-Moors. Standing in 16 acres of gardens and woodland, it is a beautiful Elizabethan mansion, extensively altered in the 19thC. Its name is said to be derived from a Scottish raider named Duncan, who chose to settle there. The Hall is now used as a hotel.

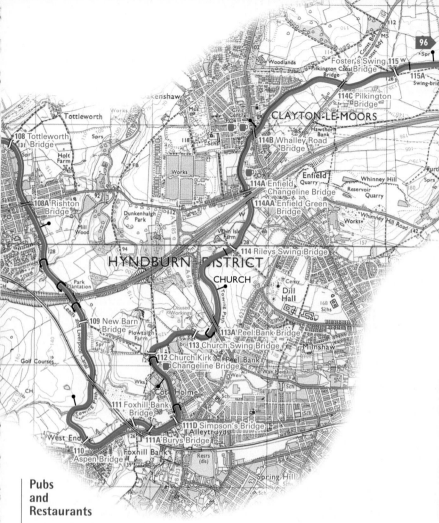

Pubs and Restaurants

Barge Inn Blackburn.
By bridge 102A. New pub with canal theme serving Thwaites real ale.

Wharf Eanam, Blackburn (01254 661029) A lively, young-persons pub, part of Eanam Wharf redevelopment. Boddingtons, Tetley's and Theakston real ales, food available *lunchtimes*. Discos *Thur–Sun evenings.*

Roebuck Rishton (01254 884500). Near bridge 108A. Theakston and guest real ales, and food *available lunchtimes Mon–Sat and all day Sun. Evening meals available on request.* Dark panelled walls, brasses and attractive pictures ensure a congenial atmosphere in this 300 year old pub which is *open all day.* Vegetarians and children catered for. Outside seating and Quiz *Thur. Weekend* live music.

Thorn Inn Church (01254 237827). East of bridge 112, behind the church. Cosy, welcoming old pub dispensing Thwaites real ale. Inexpensive bar meals and snacks *available lunchtimes (except Sat).* Traditional Sunday roasts and children's menu. Beer garden.

Hare & Hounds Whalley Road, Clayton-le-Moors (01254 233712). 250yds east of bridge 114A. Thwaites real ale and bar meals *lunchtimes and evenings, 7 days a week.* Children welcome. Garden and B & B. *Shops and take-aways nearby.*

Old England Forever Church Street, Clayton-le-Moors (01254 233435). Burtonwood real ale and sandwiches available *lunchtimes.*

Wellington Barnes Square, Clayton-le-Moors (01254 235762). Thwaites real ale. *Fri disco. Both the above are 250yds west of bridge 114B.*

Hapton

The navigation continues to wind eastwards along the side of what turns out to be the Calder Valley with the M65 motorway to the south. High ground rises on each side of the valley, and in the distance the summit of Pendle Hill (1831ft high) can be clearly seen when it is not obscured by cloud. This is an attractive length of canal, unspoilt by industry and greatly enhanced by the ever-changing views from the side of the hill along which the canal is cut, although the motorway is uncomfortably close throughout. Soon the distant mass of dwellings is recognisable as the suburbs of Burnley and the canal ducks through Gannow Tunnel (559yds long) to swing sharply over the M65.

● **Hapton**
Lancs. PO, tel, stores, station. A small and unmistakably northern town, with its regular streets of terraced houses.

Pubs and Restaurants

● **Bridge House** Hapton (01282 227473). Beside bridge 121. Thwaites real ale and bar snacks *available 12.00–20.00.* Children and vegetarians catered for. Beer garden and *Sat* entertainment.
● **Railway** Hapton (01282 779317). Along the road from the Bridge House. *Lunchtime* snacks.
● **Gannow Wharf** Gannow Lane, Burnley (01282 421908). Canalside at bridge 127A.

Boddingtons and Theakston real ales and bar food *lunchtimes and evenings.* Quiz *Wed* and live music *Fri and Sat.*
● **Mitre Hotel** 118 Westgate, Burnley (01282 423632). By bridge 129B. Worthington real ale and snacks *lunchtimes.* Live music *Wed* and disco *Mon and Thur.* B & B.

*Moorings on the
Leeds & Liverpool
Canal*

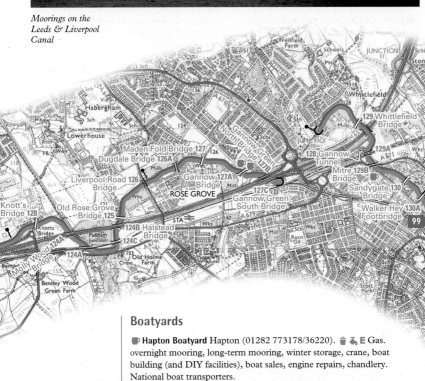

Boatyards

🛥 **Hapton Boatyard** Hapton (01282 773178/36220). 🚮 🔧 **E** Gas.
overnight mooring, long-term mooring, winter storage, crane, boat
building (and DIY facilities), boat sales, engine repairs, chandlery.
National boat transporters.

Burnley

This is an industrial stretch where the canal was once a main artery for the town and its industries. The area around bridge 130 known as the Weavers' Triangle has been recognised to be of great interest – fine warehouses, tall chimneys and loading bays flank the canal here. There is a museum in the Toll House, and a steam mill engine has been restored. The huge Burnley Embankment carries the navigation across part of the town – called 'the straight mile' it is $^3/_4$ mile long, but no less dramatic for that fact; 60ft high, it incorporates an aqueduct over a main road. The whole area of the embankment has been tidied up and the towpath opened and improved: access is now good and this, together with the British Waterways yard, makes a good mooring site. Shops are within easy reach and the attractive Thompsons Park (good play area and boating lake) can be found north of the aqueduct after bridge 130H. There is also a useful supermarket with footpath access south of bridge 130H. Now the canal negotiates a landscape which alternates between open country, towns and semi-towns, with the massive distant bulk of Pendle Hill in the background. Cobbled streets of terraced houses run down to the canal and old wharves, some disused and overgrown, are under renovation for offices and housing. There is excellent mooring immediately south of bridge 140 on the offside together with an attractive children's play ground opposite.

● **Burnley**
Lancs. All services. A large industrial northern town, which has worked hard to improve its appearance. It was once the world centre for cotton weaving. The excellent shopping centre is only 10 minutes' walk from Finsley Gate Bridge, and if you feel like a swim, a sauna or a solarium, the Thompson Recreation Centre is even closer.
Queen Street Mill Museum Harle Syke, Burnley (01282 412555). North east of Burnley Embankment, along Eastern Avenue and Briercliffe Road from the football ground. This is Britain's only working 19thC weaving mill: 300 looms powered by the 500hp steam engine 'Peace'. Virtually unchanged until it closed in 1982, the mill has now found a new lease of life, with some of the former employees back again to work the looms. Mill shop and cafe. *Undergoing extensive refurbishment at time of going to press so ring for details of opening times.*
The Weavers' Triangle The area between bridges 129B and 130B is one of the best-preserved 19thC industrial districts in the country – there are weaving sheds with 'north light' roofs, engine houses, spinning mills and well-preserved terraces of 19thC houses. An explanatory leaflet and town trail guide are available from: the

Tourist Information Centre or the Toll House Museum of local history and the cotton industry, which is also the information centre for the Weavers' Triangle. *Open 14.00–16.00 Mon, Tue, Wed, Sat, Sun Easter–Sep & 14.00–16.00 Sun only in Oct.* Free.
Townley Hall (01282 424213). On the southern outskirts of Burnley, 1$^1/_4$ miles south east of the BW yard. Set in extensive parkland with a golf course and play area, the grandiose, battlemented house dating from the 14thC was the home of the Townley family until 1902. It is now an art gallery, natural history centre and aquarium and a museum with the rooms lavishly furnished in period style. *Mon–Fri 10.00–17.00 & Sun 12.00–17.00. Closed B. Hols.* Natural history centre *also open Sat Apr–Sep.*
Tourist Information Centre Burnley Mechanics, Manchester Road, Burnley (01282 455485).
● **Brierfield**
Lancs. PO, tel, stores, garage, bank, station, cinema. A small industrial town merging into Burnley at one end and into Nelson at the other. The parish church of St Luke in Colne Road is a Victorian building with an unusually designed clock tower culminating in a steep pyramid roof.

Boatyards

British Waterways Burnley Yard Lower House Lane, Rosegrove, Burnley (01282 428680). Boating facilities to be found at the old BW yard at:

Finsley Gate, Mile End Wharf, Burnley. 🚽 🚰 ⚓ Pump-out, gas nearby, overnight mooring, slipway, toilet, telephone kiosk, good access to shops.

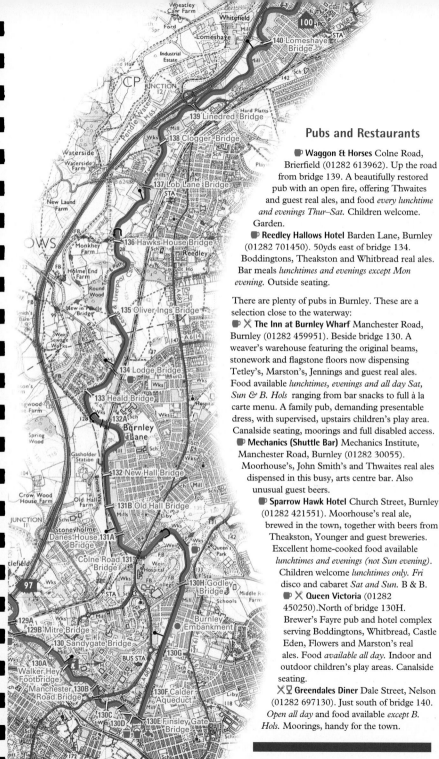

Pubs and Restaurants

🍺 **Waggon & Horses** Colne Road, Brierfield (01282 613962). Up the road from bridge 139. A beautifully restored pub with an open fire, offering Thwaites and guest real ales, and food *every lunchtime and evenings Thur–Sat*. Children welcome. Garden.

🍺 **Reedley Hallows Hotel** Barden Lane, Burnley (01282 701450). 50yds east of bridge 134. Boddingtons, Theakston and Whitbread real ales. Bar meals *lunchtimes and evenings except Mon evening*. Outside seating.

There are plenty of pubs in Burnley. These are a selection close to the waterway:

🍺 ✕ **The Inn at Burnley Wharf** Manchester Road, Burnley (01282 459951). Beside bridge 130. A weaver's warehouse featuring the original beams, stonework and flagstone floors now dispensing Tetley's, Marston's, Jennings and guest real ales. Food available *lunchtimes, evenings and all day Sat, Sun & B. Hols* ranging from bar snacks to full à la carte menu. A family pub, demanding presentable dress, with supervised, upstairs children's play area. Canalside seating, moorings and full disabled access.

🍺 **Mechanics (Shuttle Bar)** Mechanics Institute, Manchester Road, Burnley (01282 30055). Moorhouse's, John Smith's and Thwaites real ales dispensed in this busy, arts centre bar. Also unusual guest beers.

🍺 **Sparrow Hawk Hotel** Church Street, Burnley (01282 421551). Moorhouse's real ale, brewed in the town, together with beers from Theakston, Younger and guest breweries. Excellent home-cooked food available *lunchtimes and evenings (not Sun evening)*. Children welcome *lunchtimes only. Fri* disco and cabaret *Sat and Sun*. B & B.

🍺 ✕ **Queen Victoria** (01282 450250). North of bridge 130H. Brewer's Fayre pub and hotel complex serving Boddingtons, Whitbread, Castle Eden, Flowers and Marston's real ales. Food *available all day*. Indoor and outdoor children's play areas. Canalside seating.

✕ 🍴 **Greendales Diner** Dale Street, Nelson (01282 697130). Just south of bridge 140. *Open all day* and food available *except B. Hols*. Moorings, handy for the town.

Foulridge

The navigation winds as it follows the hillside; but this ceases at Nelson, where it crosses the valley on a minor aqueduct and begins to climb the pretty Barrowford Locks having finally seen off the motorway. This is a refreshing stretch, in which the canal leaves the succession of industrial towns. It rises through the seven Barrowford Locks, passing Barrowford reservoir (in which the summit level's surplus water is stored), and at the beautifully kept top lock reaches the summit level of the whole canal. Soon various feeder streams can be seen, continuously pouring vital water supplies into the navigation. Meanwhile, distant mountainous country frames beautiful old stone farms nearer at hand. Soon everything is blotted out by Foulridge Tunnel; at the other end, by the railway bridge, is an old wharf where it is possible to moor to visit the village.

BOAT TRIPS
M.V. Marton Emperor Canal trips *Sun & Tue 14.30, Easter–Sep.* Also trips through the tunnel to Barrowford. Bookings and enquiries 01282 844033. Recorded information 01282 870241

● **Nelson**

Lancs. EC Tue. MD Wed, Fri, Sat. All services.
Nelson is a conglomerate of a number of
small villages that combined in the 19thC to
form one industrial town. The centre has
been redeveloped with a large covered shopping precinct. One of Nelson's more valuable
assets is the easy access to the beautiful moors
and Forest of Pendle, behind which looms
Pendle Hill.

Tourist Information Centre Town Hall,
Nelson (01282 692890).

● **Barrowford**

Lancs. PO, tel, stores. There are still some
attractive terraces of stone cottages in this
village, which lie a short walk to the west of
the locks. The Toll House, the last intact
survivor from the old Marsden (Nelson) to
Long Preston turnpike road, together with
the 17thC Park Hill (the birthplace of Roger
Bannister, the first 'four minute miler') now
houses:

The Pendle Heritage Centre (01282 695366).
Open 10.00–17.00 every day except Xmas.

Charge. John Wesley preached from the pack-
horse bridge in the 1770s; there is a fine park
by the river containing traces of a mill dating
from 1311.

● **Foulridge**

Lancs. PO, tel, stores, take-away. Attractive
around the green, where alleys festooned with
washing lines give the place a homely air. In
the surrounding countryside are scattered the
reservoirs that feed the summit level of the
canal. There is a small museum housed in the
old warehouse on the wharf.

● **Foulridge Tunnel**

1640yds long, with no towpath, this tunnel is,
not surprisingly, barred to unapproved boats.
The hole in the hill sprang to fame in 1912
when a cow fell into the canal near the tunnel
mouth and for some reason decided to
struggle through to the other end of the
tunnel. The gallant but weary swimmer was
revived with alcohol at the Foulridge end.
Photographs in the Hole in the Wall pub
recall the incident. The tunnel roof drips
liberally.

NAVIGATIONAL NOTES

Entrance to Foulridge Tunnel is restricted and controlled by lights. Please
obey signs giving instructions.

Pubs and Restaurants

🍺 **Old Bridge Inn** Gisburn Road, Barrowford
(01282 613983). Robinson's real ale served in
a cosy village local. Traditional pub games.

🍺✕ **White Bear** Gisburn Road, Barrowford
(01282 615646). Bass, Worthington and guest
real ales together with good home-cooked
meals, *lunchtimes and evenings. Barrowford can
be accessed via a footpath near the top of
Barrowford Locks.*

✕� **Foulridge Restaurant** Foulridge Canal
Wharf (01282 869159). Attractive conversion
of the old wharf office and stables to form a tea
room and restaurant providing an appetising
range of home-cooked snacks and meals. Tea
room *open from 10.00 every day in summer and
Wed–Sun in winter.* Restaurant *open 19.00–
21.00 Wed–Sat all year.* Also incorporates a

home bakery using organic, stone-ground flour
to produce a tasty selection of speciality
breads, pies and scones.

🍺 **Hole in the Wall** Foulridge (01282 863568).
250yds east of tunnel, north end. Here is
recorded the famous cow in the canal incident.
Thirsty boaters, however, are revived with
Worthington, Boddingtons and guest real
ales together with an inexpensive range of
home-cooked food available *lunchtimes and
evenings (not Wed evening) and all day on
Sunday.* Children welcome. Beer garden, pool
and darts. B & B.

🍺 **New Inn** Foulridge (01282 864068). Carry
on past the Hole in the Wall and cross the main
road. Thwaites real ale and bar food available
lunchtimes and evenings (except Tue evening).

Barnoldswick

Meanwhile the navigation continues northward through this very fine countryside to Salterforth, crossing over the little 'Country Brook' between bridges 149 and 150. This is one of the most remote sections of the whole canal and probably the most beautiful. There is also much canal interest, for just south of bridge 153 was the junction, now disappeared, of the Rain Hall Rock Branch, essentially a linear quarry where the limestone was loaded directly from the rock face onto the boats. Walk up the road from the bridge (east) and turn right at the top where it will come into view, straddled by a tall three-arched viaduct. A mile further along one rounds a corner and is confronted by Greenberfield Top Lock (showers, camping), which introduces the beginning of the long descent towards Leeds. (The feeder from the distant Winterburn reservoir enters the canal at the top lock.) The three locks here were built in 1820 to replace the original flight (the old dry bed of the earlier route can be seen on the towpath side) and are set in beautiful uplands – for the next few miles the canal winds through scenery that is composed of countless individual hillocks, some topped by clumps of trees. Beyond are distant mountains.

Boatyards

Ⓑ **Lower Park Marina** Kelbrook Road, Barnoldswick (01282 815883). ⛽ D Pump-out, gas, winter storage, boat building and repairs (including fibreglass hulls), engine sales and repairs (including outboards), DIY facilities, chandlery, gifts, books and maps, telephone, groceries and fresh milk.

● **Salterforth**
Lancs. PO (Mon & Thur), tel, stores. A small village of narrow streets and terraced houses in an upland setting. Children will enjoy the playground north of bridge 151. Farm shop *open daily.*

● **Barnoldswick**
Lancs. EC Tue. PO, tel, stores, garage, bank. Set back from the canal, the mainstay of this town's existence is the Rolls Royce factory, where experimental work is done on aero engines. The centre of the town is compact and dominated by the modern Holy Trinity Church completed in 1960.
Bancroft Mill Engine Trust Gillians Lane, Barnoldswick (01282 865626). A 600 hp. steam engine and its two boilers, once powering the looms of Bancroft Mill, saved for preservation. Regular steaming and weaving demonstrations. Telephone for details.
Tourist Information Centre The Old Library, Fernlea Avenue, Barnoldswick (01282 817046).
Pennine Way The Pennine Way is a walking route covering over 250 miles of Pennine highland from Edale in the south to Kirk Yetholm in the north. Because of the nature of the route much of the Way is rough, hard walking, but it gives a superb view from the mountains. At East Marton the Pennine Way shares the canal towpath for a short distance – you will notice that the stones here abound with fossils.

Pubs and Restaurants

⬤ ✕ **Anchor** Salterforth (01282 813186). Canalside, at bridge 151. A traditional pub serving Bass, Worthington, Theakston and guest real ales, where a second building was built on top of the first – hence where you now drink was once the bedrooms. Wide range of good, traditional pub food served *lunchtimes and evenings.* The cellar has stalactites. Good moorings, children's menu and outdoor play area.

There are plenty of pubs in Barnoldswick.

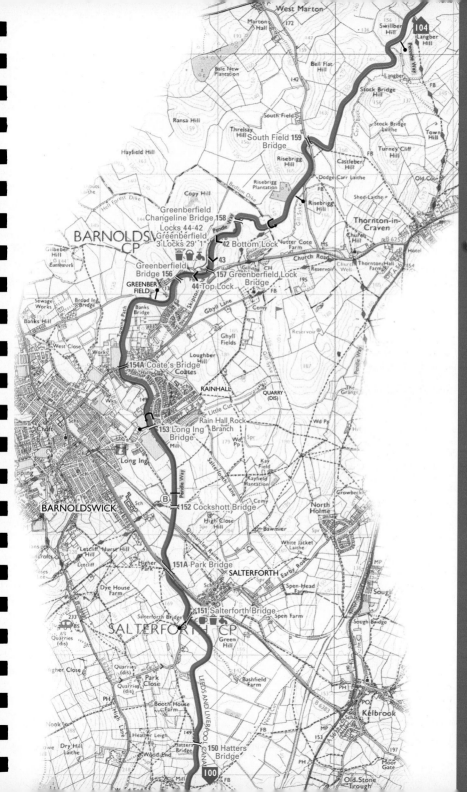

Gargrave

Around East Marton, after skirting the isolated church, the surroundings change briefly: the navigation enters a cutting, passes under a double-arched main road bridge and enters a sheltered fold housing a farm, a pub and some moorings. A steep wooded cutting leads the canal back into the rugged moorlands. There is a useful shop and restaurant at Wilkinsons Farm, together with B & B and camping, by bridge 162, which can also be reached via a lane to the side of the Cross Keys. This is another outstanding stretch, in which the navigation continues to snake extravagantly around the splendid green and humpy hills that fill the landscape. The six Bank Newton Locks lower the canal into Upper Airedale, yielding excellent views

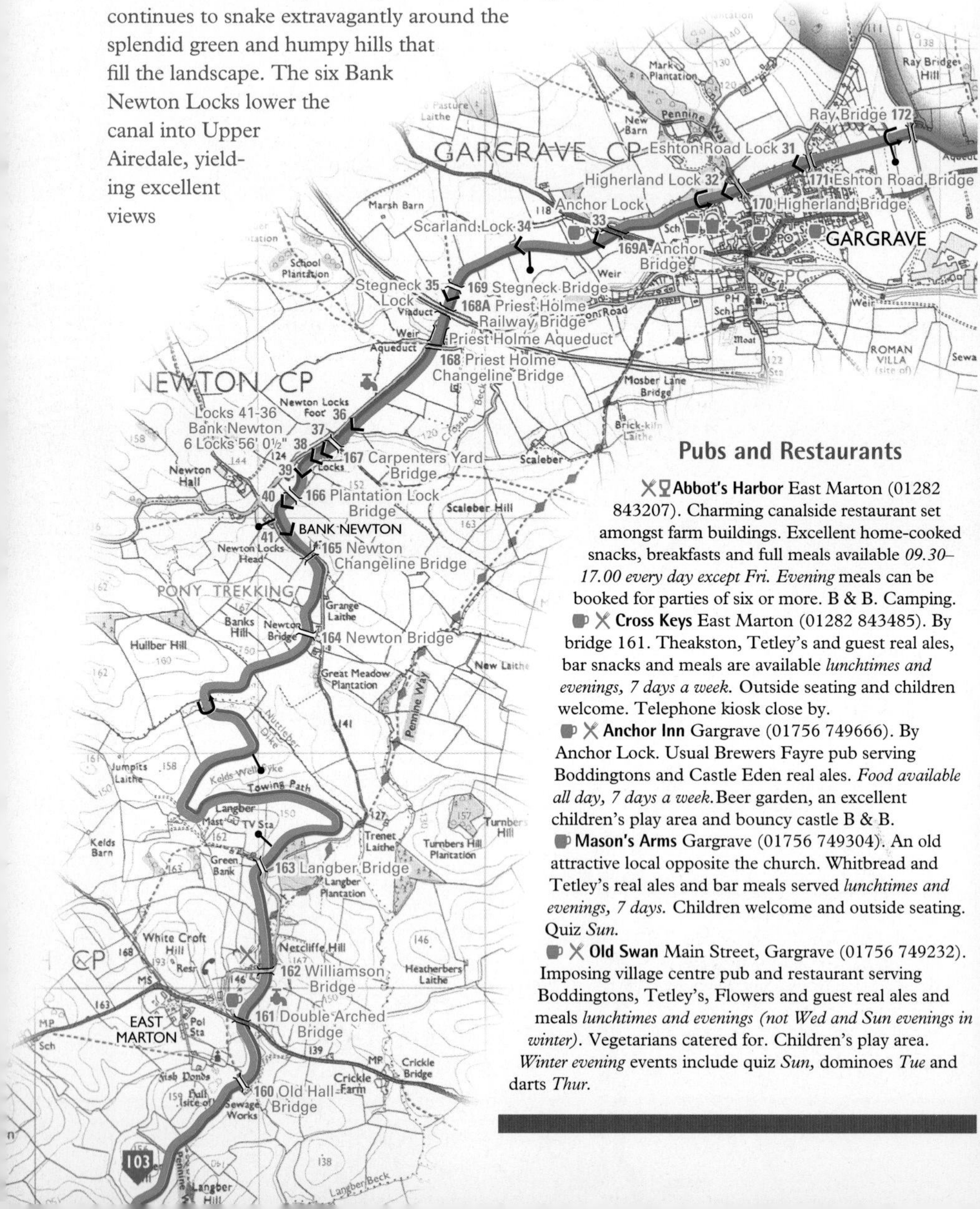

Pubs and Restaurants

Abbot's Harbor East Marton (01282 843207). Charming canalside restaurant set amongst farm buildings. Excellent home-cooked snacks, breakfasts and full meals available *09.30–17.00 every day except Fri. Evening* meals can be booked for parties of six or more. B & B. Camping.

Cross Keys East Marton (01282 843485). By bridge 161. Theakston, Tetley's and guest real ales, bar snacks and meals are available *lunchtimes and evenings, 7 days a week.* Outside seating and children welcome. Telephone kiosk close by.

Anchor Inn Gargrave (01756 749666). By Anchor Lock. Usual Brewers Fayre pub serving Boddingtons and Castle Eden real ales. *Food available all day, 7 days a week.* Beer garden, an excellent children's play area and bouncy castle B & B.

Mason's Arms Gargrave (01756 749304). An old attractive local opposite the church. Whitbread and Tetley's real ales and bar meals served *lunchtimes and evenings, 7 days.* Children welcome and outside seating. Quiz *Sun.*

Old Swan Main Street, Gargrave (01756 749232). Imposing village centre pub and restaurant serving Boddingtons, Tetley's, Flowers and guest real ales and meals *lunchtimes and evenings (not Wed and Sun evenings in winter).* Vegetarians catered for. Children's play area. *Winter evening* events include quiz *Sun,* dominoes *Tue* and darts *Thur.*

across the valley to the hills and moors beyond. The River Aire flows in from the north, accompanied by the railway line to Skipton and Leeds from Morecambe, Settle and distant Carlisle. The canal crosses the river by a substantial stone aqueduct. Meanwhile, yet more locks take the canal round Gargrave; the beauty of the area may be judged by the fact that the Yorkshire Dales National Park borders the navigation along here.

● **Gargrave**
N. Yorks. PO, tel, stores, garage, station. A very attractive and much-visited village. Holding an enviable position near the head of Airedale between the canal and the river, this place is the ideal centre for boat crews to explore the surrounding countryside. The River Aire cuts Gargrave in two, and the bridge over it forms the centre of the village. There is a charming station, and some pretty stone cottages along the green. The church is mostly Victorian, except for the tower, which was built in 1521. There is also *a cycle shop hiring bikes* and, by bridge 171, *a coal and log merchant.*
Cycle Hire Dave Ferguson Cycles, Gargrave (01756 748030/795367). Bikes available in both Gargrave and Skipton.

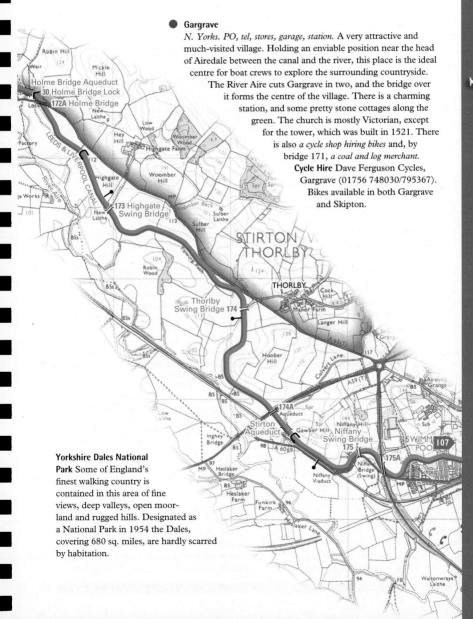

Yorkshire Dales National Park Some of England's finest walking country is contained in this area of fine views, deep valleys, open moorland and rugged hills. Designated as a National Park in 1954 the Dales, covering 680 sq. miles, are hardly scarred by habitation.

Skipton

The canal now turns south east and proceeds down Airedale, a valley which contains it from here right through to Leeds. Upper Airedale is a flat, wide valley defined by tall steep hills. The countryside is open, unploughed and very inviting to walkers, especially with the moorlands stretching away over the top of the hills. In this robust landscape the navigation hugs the hillsides just above the valley floor, enjoying a lock-free pound that is 17 miles long – although the navigator's relief at the absence of locks may be tempered by the abundance of swing bridges. Entering Skipton, which is usually bristling with pleasure boats, the navigator will see the Springs Branch, a little arm packed with moored craft, that leads off past the town centre and soon finds itself in what is virtually a ravine, overlooked by the castle more than 100ft above. (Navigation is limited – see Navigational Note 2 below). At the junction is a boatyard: next door is a restored canal warehouse. On leaving Skipton the canal continues along the hillside down the valley of the River Aire, with the main road just beside and below the navigation. Excellent views are offered up and down this splendid valley and the surrounding countryside. The village of Bradley has an attractive waterfront – the *PO stores* are situated beyond the imposing mill building. (*Visitor moorings on towpath side only.*)

Pubs and Restaurants

There is a wide choice of pubs in Skipton. This is just a selection within reach of the canal:

● ✕ **Herriots** Broughton Road, Skipton (01756 792781). Canalside, Near bridge 176. 'Modern Victorian' decor and Tetley's, Theakston and guest real ales are on offer in this bar and à la carte restaurant. A good selection of dishes and filled Yorkshire pudding snacks; vegetarian options and children catered for. Outside seating and quiz *Thur.* B & B.

● **Rose & Crown** Coach Street, Skipton (01756 792654). By the junction with the Springs Branch. Tetley's real ale and *lunchtime* food served in this town centre pub. Children welcome and outside seating.

● **Royal Shepherd** Canal Street, Skipton (01756 793178). Boddingtons, Cains, Whitbread, Tetley's and Marston's real ales available in this lively pub overlooking the Springs Branch. Bar food served *lunchtime*. Children's room and outdoor play area. Garden.

✕ ♀ **Hatters** 17 Otley Street, Skipton (01756 791534). The canal and food-loving proprietors serve a tasty range of inexpensive, home-cooked and predominantly vegetarian fare, in this rustic, continental style establishment. *Open 10.00–16.30 all year and also 17.00–20.00 for early evening meals in summer.* Tea garden.

● **Cock & Bottle** Swadford Street, Skipton (01756 794734). Exposed stone walls and beamed ceilings make this 18thC coaching inn a congenial pub in which to enjoy Boddingtons, Castle Eden, Marston's, Timothy Taylor's and guest real ales. *Open all day* and serving food *lunchtimes.* Outside seating.

✕ ♀ **Claire's Kitchen** 20 Newmarket Street, Skipton (01756 792716). Comfortable, family orientated café and bistro serving tea, coffee and snacks together with an appetising range of home-cooked meals from pastas to steaks. *Open 10.30–21.00 except Mon & Tue closed at 17.00).* Bargain three course meals *early evenings until 19.00.*

● ✕ **Bay Horse** Snaygill, (01756 792449). Near bridge 181. Big Steak establishment, aimed at the family market. Food *all day, every day* together with Tetley's, Marston's and Burton real ales. Beer garden and moorings outside. Quiz *Mon & Thurs.* Open all day.

● **King Henry VIII** Keithley Road, Snaygill (01756 796428). Not far from bridge 181. Traditional, home-cooked meals available *all day in summer and lunchtimes and evenings in winter.* Boddingtons and Tetley's real ales served in mock medieval surroundings. Vegetarian and children's menu. Outside seating and children's play area. Quiz *Thur.*

● **Slaters Arms** Crag Lane, Bradley (01535 632179). Near bridge 182A. 18thC local complete with cosy inglenook fireplace and Commercial and John Smith's real ales. Food available *lunchtimes and evenings.* Beer garden.

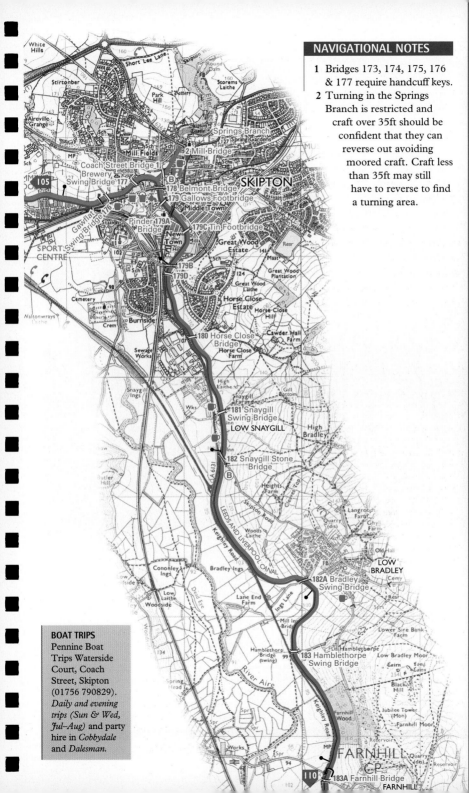

NAVIGATIONAL NOTES

1 Bridges 173, 174, 175, 176 & 177 require handcuff keys.
2 Turning in the Springs Branch is restricted and craft over 35ft should be confident that they can reverse out avoiding moored craft. Craft less than 35ft may still have to reverse to find a turning area.

BOAT TRIPS
Pennine Boat Trips Waterside Court, Coach Street, Skipton (01756 790829). *Daily and evening trips (Sun & Wed, Jul–Aug)* and party hire in *Cobbydale* and *Dalesman*.

Entrance to Springs Branch, Skipton

Boatyards

Ⓑ **Pennine Cruisers** The Boat Shop, 19 Coach Street, Skipton (01756 795478). At junction with Springs Branch. 🚮 🚾 ♿ D E Pump-out, gas, narrow boat hire, day hire craft, overnight mooring, long term mooring, winter storage, dry dock, chandlery, books, maps and gifts, boat sales, engine sales and repairs. *24hr* emergency breakdown service.

Ⓑ **Snaygill Boats** Skipton Road, Bradley, Nr Skipton (01756 795150). At bridge 182. 🚮 🚾 ♿ D E Pump-out, gas, narrow boat hire, overnight mooring, long-term mooring, chandlery, dry dock, books, maps and gifts, engine repairs, toilet, shower.

● **Skipton**

N. Yorks. MD Mon, Wed, Fri, Sat. All services (including cinema) and excellent shops. Skipton is probably the most handsome town along the whole Leeds & Liverpool Canal. It is an excellent place for visiting from the canal, for one can moor snugly and safely about one minute's walk away from the centre. It still maintains its importance as a market town, which is referred to in its name: Saxon 'Scip-tun' means sheep-town. The wide High Street is very attractive, lined with mostly Georgian houses, and headed at the northern end by the splendid castle and the well-kept graveyard of the parish church. There is an interesting water-mill beside the Springs Branch.

Church of the Holy Trinity Standing opposite the castle, it is a long battlemented church, encircled by large lawns and flourishing gardens. It is in Perpendicular style dating from the 14thC, though it was greatly renovated after suffering serious damage during the Civil War. It has a fine oak roof and a beautifully carved Jacobean font cover.

Craven Museum Town Hall, High Street, Skipton (01756 794079). Outstanding local geology and archaeology collection together with a colourful insight into life in the Craven Dales. *Open Apr–Sep Mon, Wed–Fri 10.00–17.00; Sat 10.00–12.00 & 13.00–17.00; Sun 14.00–17.00. Oct–Mar Mon, Wed–Fri 13.30–17.00; Sat 10.00–12.00 & 13.30–16.30. Free.*

Cycle Hire Dave Ferguson Cycles, Skipton (01756 795367). Bikes for hire in both Skipton and Gargrave.

● **Springs Branch**

A short (770yds) but very unusual branch that leaves the Leeds & Liverpool Canal, passes the centre of Skipton and soon finds itself in what is virtually a ravine, overlooked by the castle that towers 100ft above. The branch is navigable by small craft, and makes an interesting diversion by boat or foot. (The towpath continues past the arm, into Skipton

Woods.) It was built by the Earl of Thanet, the owner of Skipton Castle, to carry limestone away from his nearby quarry. It was extended by 240yds in 1797 from the water-mill bridge through the deep rock cutting, and 120ft-chutes were constructed at the new terminus to drop the rock into the boats from the horse tramway that was laid from the quarry to the castle. The quarry still flourishes, but the canal and tramway have not been used since 1946. Trains and lorries have replaced them. Now a picturesque backwater the Springs Branch acted for many years as a feeder to the Leeds & Liverpool Canal, taking water from Eller Beck, which runs beside it.

Skipton Castle Skipton (01756 792442). A magnificent Norman castle, with 17thC additions, that dominates Skipton High Street. After a three-year siege during the Civil War, Cromwell's men allowed the restoration of the castle, but ensured that the building could never again be used as a stronghold. The six massive round towers have survived from the 14thC and other notable features are the 50ft-long banqueting hall, a kitchen with roasting and baking hearths, a dungeon and the 'Shell Room', the walls of which are decorated with sea shells. *Open daily (closed Sun morning).* Charge.

Tourist Information Centre Old Town Hall, Sheep Street Skipton (01756 792809).

Skipton Woods Fine woods leading up the little narrow valley from the Springs Branch. For access, just keep on walking up the towpath of the branch.

Yorkshire Dales Railway Embsay Station (01756 794727). Talking timetable (01756 795189). 1 mile north of Skipton off the A59/65 bypass. Bus service from Skipton. A 4-mile round-trip either steam or diesel hauled. Museum, mining centre, picnic area, shop, cafe. *Services every hour 11.00–16.15 Sun, all year; Tue & Sat, Jul; daily except Mon & Fri during Aug; most B. Hols & Box. Day; plus various 'specials'.*

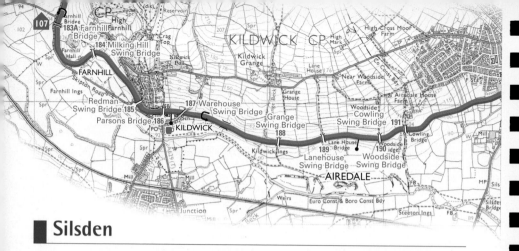

Silsden

There is a fine wooded stretch north of Kildwick; then one curves sharply round the outcrop on which crouches Farnhill Hall, a mellow stone building. The intriguing village of Kildwick has some well-restored canalside buildings now used as private residences. There are good moorings here prior to quieter country: the main road and the railway cut the valley corner while the canal takes the longer route round to Silsden. Overlooking Airedale, the green hills are very steep and beautifully wooded in places. The distant rows of chimneys, factories and terraced houses across the valley comprise Keighley; most of its industrial and suburban tentacles are quickly passed by the canal, although the constant succession of little swing bridges regularly impedes a boat's progress. This type of swing bridge is prone to intermittent stiffness due to the elements, and all require a handcuff key. There is an attractive mooring by woods, to the east of bridge 195.

- **Kildwick**
  W. Yorks. PO, stores (both in Farnhill, on the opposite side of the canal), tel. An interesting and unusual village spilling down the hillside. The streets are extremely steep; one of them goes under the canal through a narrow skewed aqueduct.
- **Silsden**
  W. Yorks. EC Tue & Sat, PO, tel, stores, garage, bank. A well-contained, stone-built industrial town spreading uphill from the canal. In addition to its proximity to the Yorkshire Dales National Park, it offers plenty of shops near the canal. The canalside warehouses are attractive; there is also an old corn mill dated 1677.
- **Keighley**
  W. Yorks. EC Tue. MD Wed, Fri, Sat. All services. Compared with some other industrial centres in the area, Keighley is a clean and pleasant town. It boasts a large new shopping centre, much modern housing and some handsome older stone terraces. The oldest part is around the parish church of St Andrew, a large perpendicular building whose main attraction is its shady churchyard.
  Cliffe Castle Spring Gardens Lane, Keighley. (01535 618230). Once the home of the Butterfield family, it has been completely restored

and now houses the museum and art gallery. Local exhibits illustrate the archaeology, natural history and industrial history of the area. There are reconstructed craft workshops and a textile room. Picturesque grounds where band concerts are held. *Open 10.00–17.00 Tue–Sat, 12.00–17.00 Sun. Closed Mon except B. Hol and on Good Friday and over Christmas. Free.*
Keighley & Worth Valley Railway (01535 645214). Talking timetable *24hrs* (01535 647777). Privately preserved by volunteers of the Keighley & Worth Valley Railway Preservation Society, the line runs for 5 miles from the British Rail station at Keighley up to Haworth, the home of the Brontë family, and Oxenhope. British Railways closed the line in 1961, but the Society eventually succeeded in reopening it in 1968 with a regular service of steam trains. In the mornings, the service is operated by diesel railbuses, but in the afternoons magnificent steam engines puff their way along the track. In the goods yard at Haworth the Society has a splendid collection of steam engines and carriages, mostly ancient. The line was made famous by the film *The Railway Children*.
Tourist Information Centre 2/4 West Lane, Howarth (01535 642329).

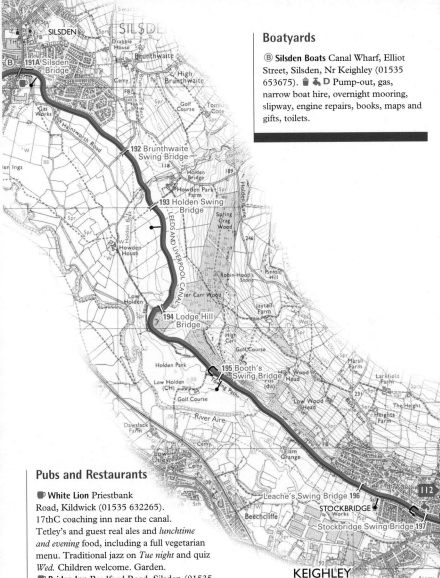

Boatyards

ⓑ **Silsden Boats** Canal Wharf, Elliot Street, Silsden, Nr Keighley (01535 653675). 🛁 🔧 D Pump-out, gas, narrow boat hire, overnight mooring, slipway, engine repairs, books, maps and gifts, toilets.

Pubs and Restaurants

🍺 **White Lion** Priestbank Road, Kildwick (01535 632265). 17thC coaching inn near the canal. Tetley's and guest real ales and *lunchtime and evening* food, including a full vegetarian menu. Traditional jazz on *Tue night* and quiz *Wed*. Children welcome. Garden.

🍺 **Bridge Inn** Bradford Road, Silsden (01535 653144). Cosy canalside local which predates the waterway serving John Smith's, Black Sheep and guest real ales. *Lunchtime and evening* meals, children's room and garden. Moorings.

🍺 **King's Arms** Bolton Road, Silsden (01535 653216). Young people's pub offering Tetley's real ale and food *lunchtimes, Mon–Fri*. Children welcome, garden. *Fri* kakaoke and *Sun* disco.

🍺 **Albert Hotel** Bridge Street, Keighley (01535 602306). Timothy Taylor real ale in an usually decorated Victorian town pub. *Open all day Fri and Sat.*

🍺 **Boltmaker's Arms** 117 East Parade, Keighley (01535 661936). Intimate, one-roomed pub dispensing Timothy Taylor real ale and at least 18 whiskies. Pub games.

🍺 **Red Pig** Church Street, Keighley (01535 605383). Popular pub displaying local artists' work and serving Commercial, Timothy Taylor and guest real ales.

There are plenty of other pubs in Keighley.

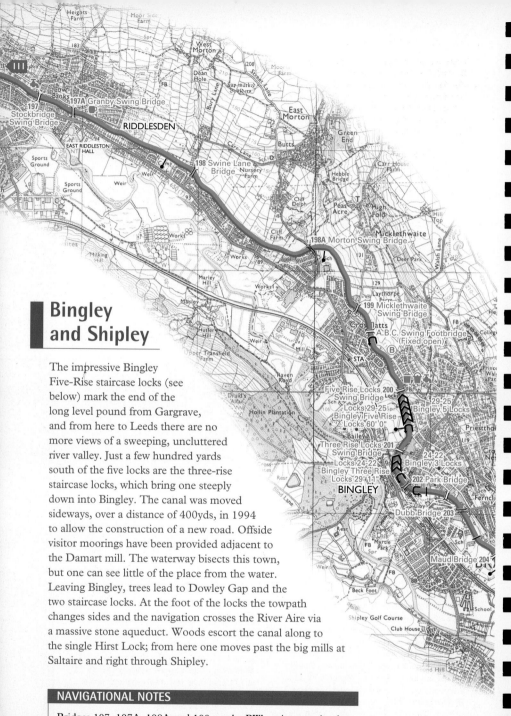

Bingley and Shipley

The impressive Bingley Five-Rise staircase locks (see below) mark the end of the long level pound from Gargrave, and from here to Leeds there are no more views of a sweeping, uncluttered river valley. Just a few hundred yards south of the five locks are the three-rise staircase locks, which bring one steeply down into Bingley. The canal was moved sideways, over a distance of 400yds, in 1994 to allow the construction of a new road. Offside visitor moorings have been provided adjacent to the Damart mill. The waterway bisects this town, but one can see little of the place from the water. Leaving Bingley, trees lead to Dowley Gap and the two staircase locks. At the foot of the locks the towpath changes sides and the navigation crosses the River Aire via a massive stone aqueduct. Woods escort the canal along to the single Hirst Lock; from here one moves past the big mills at Saltaire and right through Shipley.

NAVIGATIONAL NOTES

Bridges 197, 197A, 198A and 199 need a BW sanitary station key.
Bridge 209 needs a BW sanitary station key and a windlass.

Pubs and Restaurants

There are plenty of pubs in Bingley and Shipley.

Marquis of Granby Riddlesden (01535 607164). At swing bridge 197A. Black Sheep, John Smith's and Webster's real ales, together with traditional pub food (and curries) served *lunchtimes and all day Sun.* Vegetarians and children catered for. Beer garden and moorings outside. *PO and stores* south of bridge 197.

Brown Cow Ireland Bridge, Bingley (01274 569482). ¼ mile west of bridge 202. Timothy Taylor real ale and bar snacks available *lunchtimes and evenings. Sunday* carvery. Children and vegetarians catered for. Regular *Mon* jazz nights. Outside seating. B & B.

Ferrands Arms Queen Street, Bingley (01274 563949). 250yds south of bridge 202. Timothy Taylor and Tetley's real ales and bar meals available *lunchtimes and evenings.* Children welcome *until 20.00.* Outside seating.

Fishermen's Dowley Gap, Bingley (01274 564238). Canalside, above Dowley Gap locks. Stones, Worthington and Bass real ales and bar meals served *lunchtimes and evenings (except weekend evenings).* Vegetarians and children catered for. Garden.

X Boathouse Inn Victoria Road, Saltaire (01274 590408). Between river and canal at bridge 207A. Flying in the face of a century and a quarter of local tradition this is the first licensed premises in Saltaire, dispensing Theakston and Courage real ales. Tastefully developed from the riverside boathouse built by Sir Titus Salt in 1871, for the recreation of his workforce (a base for rowing boats and a steamer) the pub is furnished with memorabilia and offers a full à la carte menu and a tasty range of bar snacks, available *lunchtimes and evenings (not Sun evening).* Vegetarian menu and traditional *Sunday* lunches. Children welcome in the restaurant. Riverside terrace and beer garden.

Sun Hotel Westgate, Shipley (01274 589159). 250yds south of bridge 207C. Tetley's and Mansfield real ales and *lunchtime* bar food. Outside seating and children welcome. Regular entertainment nights, including live bands. B & B.

BOAT TRIPS
Apollo Canal Cruises have a water bus operating a scheduled Metro service *up to twice daily in summer.* They also offer *lunchtime and supper* cruises *throughout the year* aboard their restaurant boat *Water Prince* and waterbus *Apollo.* Ring for details on 01274 595914.

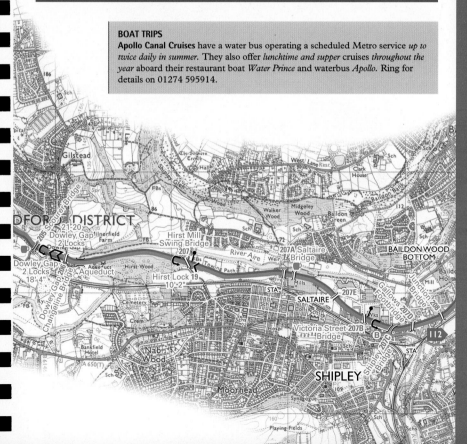

Bingley Five-Rise Locks

Boatyards

Ⓑ **Hainsworth Boatyard** Fairfax Road, Bingley (01274 565925). 200yds above the five-rise. 🛎 🛥 **D** Pump-out, gas, overnight mooring, long-term mooring, winter storage, slipway, chandlery, boat building, boat sales and repairs, engine repairs, *24 hr* emergency call out, toilets. National boat transporters.

Ⓑ **Apollo Canal Cruises** Wharf Street, Shipley (01274 595914). 🛎 🛎 🛥 Pump-out, long term mooring, toilets, showers, telephone.

● **Baildon**

W. Yorks. EC Tue. All services. 1¹/₂ miles north of Shipley. A very old industrial town huddled on a hilltop on the edge of Baildon Moor. Stretching from Baildon to Bingley is The Glen, a wooded valley that curves below the heights of the moor. A splendid scenic tramway carrying two tramcars connects the coach road to the higher parts of Baildon Moor. (In summer a frequent service operates, but in winter it is arranged only to suit the needs of residents at the upper level.)

Shipley

W. Yorks. EC Wed. MD Fri, Sat. All services. A dark stone town built on a generous scale and based on textile and engineering industries. There are powerful-looking mills to be seen, as well as the town hall and a suitably battlemented Salvation Army citadel. Shipley is lucky enough to be on the edge of Baildon Moor and Shipley Glen. The 3-mile-long Bradford Canal used to join the Leeds & Liverpool in Shipley, by bridge 208, but this has all been filled in for years.

● **Saltaire**

W. Yorks. Stores, BR station. An estate village that owes its existence to the Utopian dream of Sir Titus Salt, a wealthy Victorian mill owner. He was so appalled by the working and living conditions of his workers in Bradford that he decided to build the ideal industrial settlement. This he did in 1850 on the banks of the canal and the River Aire – hence the name Saltaire. He provided every amenity including high standard housing, but no pub – for he was a great opponent of strong drink. The village has changed little since those days (save the recent addition of a pub!); everything is carefully laid out and the terraced houses are attractive in an orderly sort of way. There is an Italianate church near the canal, and a large park beside the river. Admirers of David Hockney's work should visit the art gallery.

Museum of Victorian Reed Organs and Harmoniums Victoria Hall. Victoria Road, Saltaire (01274 585601). Music and musical nostalgia. *Open every day 11.00–16.00 except Xmas and New Year.* Charge.

Salt's Mill Saltaire (01274 531163). The 1853 Gallery showing David Hockney's work; an inexpensive diner and several furniture and furnishing retail outlets. *Open every day 10.00– 18.00 except Xmas.*

Tourist Information Centre 2 Victoria Road, Saltaire (01274 774993).

● **Bingley**

W. Yorks. EC Tue, MD Fri. All services. An industrial town now known nationally as a centre for thermal underwear. Standing at the south-east end of it amidst several old cottages is the large parish church of Holy Trinity, with its massive spire conspicuous from the canal.

Bingley Five-Rise Locks A very famous and impressive feature of the canal system built in 1774 in 'staircase' formation. They are all joined together rather than being separated by pounds of 'neutral' water. The top gates of the lowest lock are the bottom gates of the lock above, and so on. This means it is not possible to empty a lock unless the one below is itself empty. The rapid elevation thus resulting is quite daunting. Locks opening times vary (see latest edition of BW Navigation Guide or ring 01274 611303) and may be used only under the supervision of the lock keeper. The BW Sanitary Station is housed in a handsome old stable, where towing horses were once rested.

East Riddlesden Hall (01535 607075). *NT property.* Just south of swing bridge 197A. A 17thC stone manor house complete with tithe barn. Fine collection of furniture, paintings and armour. *Open Apr–Oct 12.00–17.00, Sat–Wed; also Fri in Jul & Aug. Last admission 16.30.* Tea room. Events. Charge.

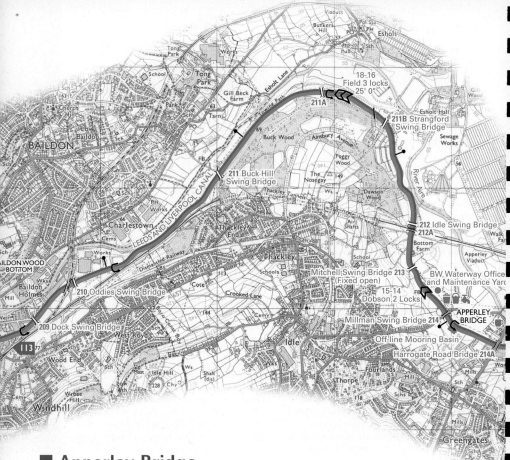

Apperley Bridge

This section sees the end of the wide open moorlands that frame the scenery further upstream: from now on, industry and housing begin to feature more as one approaches the outskirts of Leeds. The navigation, however, is thankfully sequestered from these intrusions into the landscape. Leaving Shipley, the adjacent railway cuts through a 500ft high hill in two mile-long tunnels. The canal goes all the way round this delightfully wooded hill, tenaciously following the Aire Valley. Halfway round the long curve are Field Locks. Beyond the main railway bridge is a British Waterways maintenance yard at the head of Dobson Locks. This is also the local Waterway Office housed in a former canal warehouse. Temporarily traversing a built-up area, the navigation emerges yet again onto a wooded hillside overlooking the still rural and charming valley that contains the River Aire.

NAVIGATIONAL NOTES

Bridge 214 needs a BW sanitary station key.
Bridge 215 is padlocked open to the canal.

● **Rodley**
W. Yorks. PO, tel, stores. A useful village on the canal bank. There are two pubs, several shops and good visitor moorings.

Pubs and Restaurants

🍺 **Shoulder of Mutton** Otley Road, Baildon (01274 584071). ¼ mile east of bridge 210. Tetley's and Theakston real ales and *lunchtime* bar meals. Food also available *evenings Wed–Sat*. Vegetarian menu. Garden and children's swings. Disabled access.

🍺 **Woolpack** Esholt, Shipley (01274 582425). As featured in the TV series Emmerdale. From bridge 211 follow the footpath to the main road, turn right, then take the turning to the right signposted Esholt. Castle Eden, Boddingtons and guest real ales together with *lunchtime snacks (not Sun)* served in this well known pub. Children's room and garden. Quiz *Thur*.

🍺 ✕ **George & Dragon** Apperley Bridge (01274 612015). 200yds north east of bridge 214A. A Porterhouse restaurant with three bars, built around an old oak tree which still grows through the ceiling. Tetley's real ale and meals (*L & D*).

🍺 **Rodley Barge** Rodley, Leeds (0113 257 4606). Unpretentious canalside pub by bridge 217 serving Bass and Tetley's real ales. Inexpensive home-cooked bar meals available *lunchtimes Mon–Fri* and pie and peas available *whenever open*. Children and vegetarians catered for. Canalside beer garden and moorings. Quiz *Mon*. Open all day Fri–Sun.

🍺 ✕ **Owl Hotel** Town Street, Rodley (0113 256 5242). John Smith's and Theakston real ales together with bar and restaurant meals served *lunchtimes and evenings (not Sat & Sun evenings)*. Vegetarian menu. Children's play area and farm animals. Garden and jazz *Sun*.

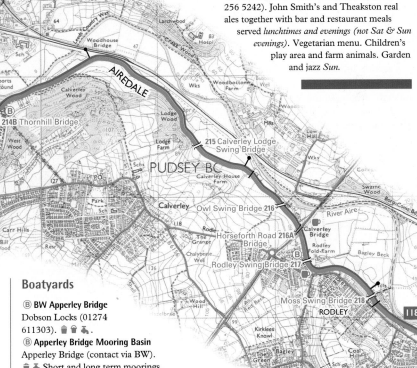

Boatyards

Ⓑ **BW Apperley Bridge** Dobson Locks (01274 611303). 🚾 🚿 ♿.

Ⓑ **Apperley Bridge Mooring Basin** Apperley Bridge (contact via BW). 🚿 ♿ Short and long term moorings.

Ⓑ **Swiftcraft** The Boathouse, Parkin Lane, Apperley Bridge, Bradford (01274 611786). By bridge 214B. Ⓓ Gas, overnight mooring, long-term mooring, winter storage, chandlery, books and maps, engine sales and repairs, toilets, telephone.

Ⓑ **Rodley Boat Centre** Canal Wharf, Canal Road, Rodley, Leeds (0113 257 6132). By bridge 216A. 🚾 🚿 ♿ Ⓓ Ⓔ Pump-out, gas, narrow boat hire, day hire craft, overnight mooring, long-term mooring, winter storage, slipway, chandlery, books and maps, boat building and repairs, boat sales, engine sales and repairs, generators and electrics.

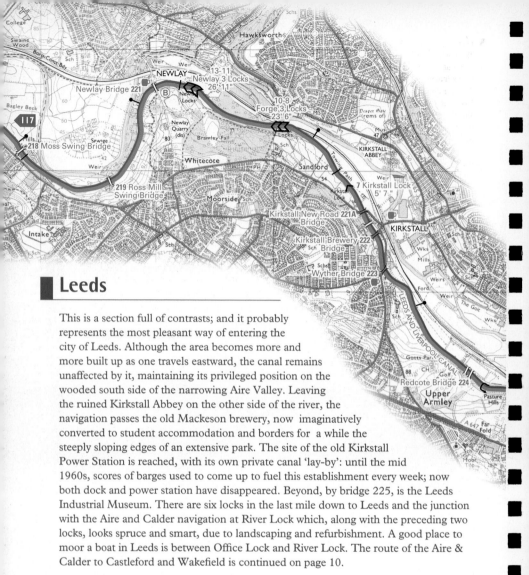

Leeds

This is a section full of contrasts; and it probably represents the most pleasant way of entering the city of Leeds. Although the area becomes more and more built up as one travels eastward, the canal remains unaffected by it, maintaining its privileged position on the wooded south side of the narrowing Aire Valley. Leaving the ruined Kirkstall Abbey on the other side of the river, the navigation passes the old Mackeson brewery, now imaginatively converted to student accommodation and borders for a while the steeply sloping edges of an extensive park. The site of the old Kirkstall Power Station is reached, with its own private canal 'lay-by': until the mid 1960s, scores of barges used to come up to fuel this establishment every week; now both dock and power station have disappeared. Beyond, by bridge 225, is the Leeds Industrial Museum. There are six locks in the last mile down to Leeds and the junction with the Aire and Calder navigation at River Lock which, along with the preceding two locks, looks spruce and smart, due to landscaping and refurbishment. A good place to moor a boat in Leeds is between Office Lock and River Lock. The route of the Aire & Calder to Castleford and Wakefield is continued on page 10.

Pubs and Restaurants

🍺 **Abbey** Newlay, Leeds (0113 258 1248). 50yds downhill from bridge 221. Whitbread, Boddingtons, Castle Eden and guest real ales. Bar snacks *lunchtimes (not Wed and Sun)*. Children and vegetarians catered for. Quiz *Sun*.

🍺 **Old Bridge Inn** Kirkstall, Leeds (0113 274 9508). 100yds east of bridge 222. Tetley's, Boddingtons, Stones and Theakston real ales. Meals available *lunchtimes and evenings (not Sun evening)*. Excellent *Sunday lunches*. This welcoming old pub is open all day and in past times is

reputed to have served as both mortuary to the monks at nearby Kirkstall Abbey and, more recently, the police cells. Riverside seating beside a very attractive cast-iron bridge over The Aire. Children and vegetarians catered for. Regular *summer* barbecues. Quiz *Tue*.

🍺 **Warrens** Armley, Leeds (0113 275 1669). Modern, housing-estate pub serving Tetley's and Stones real ales. Outside seating area. Disco every night.

See also page 10

● **Leeds**
W. Yorks. MD Tue, Fri, Sat. All services. See
also page 10.
Leeds Industrial Museum Armley Mills, access
from bridge 225A. (0113 263 7861). There
have been corn and fulling mills on this site
since at least 1559, with the present building
dating from 1805. When built it was the most
advanced in the country and it now houses a
superb range of real-life exhibits demonstrating
the local textile, heavy engineering, tanning
and printing trades. There are working cranes,
locomotives and waterwheels, and a cinema of
the 1920s. The little stone bridge over the
canal here dates from around 1770. *Open
Tue–Sat 10.00–17.00 & Sun 13.00–17.00.*
Small charge.

Kirkstall Abbey The large elegant ruins of a
Cistercian abbey founded in the 12thC. The
remaining walls narrowly escaped demolition
in the late 19thC, but are now carefully preserved surrounded by a small, attractive park.
Abbey House Museum (0113 275 5821). Just
near the abbey is the splendid folk museum
illustrating the life and work of the people of
Yorkshire during the last 300 years. As well as
exhibiting toys, costumes and pottery, it houses
three streets of fully furnished 19thC shops,
cottages and workshops, including those of a
saddler, chemist, tanner and blacksmith. *Open
Tue–Sat, 10.00–17.00 & Sun 13.00–17.00.*
Small charge.
Tourist Information Centre City Station, Leeds
(0113 242 5242).

NAVIGATIONAL NOTES

Passage between Newlay 3 Locks and
Forge 3 Locks is only allowed under
supervision of BW staff. See latest
edition of BW Navigation Guide for
opening hours or ring 01274 611303.

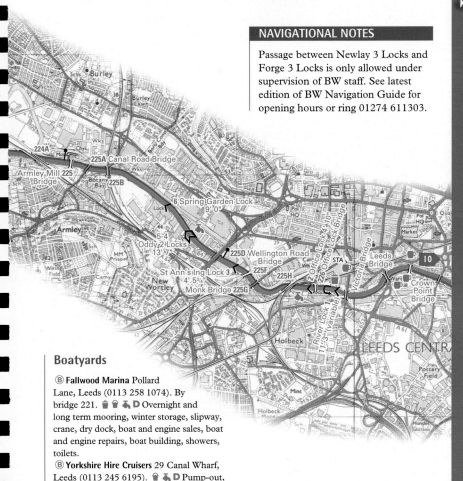

Boatyards

Ⓑ **Fallwood Marina** Pollard
Lane, Leeds (0113 258 1074). By
bridge 221. 🚽 🚿 ⚓ **D** Overnight and
long term mooring, winter storage, slipway,
crane, dry dock, boat and engine sales, boat
and engine repairs, boat building, showers,
toilets.
Ⓑ **Yorkshire Hire Cruisers** 29 Canal Wharf,
Leeds (0113 245 6195). 🚿 ⚓ **D** Pump-out,
overnight mooring.

Bosley Locks (see page 125)

MACCLESFIELD CANAL

MAXIMUM DIMENSIONS	*MARPLE JUNCTION*
Length: 70'	(Peak Forest Canal): 27³/4
Beam: 7'	
Headroom: 7'	Locks: 13
MILEAGE	**MANAGER**
HARDINGS WOOD JUNCTION	0161 427 1079
(Trent & Mersey Canal) to	
Congleton Wharf: 5³/4	
Bosley Top Lock: 11¹/2	
Macclesfield: 17	
Bollington: 20	

Since the completion of the Trent & Mersey Canal in 1777, there existed a demand for an alternative canal link between the Midlands and Manchester. A more direct line through the manufacturing town of Macclesfield was an obvious choice of route. However, it was not until 1825 that Thomas Telford was asked by promoters of the canal to survey a line linking the Peak Forest Canal and the Trent & Mersey Canal. The 28-mile line he suggested was the canal that was built, from Marple to just north of Kidsgrove, but Telford did not supervise the construction, leaving to go and build the Birmingham & Liverpool Junction Canal (now the Shropshire Union). William Crosley was the canal's engineer.

The canal, which runs along the side of a tall ridge of hills west of the Pennines, bears the distinctive mark of Telford's engineering. Like the Shropshire Union, the Macclesfield is a 'cut and fill' canal, following as straight a course as possible, and featuring many great cuttings and embankments. Apart from the stop lock at Hall Green whose 1ft rise was insisted upon as a water preservation measure by the Trent & Mersey Canal Company – to whose Hall Green Branch the Macclesfield Canal connected at the stop lock – all the locks are grouped into the flight of 12 at Bosley. The canal is fed from nearby reservoirs, at Bosley and Sutton.

In spite of intense competition from neighbouring railways and the Trent & Mersey Canal, the Macclesfield carried a good trade for many years. Much of this was coal, and cotton from the big mills established along its northern reaches.

After its purchase in 1846 by the Great Central Railway Company, the canal began a slow, but steady decline. The Macclesfield Canal today is an extremely interesting cruising waterway, and forms part of the popular 100-mile 'Cheshire Ring' canal circuit. Look out for the original, and very large, stone milestones showing distances from Hall Green stop lock (the original end of the canal) and Marple. These were removed during the Second World War in fear of helping invading forces. They have been lovingly restored to their former glory by the Macclesfield Canal Society.

Macclesfield Canal Introduction

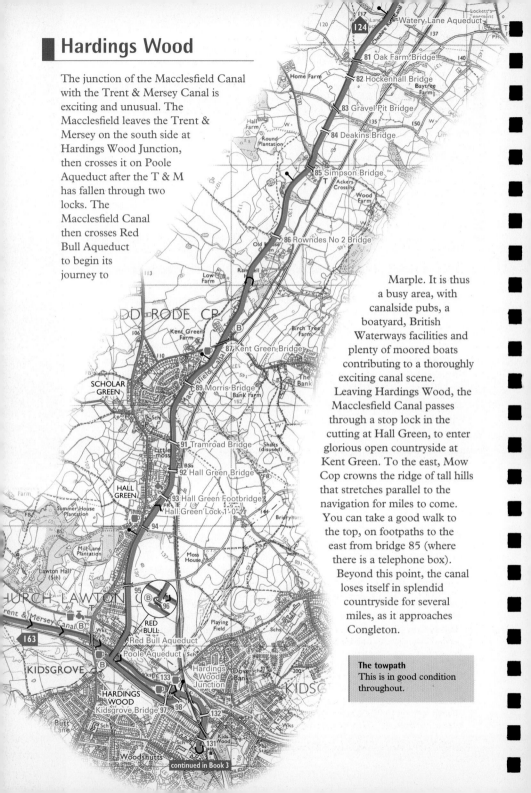

Hardings Wood

The junction of the Macclesfield Canal with the Trent & Mersey Canal is exciting and unusual. The Macclesfield leaves the Trent & Mersey on the south side at Hardings Wood Junction, then crosses it on Poole Aqueduct after the T & M has fallen through two locks. The Macclesfield Canal then crosses Red Bull Aqueduct to begin its journey to Marple. It is thus a busy area, with canalside pubs, a boatyard, British Waterways facilities and plenty of moored boats contributing to a thoroughly exciting canal scene.

Leaving Hardings Wood, the Macclesfield Canal passes through a stop lock in the cutting at Hall Green, to enter glorious open countryside at Kent Green. To the east, Mow Cop crowns the ridge of tall hills that stretches parallel to the navigation for miles to come. You can take a good walk to the top, on footpaths to the east from bridge 85 (where there is a telephone box).

Beyond this point, the canal loses itself in splendid countryside for several miles, as it approaches Congleton.

The towpath
This is in good condition throughout.

continued in Book 3

● **Little Moreton Hall**
NT property. (01260 272018). 3/4 mile west of canal. You can moor by bridge 86 and follow the signposted footpath from here. This fabulous moated house is an outstanding example of black-and-white-timbered architecture and is well worth the walk from the canal. It was built between 1559 and 1580, with carved gables and ornate windows and has scarcely changed since. It contains a fine collection of oak furniture and pewter. Restaurant. *Open 1st April to end Oct, Wed–Sun 12.00–17.30. Nov–Dec, weekends only.* Charge.

● **Mow Cop**
NT property. Walk east from bridge 85. A hill nearly 1100ft above sea level, which gives a magnificent view across the Cheshire Plain, beyond Stoke and into Wales, which looks particularly good at night. On top of the hill is Mow Cop Castle, an imitation ruin built in 1750. It was on this spot that the primitive Methodists held their first meeting in 1807. The meeting lasted 14 hours.

● **Kent Green**
Ches. Tel, stores.

NAVIGATIONAL NOTES

The Macclesfield Canal is generally quite shallow, and mooring is usually only possible at recognised sites.

Boatyards

Ⓑ **David Piper** Red Bull Basin, Church Lawton, Kidsgrove (01782 784754). By Red Bull Aqueduct. 🛆 D Pump-out, gas, overnight and long-term mooring, winter storage, boat sales, slipway, boat sales, chandlery, books and maps, boat building, boat and engine sales and repairs, breakdowns welcome.

Ⓑ **Heritage Narrowboats** Kent Green, Scholar Green, Kidsgrove (01782 785700). 🛆 D E Pump-out, gas, narrow boat hire, day hire craft, overnight mooring (not in winter), long-term mooring, slipway, cradle, chandlery, books and maps, engine repairs, provisions.

Pubs and Restaurants

🍺 **Blue Bell** Canalside, at Hardings Wood Junction (01782 771371). Friendly one bar local serving Boddingtons, Whitbread and Castle Eden real ales. Bar snacks *lunchtimes only every day except Sun.* Children welcome. Outside seating to the rear. Regular entertainment and quiz nights.

🍺 **The Tavern** Canalside by bridge 133, Hardings Wood Road (01782 775382). Serves Tetley's real ale and other guest beers. Food *lunchtimes and evenings, 7 days a week,* with vegetarian menu. Large garden. Children welcome. Nightly entertainment.

🍺 **Red Bull Hotel** By lock 43 on the Trent & Mersey, Red Bull Basin (01782 782600). A popular pub, where children are welcome, close to Hardings Wood Junction, serving Robinson's real ale (with guests from Robinson's) and bar meals *lunchtimes and evenings,* with vegetarian menu. Canalside seating area. Regular quiz nights.

🍺 **Bleeding Wolf Hotel** Hall Green (01782 782272). Near bridge 94. A large and lively thatched country pub offering Robinson's real ale and food *lunchtimes and evenings (not Mon evening),* with vegetarian options. Outside seating and children's play area. *PO, tel, garage and stores* nearby.

🍺 **Rising Sun** Station Road, Scholar Green, (01782 776235). Near the canal. A fine pub offering Thwaites, Marston's and guest real ales, and excellent food *lunchtimes and evenings, 7 days a week.* Children welcome *until 21.00.* Patio.

Congleton

The canal continues north east, crossing Watery Lane Aqueduct. To the east the ever-present range of hills is a reminder that the Pennine Chain lies just beyond. Passing a golf course, the embanked wharf that overlooks Congleton soon appears, with an aqueduct over the road that runs down into the town. The warehouse at the wharf, once handsome, now looks forlorn, and ripe for development. There is a useful grocers and off-licence a short distance south (uphill) of here. A beautifully elegant 'roving' bridge, 76, follows. These are known locally as 'snake bridges' and, in the days of horse drawn boats, changed the towpath from one side to the other without having to un-hitch the horse. Past Congleton railway station, the canal is carried on a high embankment – a common feature of the Macclesfield – across a narrow valley, affording a good view westward of the tall and elegant railway viaduct crossing the same valley. Meanwhile the looming fell known as The Cloud, over 1000ft high and with remains of ancient earthworks, is given a wide berth as the navigation continues on its lonely lock-free course through this very fine landscape. There is a good walk to the top of The Cloud along footpaths east of bridge 71. The canal then continues its lonely course, turning east to cross the River Dane on an embankment – not very impressive from the boat, but superb when viewed from the river – and arrives at the foot of Bosley Locks, in a really delightful setting which is semi-wooded and semi-pastoral. There are good, quiet moorings here.

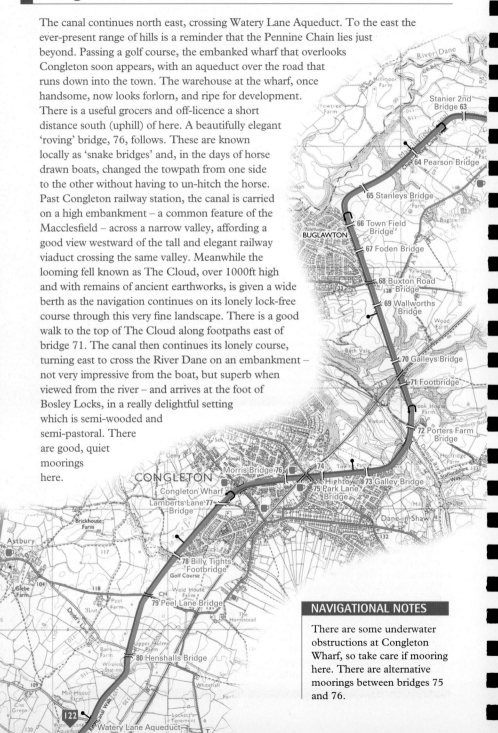

NAVIGATIONAL NOTES

There are some underwater obstructions at Congleton Wharf, so take care if mooring here. There are alternative moorings between bridges 75 and 76.

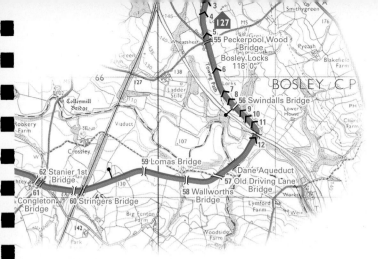

● **Astbury**
Ches. PO, tel, stores. About 1 mile north west
of bridges 79 and 80. A pretty village set just
off the A34. St Mary's Church is amazing: its
light interior and wide aisles are complemented
by generous battlements along the roof and a
tower standing quite separate from the body
of the church.
Astbury Meadow Garden Centre Just along the
main road from the village (01260 276466).
Plants, falconry and nice tea rooms. Entry fee
to the falconry. *Open daily, in summer
09.00–18.00 and in winter 09.00–17.00, and on
Sun and B. Hols 09.30–18.00.*
● **Congleton**
Ches. EC Wed. MD Tue, Sat. All services. A
compact, busy market town.

Congleton Tourist Information Centre Town
Hall, High Street (01260 271095).
● **Bosley Locks**
Effectively the only locks on all the 27 miles
of the Macclesfield Canal, these splendid
constructions are deep, raising the canal level
by fully 118ft to well over 500ft above the
sea. Each lock has a pair of mitred top gates
instead of only a single one. They are a good
example of Telford's practice of grouping
locks together in flights; here are 12 in
1 mile.
● **Bosley Reservoir**
1 mile east of Bosley Locks, along the A54. A
canal reservoir with a wide variety of land and
water birds. Excellent rambling and picnic
area.

Pubs and Restaurants

● ✕ **Egerton Arms** Astbury (01260 273946).
A handsome village pub opposite the church,
serving Robinson's real ale. Food is available
in the restaurant *lunchtimes and evenings, 7 days
a week*, with vegetarian dishes as an option.
Children are welcome, and there is a garden
with a play area. B & B.
● **Wharf** Near Congleton Wharf, Canal Road
(01260 272809). Greenalls real ale in a very
pleasant red-brick pub, decorated with flowers
in the summer. Food *lunchtimes and evenings, 7
days a week*, with a vegetarian menu. There is a
children's playground in the garden.
● **The Moss** South of Congleton Wharf, Canal
Road (01260 273583). Serves Marston's real
ale. Food *lunchtimes and evening, but not Sun
evening*, with a vegetarian menu. Children's
play area.
● **Queen's Head** Park Lane, Congleton (01260
272546). Canalside at bridge 75. A comfort-

able pub serving Tetley's real ale, and offering
food *lunchtimes and evenings, every day*. Large
garden with swings, and children welcome
before 20.00. Grocers and off-licence close-by.
● **Railway** Biddulph Road (01260 273643).
Near Congleton station, by bridge 75. A large
family real ale pub offering Bass and M & B,
and food *all day Mon–Sat*, with a vegetarian
menu. Children's play area. Occasional
entertainment.
● ✕ **Robin Hood** The Rookery (01782
784576). South west of bridge 61. Tetley's
real ale is served in this very friendly and
comfortable country pub, which dates from
1787 and was once the Buglawton Court
Room. The shelves are liberally sprinkled with
local guide books and leaflets, and outside
there is a nice, sheltered, garden. Meals are
served *lunchtimes & evenings*.

Oakgrove

The Macclesfield Canal completes the climb of Bosley Locks and resumes its lonely journey through open, attractive countryside. Approaching Oakgrove the foothills and mountains of the Pennines, some over 1200ft high, spill right down to the canal. The swing bridge at Oakgrove was once a notorious obstacle on the canal, often requiring two very strong individuals to prise it open. Thankfully those days have long passed. The navigation now follows the contour of the land as it begins to swing around the hills, passing the large flat expanse of Danes Moss and approaching Macclesfield, now clearly visible to the north. If you choose to moor by Gurnett Aqueduct to visit the pubs nearby, take a look at the plaque on a cottage wall 25 yards to the east. It commemorates the training here of James Brindley between 1733–40, the canal builder and civil engineer, apprenticed to Abraham Bennett. Just beyond the aqueduct, bridge 43 is a superb example of a typical 'snake bridge'.

Oakgrove A delightful spot with a pub and a superb backcloth of tall, green hills which are ideal for energetic walks. The lane west of the bridge leads to Gawsworth. Sutton reservoir is just north.

Gawsworth
Ches. PO. 2 miles west of Oakgrove. A refreshingly unspoilt village with several small lakes and a lovely 13thC church, approached by a long avenue of elm trees. Facing the church is the old rectory, a half-timbered house built by Rector Baguley in 1470.
Gawsworth Hall (01260 223456). Close to the church, this is a beautiful black-and-white manor house, parts of which date from Norman times. It was once the home of Mary Fitton, possibly the Dark Lady of Shakespeare's sonnets. The park encloses a medieval jousting ground, and there is a *summer season* of open-air theatre. *Open early Apr–early Oct, daily 14.00–17.30, last admission 17.00.* Charge. Tea room.

Maggoty's Wood In this pleasant wood just outside the village is the grave of the eccentric fiddler and playwright, Maggoty Johnson. After being totally rejected by London critics he returned to Gawsworth where he died in 1773, having ordered that he should be buried far from the vulgar gentry who did not appreciate his genius.

Sutton Reservoir
Close to the canal north of bridge 49, this reservoir holds up to 94 million gallons of water. There is a private sailing club, and the public are welcome to ramble and picnic here.

Superbowl Brindley Way, Lyme Green Business Park (01625 616438). By bridge 45. Maybe you, or your children, would enjoy some 10-pin bowling. *Open every day 10.00–24.00.* Charge for bowling only. Fully licensed bar and *food* with pizzas and burgers *all day*, diner *open 11.00–16.00.* Parties welcome.

Pubs and Restaurants

Fools Nook Leek Road, Sutton (01260 252254). Just east of bridge 49. An inviting country pub, where wooden beams and comfy settles immediately make you feel at home. Boddingtons real ale and good meals *lunchtimes and evenings*, from an extensive menu with vegetarian options. Very pleasant courtyard at the rear. Children welcome.

Church House Church Lane, Sutton Lane Ends (01260 252436). Well worth the 1/2 mile walk from Gurnett Aqueduct to enjoy this friendly and comfortable village local serving Boddingtons, Wadworth and Robinson's real ale and good food *lunchtimes and evenings*. Garden with children's playthings.

Old Kings Head Bradley Smithy, Gurnett (01625 423890). Below the aqueduct. Once a coaching house and smithy dating from 1695, this comfortable beamed pub serves Boddingtons, Robinson's and guest real ales and meals *lunchtimes and evenings, 7 days a week.* Children's play area in the garden.

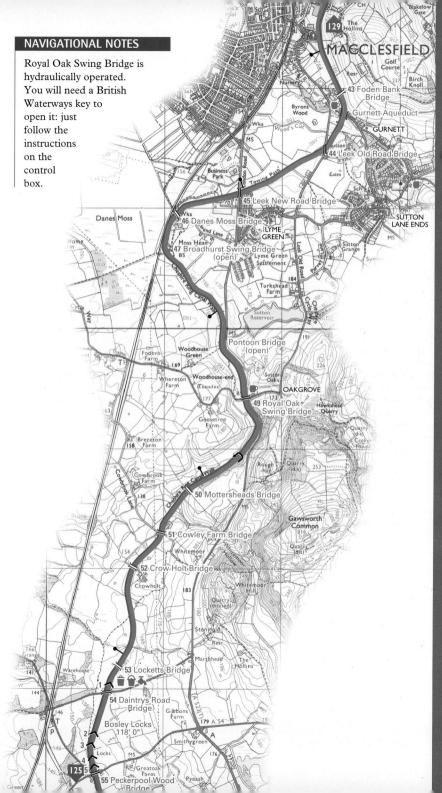

NAVIGATIONAL NOTES

Royal Oak Swing Bridge is hydraulically operated. You will need a British Waterways key to open it: just follow the instructions on the control box.

Macclesfield

Leaving green and hilly countryside, the navigation enters the outskirts of Macclesfield, where some new housing incorporates a canal crane. A very wide stretch of water is overlooked by a vast and beautifully restored flour mill, marking the site of the original Macclesfield Canal Company. This Hovis Mill was built in the 1820s, and was the birthplace of the famous flour. The word Hovis is derived from the Latin 'hominisunvis' meaning 'power to the man'. Note the archway entrance off the canal, now blocked. The town itself is down the hill; the best place to moor is south of bridge 37, which is also handy for shops and bottled gas. The tree-lined canal continues northwards to Bollington, passing through glorious open countryside with views of the hills all around, to the Adelphi Mill, once a silk mill and now converted into offices and a pub. A 60ft-high embankment and two aqueducts then carry the navigation across the valley towards the huge Clarence Mill, a textile mill now converted into thriving small manufacturing units.

Pubs and Restaurants

Macclesfield and Bollington have been described as *one of the seven wonders of the real ale enthusiast's waterways*, with *over 80 such pubs* within striking distance of the canal.

Bee Hive Macclesfield. South-west of bridge 41. Cosy Boddingtons real ale local serving *lunchtime food every day*. Children's room. Garden.

Dolphin Inn Macclesfield. West of bridge 40. Robinson's real ale in a friendly local with an open fire. Food at *lunchtime. PO box and telephone* nearby.

Navigation Black Road (01625 611249). South-east of bridge 38. Victorian local built for the original canal navvies. Tetley's and Bass real ale and bar snacks available. Children welcome. Outside seating. Regular entertainment.

Puss in Boots Buxton Road (01625 423261). Canalside at bridge 37. Comfortable pub with an open fire and garden, serving Boddingtons real ale and food *lunchtimes and evenings (not Sat and Sun evenings)* with a vegetarian menu. Children welcome.

Bridgewater Arms Hotel Buxton Road (01625 422660). West of bridge 38. A sturdy corner house serving Wilson and John Smith's real ales. Children welcome. Outside seating. *PO* nearby.

Britannia Hurdsfield. West of bridge 34. Unspoilt and attractive terraced pub serving Burtonwood real ale. Pub games. *PO, tel, stores and Chinese take-away* close-by.

Three Crowns Higher Hurdsfield. East of bridge 34. A tiny Victorian stone terraced pub with a garden. Robinson's real ale.

Barge Inn In part of the old Adelphi Mill, Grimshaw Lane, Bollington (01625 560510). A canalside free house serving a variety of real ales and food *lunchtimes and evenings, except Mon evenings*, in the chargrill restaurant. Vegetarian and children's menus. Regular entertainment. B & B.

Dog & Partridge Palmerston Street, west of Bollington Aqueduct (01625 572177). A sociable village pub with an open fire offering Robinson's real ale and sandwiches *all day*. Outside seating and regular entertainment. Children welcome.

Vale Inn Bollington (01625 575147). Down the road from bridge 26, or through the woods (take a torch if it's dark) opposite Clarence Mill, just 250 yards from the canal. Thwaites and Taylor real ales in a very fine terraced stone pub with an open fire. Food *lunchtimes and evenings (not all day Mon or Sun evenings)*. Children welcome. Garden.

BOAT TRIPS
The White Nancy Cruising Restaurant A restaurant boat operating from Bollington Wharf, Grimshaw Lane. Book well in advance on 01663 763936. Private bookings for up to 12 people from mid-Feb to Christmas.

Boatyards

(B) **Macclesfield Canal Centre** Swettenham Wharf, Brook Street, Macclesfield (01625 420042). 🛏 🛏 🔧 D E Pump out, gas, narrow boat hire, overnight mooring, long-term mooring, winter storage, slipway, crane available, chandlery, public telephone, books, maps and gifts, boat sales, engine sales and repairs, toilets and showers, restaurant boat.

(B) **Peak Forest Cruisers** The Wharf, Buxton Road, Macclesfield (01625 424172). Narrow boat hire (2 boats available for week or weekend hire), long-term mooring. *Nearby* 🔧 one either side of Bridge 37.

British Waterways Swettenham Street Yard 0161 427 1079.

(B) **Bollington Wharf Leisure** Grimshaw Lane, Bollington (01625 575811). 🛏 🛏 🔧 D Pump-out, gas, day boat hire, overnight and long-term mooring, engine sales, boat and engine repairs, boat fitting, telephone, toilets, showers, refreshments, chandlery, books and maps, gifts, provisions, pets corner and picnics.

(B) **Kerridge Dry Dock** Bollington (01625 574287). Between bridges 28 and 29. 🔧 D Pump-out, long-term mooring, winter storage, boat building, boat sales, engine sales and repairs.

● **Macclesfield**
Ches. MD Tue, Fri, Sat. All services. Earliest records of a settlement are to be found in the Domesday Book, when the area was detailed as part of the land of Earl Edwin of Mercia. The town grew rapidly until it became the most important town in east Cheshire, being recognised as a borough in 1220. At that time it was the administrative centre for the Macclesfield Forest, and was granted its charter in 1261. Following set-backs resulting from the Battle of Flodden Field in 1513, the town was granted a new charter in 1595, this being replaced by another, granted by Charles II, in 1684. Now the town is an interesting combination of a thriving silk manufacturing centre and old market town, with cobbled streets and a picturesque medieval Market Place, encircled by busy modern roads. There are several fine classical buildings, making the most of the local stone, and detailed in the fine Town Trail leaflet available at the Tourist Information Centre. In the 18thC the town was one of the leading silk producing centres and is still important for its textile and pharmaceutical industries. One interesting feature of the town is the Unitarian Chapel in King Edward Street, approached through a narrow passage and guarded by a lovely wrought-iron gate: it is dated 1689 and is 'for William and Mary's subjects dissenting from the Church of England'.
St Michael's Church Market Place. Very little remains of the original structure founded in 1278 by Queen Eleanor and then known as All Hallows, although the Savage Chapel, the oldest stone building in the town, survives. The church still contains many fine monuments.
Paradise Mill Park Lane (01625 618228). Built between 1820–60, this handloom silk-weaving mill finally closed down in 1981. Here you can see Jacquard handlooms in action, authentic room settings and an exhibition of a whole

wealth of material connected with one of Macclesfield's major industries. *Open Tue–Sun 13.00–17.00, (Nov to March, 13.00–16.00). Closed Mon.* Charge (*buying a joint ticket for this and the Silk Museum results in a saving*).
Silk Museum & Macclesfield Heritage Centre Roe Street (01625 613210). The first museum in the country devoted entirely to the study of the silk industry: audio visuals, costume, textiles, room settings and even parachutes. Visit also The Heritage Centre in the old 1813 Sunday School building. *Open Tue–Sat 11.00–17.00 and Sun 13.00–17.00.* Charge (*see above*). *Tea room and shop.*
Macclesfield Leisure Centre Priory Lane (01625 615602). Three swimming pools, six squash courts and a host of other facilities. Entertainment in the 1200–seat hall and the Priory Suite.
The Middlewood Way A 10-mile footpath and cycleway, along the course of the old Macclesfield, Bollington and Marple Railway which opened in 1869. It was converted for recreational use in 1985. Information and leaflets from Macclesfield Leisure Services on 01625 504509.
Macclesfield Tourist Information Centre Town Hall, Market Place (01625 504114). Extremely helpful and containing a wealth of information about the town and surrounding area.

● **Bollington**
Ches. EC Wed. PO, tel, stores, garage, bank. There is a good view of this stone-built town from the huge canal embankment that cuts across it. From here it is only a mile to the boundary of the Peak District National Park. The white tower on the ridge south of the town is called White Nancy. One popular story is that it was built to commemorate the battle of Waterloo by a member of the Gaskell family and took its name from one of the ladies of the family called Nancy.
The Macclesfield Groundwork Discovery Centre Adelphi Mill Gate Lodge, Grimshaw Lane,

Bollington (01625 572681). Tourist information, walks, canoe and cycle hire, and an exhibition. *Open Mon–Fri 14.00–16.30, and Sun 10.00–16.30.* **Bollington Leisure Centre** Heath Road (01625 574774). Squash courts, a swimming pool and other facilities.

BOAT TRIPS
Mary Sunley Available for trips and charter from Bollington Wharf. Ring 01625 575811 for details.

Canal embankment at Bollington

Higher Poynton

This isolated stretch is typical of the Macclesfield Canal and in its beautifully quiet, rural isolation it represents much of the charm that most canals possess. Winding northwards along the summit level at over 500ft above the sea, the navigation generally follows the contours of this upland country, but crosses several valleys on embankments with fine aqueducts. There is a fine shady, wooded section between bridges 22 and 21, and good moorings between bridges 20 and 19. There are few centres of population near the canal, just the odd pub here or there, and the countryside is quite unspoilt. Around Higher Poynton the canal becomes wider, the result of ancient subsidence from a coal-mine, which necessitated the continual raising of the canal banks and bridges to hold the water in the sinking canal. Be sure to adhere to the main channel here. An old branch near bridge 15 used to lead to the mine; now it is used by a boatyard.

● **Higher Poynton**
Ches. PO, tel, stores, garage. Considered by some to be the most pleasant moorings on the canal, where the wide water supports large families of ducks, geese and swans. There is a recreation field adjacent, and a handy pub.
The Anson Museum Anson Road, Poynton (01625 874426). A working display of early internal combustion engines, with emphasis on those made in the Manchester area. *Open May–Oct, Sun only 11.00–17.00.*
Lyme Park *NT property* Ring Macclesfield TIC for details. 2 miles east of Higher Poynton. Pedestrian entrance at West Parkgate, 1/4 mile south east of bridge 17 or footpath from bridge

15. In the centre of an extensive park containing deer is a magnificent Elizabethan house that belonged to the Legh family from the 14thC until 1947, when it was handed over to the nation as payment of death duties. It has a fine interior containing many works of art, and four Chippendale chairs claimed to be covered with material from a cloak worn by King Charles I at his execution. There is an adventure playground for the children. Refreshments available. Hall: *opens 1st Apr to 31st Oct, Sat–Wed 13.30–17.00. Park opens all year round from 08.00 to dusk. Garden: 1st Apr to 31st Oct, 11.00–17.00 and Nov–17th Dec weekends only, 12.00–16.00.* Charge.

Pubs and Restaurants

🍺 ✕ **The Windmill Inn** Holehouse Lane, Whiteley Green (pub – 01625 573189, carvery – 01625 574222). 250yds west of bridge 25. Large open-plan pub in a former cotton mill, with an open fire, built in 1675. Tetley's real ale and food *lunchtimes and evenings*, with a vegetarian menu. Children welcome. Garden. Regular entertainment with jazz, folk and country music. The carvery is *open for Sat D and Sun L.* There is a useful post box in the wall.

🍺 **Miners Arms** Near bridge 18, Wood Lane North, Four Lane Ends (01625 872731). A big, bustling, lively and thriving country pub which is pleasantly family orientated, having extensive gardens and amusements for children. Boddingtons real ale and a varied menu *lunchtimes and evenings, and all day at weekends*, with vegetarian and children's menus.

🍺 **Boar's Head** Shrigley Road North, Higher Poynton (01625 878325). Down the hill from bridge 15. An imposing red-brick pub serving Boddingtons real ale and bar meals and snacks *lunchtimes only*. Beer garden.

Boatyards

Ⓑ **Lyme View Marina** Adlington Basin, Poynton (01625 874638). 🛒 🛒 ⚓ **D** Pump-out, gas, narrow boat hire, overnight and long-term mooring, slipway, engine repairs, licensed cafe, chandlery, coal sales.

Ⓑ **Barton Boat Services** In the grounds of Lyme View Marina (01625 850984). Builds customised boat interiors.

Ⓑ **Midships Marine Supplies** In grounds of Lyme View Marina, contact through the Marina. Chandler.

Ⓑ **Constellation Cruises** Lyme Road, Higher Poynton, Stockport (01625 873471). Near bridge 15. ⚓ **D** Gas, day hire craft, overnight and long-term mooring, books, maps and gifts, boat building and fitting.

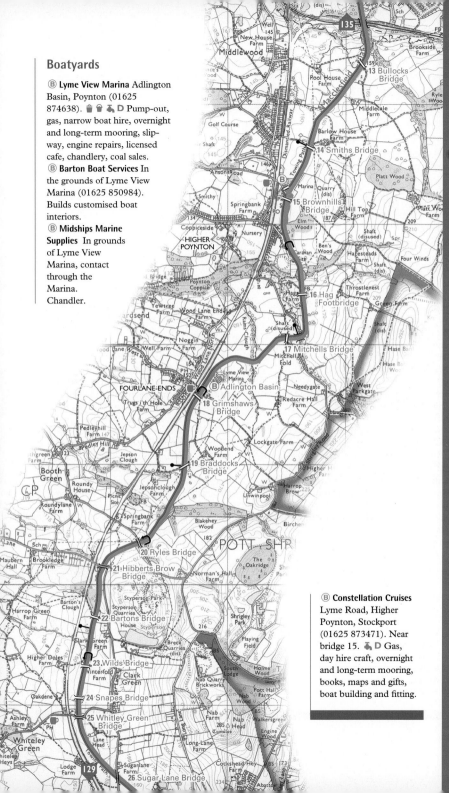

Marple Junction

Another massive embankment and a tall aqueduct, this time over a railway, are crossed on the way into High Lane. The canal proceeds northwards in a cutting through High Lane, passing the junction with the short High Lane Arm – well protected and now used as a club mooring site – and a children's play-park. There are moorings between the arm and bridge 11, with shops close by. Beyond the town is a restored mill; then open country intervenes, offering views westward of Stockport and the southern outskirts of Manchester. There is a useful shop, the Doodfield Stores, down the hill from bridge 6. At bridge 3 there are two grocers and a fish & chip shop. Goyt Mill appears, thankfully restored and now housing workshops, heralding the start of Marple, a busy boating centre much enjoyed by the citizens of Manchester. The area of the junction with the Peak Forest Canal is delightful: an old turnover bridge, mellow wharf buildings and the nearby flight of Marple Locks are framed by the distant mountainous country across the Goyt Valley. The canal here is 500ft above sea level.

● **High Lane**
Gt Manchester. PO, tel, stores, garage, station, fish & chips. More a spread than a village; good moorings and useful for supplies. High Lane is effectively at the south-east corner of the Manchester conurbation, and is quite indistinguishable from its neighbours. The very long Disley railway tunnel passes deep underneath the place.

● **Marple**
Gt Manchester. All services. A typical residential town, serving as a dormitory base for Stockport and Manchester. Elements of the old village can still be seen, buried amongst the suburbia, but much the most attractive part is by the canal. The rugged Ludworth Moor is not far away, where 'Robin Hood's Picking Rods' still stand, the supposed remains of a Celtic Druid's temple.

● **Marple Locks**
The 16 locks at Marple were not built until 1804, four years after the rest of the Peak Forest canal was opened. The one-mile gap thus left was bridged by a tramway, while the Canal Company sought the cash to pay for the construction of a flight of locks. This was obviously a most unsatisfactory state of affairs, since limestone from Doveholes had to be shifted from wagon to boat at Buxworth Basin, from boat to wagon at Marple Junction, and back into boat again at the bottom of the tramway. Not surprisingly, a container system was developed – using iron boxes with a 2-ton payload – to ease the triple transhipment. However, this was no long-term solution, and when the necessary £27,000 was forthcoming the company authorised construction of the flight of locks. Today they stand comparison with any flight on the network. Note especially Samuel Oldknow's superb warehouse, by lock 9 opposite the lock keeper's house, now tastefully converted to offices.

Pubs and Restaurants

● **Bull's Head** Market Street, High Lane. At bridge 11. (0161 427 1250) A lovely comfy, cosy, friendly, local's pub with an open fire, settles and bookshelves. Boddingtons real ale and excellent *lunchtime* food in generous quantities. Canalside terrace.

● ✕ **Ring O'Bells** Marple (0161 427 2300). By bridge 2. A very comfortable and friendly pub with a chiming grandfather clock. The waterways bar is recommended. Serving Robinson's real ale and good food *lunchtimes and evenings, except Sun when food is available in the evening only.* Excellent children's menu. Garden. Telephone kiosk outside.

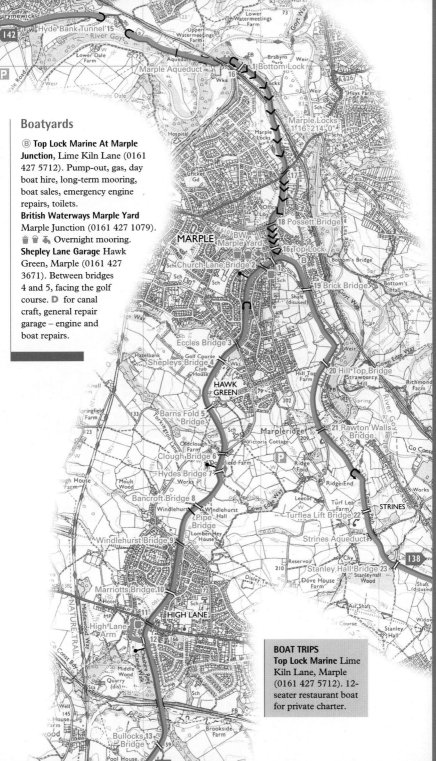

Boatyards

Ⓑ **Top Lock Marine At Marple Junction**, Lime Kiln Lane (0161 427 5712). Pump-out, gas, day boat hire, long-term mooring, boat sales, emergency engine repairs, toilets.

British Waterways Marple Yard Marple Junction (0161 427 1079). 🚽🚿♿ Overnight mooring.

Shepley Lane Garage Hawk Green, Marple (0161 427 3671). Between bridges 4 and 5, facing the golf course. **D** for canal craft, general repair garage – engine and boat repairs.

BOAT TRIPS
Top Lock Marine Lime Kiln Lane, Marple (0161 427 5712). 12-seater restaurant boat for private charter.

Marple, a busy boating centre on the Macclesfield Canal

PEAK FOREST AND ASHTON CANALS

MAXIMUM DIMENSIONS	MILEAGE
Length: 70'	*ASHTON CANAL*
Beam: 7'	Duckinfield Junction to
Headroom: 6'	Ducie Street Junction: 6½
	Locks: 18
MANAGER	*PEAK FOREST CANAL*
0161 273 4686	Whaley Bridge to
	Marple Junction: 6½
	Dukinfield Junction: 14½
	Locks: 16

THE ASHTON CANAL

Authorised in 1792 and opened shortly afterwards, the Ashton was a strong rival of
the Rochdale Canal – with which it connects in Manchester. The two canals were
constructed simultaneously, partly to tap the big coal producing area around Oldham.
The Ashton also opened a new trade route from Manchester to the textile mills of
Ashton, while the Rochdale served as a broad canal link over the Pennines between the
Mersey and the rivers of Yorkshire. In 1831 completion of the narrow Macclesfield
Canal made the Ashton part of a through route from Manchester to the Potteries.
The 1830s saw the peak of the Ashton Canal's prosperity. The canal company sold out
to the forerunner of the Great Central Railway Company in 1846, who continued to
maintain and operate the canal. Traffic declined in the present century and by 1962 it
was unnavigable. A determined effort by the Peak Forest Canal Society, the IWA, local
councils and the BWB (as was) resulted in its reopening in 1974.

THE PEAK FOREST CANAL

This canal runs from the Ashton Canal at Ashton through Marple to Whaley Bridge
and Buxworth. Authorised by Act of Parliament in 1794, it was aimed at providing an
outlet for the great limestone deposits at Doveholes, south east of Whaley Bridge.
However, since Doveholes is over 1000ft above sea level, the canal was terminated at
Buxworth, and the line was continued up to the quarries by a 6½-mile tramway.
The canal was completed by 1800 except for the flight of locks at Marple, which were
not built until 1804. A second, temporary, tramway bridged this gap in the meantime.
Buxworth soon became a busy interchange point where the wagons bringing the stone
down from Doveholes tipped their load either into canal boats or into lime-kilns. This
traffic, and the boats bringing coal *up* the canal for firing the kilns, accounted for the
greatest proportion of the canal company's revenue.
The Peak Forest was also boosted by the opening of the Macclesfield Canal to Marple
top lock in 1831 making it part of a new through route from Manchester to the
Potteries. The Cromford & High Peak Railway was opened in 1831, joining up Whaley
Bridge with the Cromford Canal on the far side of the Peak District.
By the early 1840s the Peak Forest Canal was suffering from competition from the
Trent & Mersey Canal Company and two new railways. It was leased in perpetuity to
the Sheffield, Ashton-under-Lyne & Manchester Railway, later the Great Central. In
1922 the Buxworth traffic finished, while (through) traffic on the 'lower' Peak Forest
Canal had disappeared by the last war. Along with the Ashton, full navigation was
restored in 1974, with the Buxworth line currently undergoing restoration.

Upper Peak Forest

The Upper Peak Forest Canal leads
off to the north west; and it rapidly
becomes apparent that this is a navigation
set in a robust, handsome landscape. Clinging
desperately to a wooded mountainside overlooking
the steep, wide Goyt Valley, it winds its precarious way
to New Mills. The trains that traverse the opposite side of
the valley look like tiny models on the distant, massive mountains.
The former Whaley Bridge Branch, now the main line, terminates in a small
basin at the north end of the town. There is a building here of great interest to
industrial archaeologists: it covers a dock and was built in 1832 at this, the junction
of the Peak Forest Canal and the Cromford & High Peak Railway. Here transhipment
between canal boat and railway wagon could take place under cover. The former
railway's Whaley Bridge inclined plane (now a footpath) rises to the south of this
historic building. South of bridge 34 the canal splits: the original main line, at present
closed beyond the bridge, turns east across the Goyt on an aqueduct to Buxworth (its
name changed from the supposedly less desirable Bugsworth) with its fascinating basin
complex overlooked by a fine pub. The A6 road and the railway are always close to the
navigation, but they detract not at all from its isolation. There are charming stations at
New Mills, Furness Vale and Whaley Bridge: from these one may take a magnificent
railway trip past two canal-feeding reservoirs and over the hills to the summit, 1200ft
above sea level, then down to the old Roman town of Buxton, now unfortunately the
end of the line. The canal continues north-west along the mountainside towards
Whaley Bridge. It is an enchanting stretch, passing plenty of woods, pastures and
grazing horses. As you approach New Mills you will notice the smell of sweets in the
air – Matlows, the makers of 'Swizzles', have their factory here. Near Disley, another
railway pops out of the long Disley Tunnel, way below the canal; while yet another
line appears above and beside the canal, from High Lane. Thus around New Mills
the valley contains three very picturesque railways. One of the pleasant features of
this terrain is the easy co-existence of woods, fields and a canal on the one hand, and
a certain amount of industry on the other. There are good moorings at bridge 24,
where a public footpath gives easy access to Strines.

BOAT TRIPS
Judith Mary Unicorn Marine, The Wharf, Canal Street, Whaley Bridge (01663 734737).
A fine 70ft, 42 seater narrow boat available for private charter *all year*. Fully licensed.

NAVIGATIONAL NOTES

1 You will need a Leeds & Liverpool type padlock key for the locks on this and the Ashton Canals. These can be obtained from the Canal Manager's Office, BW, Top Lock, Marple, Manchester (0161 427 1079) and the Rochdale Canal Co (0161 236 2456).
2 Bridge 24 is windlass operated.
3 The canal on this section is very shallow – take it slowly and appreciate the surroundings fully.

The towpath
This is in good condition throughout.

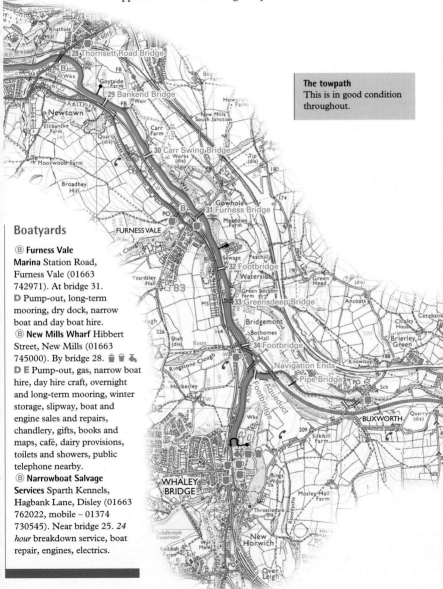

Boatyards

Ⓑ **Furness Vale Marina** Station Road, Furness Vale (01663 742971). At bridge 31.
D Pump-out, long-term mooring, dry dock, narrow boat and day boat hire.
Ⓑ **New Mills Wharf** Hibbert Street, New Mills (01663 745000). By bridge 28.
D E Pump-out, gas, narrow boat hire, day hire craft, overnight and long-term mooring, winter storage, slipway, boat and engine sales and repairs, chandlery, gifts, books and maps, café, dairy provisions, toilets and showers, public telephone nearby.
Ⓑ **Narrowboat Salvage Services** Sparth Kennels, Hagbank Lane, Disley (01663 762022, mobile – 01374 730545). Near bridge 25. *24 hour* breakdown service, boat repair, engines, electrics.

● **Whaley Bridge**
Derbs. EC Wed. PO, tel, stores, garage, station, laundrette, fish & chips, banks. Built on a steep hill at the end of the canal, with good views across the Goyt valley, this is now a quiet and pleasant place, a new by-pass having removed much of the traffic. The beautiful nearby hills are, however, more noteworthy than the town.

Cromford & High Peak Railway In the early 1820s a physical connection was planned between the Peak Forest Canal at Whaley Bridge and the Cromford Canal, way over to the south east on the other side of the Peak District, using a junction canal. However a canal would have been impracticable through such mountainous terrain, and so a railway was constructed. Known as the Cromford & High Peak Railway, it was opened throughout in 1831, 33 miles long. With a summit level over 1200ft above the sea, this extraordinary standard-gauge goods line was interesting chiefly for its numerous slopes and inclined planes, up which the wagons were hauled by either stationary or tenacious locomotive steam engines. (The steepest gradient on the line was 1 in 7.) The C & HPR closed in 1967; much of the route is now being turned into a public footpath and bridleway. Around Whaley Bridge one may still see the remains of the short inclined plane (now a footpath) which brought the goods down the hill, then through the town to the wharf at the terminus of the Peak Forest Canal.

Toddbrook Reservoir Just south of Whaley Bridge. A very pleasant area for picnicking and walking. Private sailing club; fishing rights on this BW reservoir are exercised by an angling club.

● **Buxworth**
Derbs. PO, tel, stores. The main feature in Buxworth is the fascinating old terminal basin system. This used to be a tremendously busy complex, and is of great interest to industrial archaeologists. The canal line to Buxworth (once Bugsworth) was built to bring the canal as near as possible to the great limestone quarries at Doveholes, a plate tramway being constructed in 1799 via Chapel Milton to complete the connection. Known as the Peak Forest Tramway, this little line, 6½ miles long, brought the stone down the hills to Buxworth, where it was transhipped into waiting canal boats. Throughout the history of the line, the wagons on the tramway were drawn exclusively by horse-power – except for a 500yd inclined plane in Chapel-en-le-Frith, where the trucks were attached to a continuous rope so that the descending trucks pulled empty ones up the 1 in 7½ slope. The tramway was closed by 1926, and the sidings and basins at Buxworth have been disused and overgrown since that time. However the Inland Waterways Preservation Society and BW are working towards a complete restoration of the complex. See the notice board by the bridge for the latest information.

● **Furness Vale**
Derbs. PO, tel, stores, garage, station. A main road (A6) village, useful for supplies.

● **New Mills**
Derbs. PO, tel, stores, garage, banks, laundrette, stations. A mostly stone-built town on the Cheshire/Derbyshire border: its industries include textile printing, engineering and engraving. A boatyard occupies old canal buildings to the east of bridge 28.

● **Disley**
Ches. PO, tel, stores, garage, station. On the south bank of the canal. The centre of the village is quite pretty, spoilt slightly by the A6 traffic. The village is up the hill, south west of bridge 26. The attractive church stands among trees above the little village square. It was greatly renovated in the last century, but the ancient tower with the griffin leering down at passers-by dates from the 16thC. Vehicular and pedestrian access to Lyme Park (see page 132) is from the A6 near Disley, 1½ miles south west of bridge 26.

● **Strines**
Gt Manchester. PO, tel, stores, station. A useful place for supplies.

A SILK PURSE FROM A SOW'S EAR

The Ashton Canal is now a part of 'The Cheshire Ring', a superb 100-mile cruising circuit which can be comfortably completed in a week. Those with extra energy, or a day or two more, can add in a diversion along the Peak Forest Canal, and their efforts will reap just reward. The ability to cruise these waterways is due to those who campaigned between 1959 and 1974 to clear and restore canals that had become both an eyesore and a danger. Extensive lobbying resulted in the formation of the Peak Forest Canal Society, and with the staging of the 1966 IWA National Rally at Marple restoration gained momentum. 'Operation Ashton', held over a weekend in September 1968, saw 600 waterway enthusiasts clear more than 2000 tons of rubbish from the canal. Local people were amazed, and began to realise that what had long been regarded as an eyesore and a danger could now become a valuable local amenity. *The corner had been turned.* Following a rally on the Rochdale Canal at Easter 1971, local authorities and the British Waterways Board (as it then was) decided to proceed with full restoration of the Ashton and Peak Forest Canals. We owe a great debt to all those involved.

Cromford & High Peak Railway

Pubs and Restaurants

🍺 **Railway** Whaley Bridge (01663 732245). Robinson's real ale, bar meals and snacks *all day every day* in a fine straightforward pub. Children welcome.

🍺 **The Goyt Inn** Bridge Street, Whaley Bridge (01663 732840). Attractive backstreet pub with a garden. Vaux ales.

🍺 **Navigation** Johnson Street, Whaley Bridge (01663 732308). Near the canal terminus. Pub with a narrow boat theme serving Boddingtons real ale and food *all day.* Children welcome in afternoons. Garden. Regular jazz nights.

🍺 ✕ **Jodrell Arms** Whaley Bridge (01663 732164). Webster's and John Smith's real ale, bar meals *lunchtimes and evenings* with vegetarian option. Children welcome. Regular entertainment from jazz to folk nights. On site Indian Balti restaurant *open 17.00–midnight.* B & B.

🍺 ✕ **Navigation** Buxworth (01663 732072). By the canal terminus, this is a superbly situated pub overlooking the old basins. Marston's, Webster's and a guest real ale, food *all day.* Several very comfortable bars, one with a canal theme, plus a restaurant and family room. Garden with playground. Games and events. B & B.

🍺 **Dog & Partridge** Bridgemont (01663 732284). Near the junction to Buxworth Basin. A local pub serving real ale. Food. Children welcome.

🍺 **The Crossing** By the level crossing, up the hill from bridge 31. Robinson's real ale and food *lunchtimes and evenings.*

🍺 **Soldier Dick** Buxton Road, Furness Vale (01663 743868). Just past The Crossing pub from Bridge 31. A road house serving Bass and guest real ales and food *lunchtimes and evenings,* with good vegetarian menu. Children welcome. Outside seating. Regular food theme nights. B & B.

🍺 ✕ **The Beehive** Albion Road, New Mills (01663 742087). Just along the lane opposite New Mills Wharf, by bridge 28. A welcoming stone-built pub run by canal enthusiasts. A variety of good real ale is always available including Boddingtons and Flowers, together with home-cooked bar meals *lunchtimes and evenings.* Booking is advisable for the restaurant. Children are welcome.

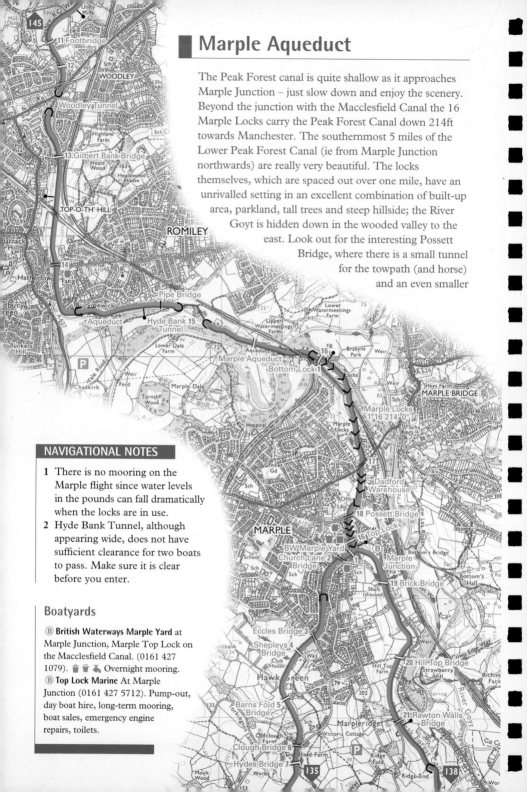

Marple Aqueduct

The Peak Forest canal is quite shallow as it approaches Marple Junction – just slow down and enjoy the scenery. Beyond the junction with the Macclesfield Canal the 16 Marple Locks carry the Peak Forest Canal down 214ft towards Manchester. The southernmost 5 miles of the Lower Peak Forest Canal (ie from Marple Junction northwards) are really very beautiful. The locks themselves, which are spaced out over one mile, have an unrivalled setting in an excellent combination of built-up area, parkland, tall trees and steep hillside; the River Goyt is hidden down in the wooded valley to the east. Look out for the interesting Possett Bridge, where there is a small tunnel for the towpath (and horse) and an even smaller

NAVIGATIONAL NOTES

1 There is no mooring on the Marple flight since water levels in the pounds can fall dramatically when the locks are in use.
2 Hyde Bank Tunnel, although appearing wide, does not have sufficient clearance for two boats to pass. Make sure it is clear before you enter.

Boatyards

Ⓑ **British Waterways Marple Yard** at Marple Junction, Marple Top Lock on the Macclesfield Canal. (0161 427 1079). Overnight mooring.
Ⓑ **Top Lock Marine** At Marple Junction (0161 427 5712). Pump-out, day boat hire, long-term mooring, boat sales, emergency engine repairs, toilets.

one for the boatman, leading down to the lock. At the foot of the locks, where the River Goyt is crossed, there is the superb spectacle of a major canal aqueduct with an even bigger railway viaduct alongside. West of here a narrow stretch was once Rose Hill Tunnel, long since opened out. The canal then traverses a wooded hillside before diving into Hyde Bank Tunnel, 308yds long. The towpath is diverted over the hill, passing a farm. On the other side, a couple of minor aqueducts lead the canal northwards, away from the Goyt Valley and past Romiley, Bredbury and Woodley, where there is a narrow 176yd-long tunnel, this time with the towpath continued through it. There is a swimming pool close to the canal at bridge 14.

● **Marple**
Gt Manchester. All services. Once a famous hat-making centre, the town is most interesting by the canal. There are shops just downhill from bridge 17.

● **Marple Locks**
The 16 locks at Marple were not built until 1804, four years after the rest of the navigation was opened. The one-mile gap thus left was bridged by a tramway, while the Canal Company sought the cash to pay for the construction of a flight of locks. This was obviously a most unsatisfactory state of affairs, since the limestone from Doveholes had to be shifted from wagon to boat at Buxworth Basin, from boat to wagon at Marple Junction, and back into boat again at the bottom of the tramway. Not surprisingly, a container system was developed – using iron boxes with a 2-ton payload – to ease the triple transhipment. However, this was no long-term solution, and when the necessary £27,000 was forthcoming the company authorised construction of the flight of locks. Today they stand comparison

with any flight on the network. Note especially Samuel Oldknow's superb warehouse, by lock 9 opposite the lock keeper's house, now tastefully converted to offices.

● **Marple Aqueduct**
Deservedly scheduled as an ancient monument, this three-arched aqueduct over the River Goyt is a very fine structure, in an exquisite setting almost 100ft above the river. Designed by Benjamin Outram its construction utilises circular pierced shoulders above each arch to reduce the weight of the rubble filling whilst providing a decorative feature. Contrast and interest are further added by the use of two different colours of gritstone in the parapets and ledges.

● **Romiley**
Gt Manchester. All services. A useful place for supplies.

> **BOAT TRIPS**
> *Top Lock Marine* Lime Kiln Lane, Marple (0161 427 5712). 12-seater restaurant trip boat for private charter.

Pubs and Restaurants

🍺✕ **Ring O'Bells** Marple (0161 427 2300). By bridge 2. A very comfortable and friendly pub with a chiming grandfather clock. The waterways bar is recommended. Serving Robinson's real ale and good food *lunchtimes and evenings, except Sun when food available in the evening only.* Excellent children's menu. Garden. Telephone kiosk outside.

🍺✕ **The Navigation Hotel** By lock 13, Stockport Road, Marple (0161 427 2270). Useful for 'lock wheelers' (remember, there is no mooring on the flight!). A large comfortable Robinson's pub. Food, *lunchtimes and evenings,* with vegetarian menu in a dining room. Children welcome.

🍺 **Duke of York Hotel** 250yds east of bridge 14, Stockport Road, Romiley (0161 430 2806).

John Smith's real ale. Food *lunchtimes and evenings,* with vegetarian option and a *weekend restaurant.* Occasional entertainment and quiz nights. Outside seating.

✕ **Bridge Café** Stockport Road, Romiley (0161 430 5937). Moor north of bridge 14. A friendly and welcoming café decorated in canal style and with a pretty garden to the rear, offering reasonably priced, authentic, home-made food including vegetarian dishes. Fresh vegetables, Scotch salmon, hams and turkeys roasted on the premises. *Open Mon–Fri 9.00–15.00, breakfast through to lunch; gourmet evenings for group bookings only (minimum 12).* Bring your own wine. Swimming pool adjacent and shops and services close by.

Hyde

The canal continues northward through a landscape which becomes less rural, but just as interesting. At bridge 7 the towpath changes sides; the building nearby is the headquarters of the Peak Forest Canal Society. Bridge 6 is a pretty roving bridge, grown wider over the years. Beyond is a wharf with some well-restored buildings and good moorings on either side. To the north the industrial tentacles of Hyde – Greater Manchester – ensnare the canal traveller. The approach to Dukinfield Junction and Portland Basin is very pleasant. The towpath is tidy, with plenty of grass, trees and seats. A Llangollen-type lift bridge, an aqueduct over the River Tame and a stone roving bridge provide plenty of canal interest. Portland Basin was constructed to allow boats to make the sharp turn here, and was nicknamed the 'weavers rest', since so many weavers had reputedly drowned themselves here during hard times, such as the famine of 1860 and the depression of the 1930s. The warehouse which faces you across the junction, built in 1834, has been restored as a canal heritage centre and museum, and is well worth visiting. Heading off to the south west, the Ashton Canal takes you into Manchester proper: to the west is a two mile restored section of the Huddersfield Narrow Canal, including three locks, reaching as far as Stalybridge. This is a fine, solid industrial section of waterway, with steaming factories, tall chimneys and a good clear towpath. If you pass Dukinfield Junction during *July*, you may see the colourful Ashton Canals Festival, which has been running successfully for over 10 years now. Portland Basin is a recommended mooring place for those on the Cheshire Ring.

● **Ashton-under-Lyne**
Gt Manchester. All services. Walk north-west from Portland Basin and you will find the church of St Michael, which was begun by Sir John de Assheton in the early 15thC and completed by his great grandson before 1516. The church is large, with a tall west tower rebuilt by Crowther in 1886–8. Particularly notable is the stained glass, depicting the Life of St Helena and dating from the 15th–16thC. A market was granted to the town in 1284, but by 1801 the population still numbered only 4800. It then expanded rapidly, due to the growth of cotton weaving in the area, and by 1851 numbered over 30,000.
Portland Basin Heritage Centre and Museum
Portland Basin, Ashton-under-Lyne (0161 343 1978). The museum, housed in the superb warehouse built in 1834, tells the rich story of Tameside's social and industrial history by drawing on the very different facets of local life. The water-wheel outside was installed around 1840 to power hoists inside the warehouse. Water reaches the wheel by a leat which runs underground across the front of the warehouse, and used to drain through a tail race to the river. Now the water is returned to the canal. The wheel is constructed from cast and wrought iron, and measures 3ft wide by 24ft diameter, and cost £1078 0s 6p when built. It was restored and re-built 1987–88. *Open Apr 1st–Sept 30th, Tue–Sun 10.00–18.00. Oct 1st–Mar 30th, Tue–Sun 10.00–16.00. B. Hols 12.00–18.00.* Admission free.
The Astley Cheetham Art Gallery Stalybridge (0161 338 2708). Above Stalybridge Library, this small exhibition features the work of Turner, Cox, Burne-Jones and local artists including Harry Rutherford. Programme changes monthly. *Open 13.00–19.30, Sat 09.00–16.00, closed Thur & Sun.* Free.

Boatyards

Ⓑ **Warble Narrowboats** Warble Wharf, Broadway, Hyde (0161 367 9205). 🔧 D E Pump-out, gas, overnight and long-term mooring, winter storage, crane (20 ton), boat building and fitting, boat and engine sales and repairs, public telephone nearby, toilets.

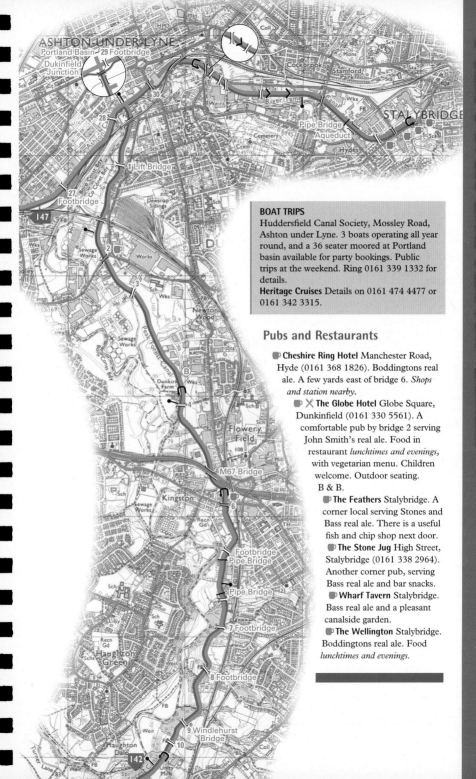

BOAT TRIPS

Huddersfield Canal Society, Mossley Road, Ashton under Lyne. 3 boats operating all year round, and a 36 seater moored at Portland basin available for party bookings. Public trips at the weekend. Ring 0161 339 1332 for details.

Heritage Cruises Details on 0161 474 4477 or 0161 342 3315.

Pubs and Restaurants

Cheshire Ring Hotel Manchester Road, Hyde (0161 368 1826). Boddingtons real ale. A few yards east of bridge 6. *Shops and station nearby.*

The Globe Hotel Globe Square, Dunkinfield (0161 330 5561). A comfortable pub by bridge 2 serving John Smith's real ale. Food in restaurant *lunchtimes and evenings*, with vegetarian menu. Children welcome. Outdoor seating. B & B.

The Feathers Stalybridge. A corner local serving Stones and Bass real ale. There is a useful fish and chip shop next door.

The Stone Jug High Street, Stalybridge (0161 338 2964). Another corner pub, serving Bass real ale and bar snacks.

Wharf Tavern Stalybridge. Bass real ale and a pleasant canalside garden.

The Wellington Stalybridge. Boddingtons real ale. Food *lunchtimes and evenings.*

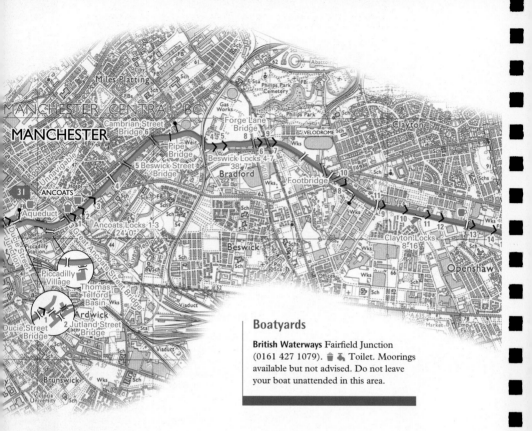

Boatyards

British Waterways Fairfield Junction
(0161 427 1079). 🚽 🛁 Toilet. Moorings
available but not advised. Do not leave
your boat unattended in this area.

▌ Droylsden

From start to finish, the Ashton Canal passes through a densely built-up area in
which the canal is conspicuous as a welcome relief from the townscape that flanks it.
Its clear water, its excellent towpath, its functional but dignified old bridges and the
peace that generally surrounds it make it a haven for local school children, anglers,
walkers and idlers, and for anyone else who enjoys an environment that is quite
separate from and unrelated to ordinary daily life. The rare pleasure, afforded only by
an English canal, of stepping out of a city suburb into the peaceful and unpretentious
atmosphere of the 18thC is once again, with gradual restoration work, becoming
available to all. At Fairfield Junction the top lock of the 18 which climb from Ducie
Street Junction is encountered. It is a picturesque canal scene here with traditional
buildings, including a shed dated 1833 standing over a canal arm, giving the area a
quiet dignity. There is also a useful sanitary station. Descending the locks, you may
wish to look out for the remains of several old canal arms: one of the more important
was the 5-mile Stockport Branch, leaving from Clayton Junction, just below lock 11.
The canal now falls through the remaining locks into Manchester. The surroundings
are brightened by the well-cared-for Beswick flight, but eventually become industrial
until the canal is totally hemmed in by the back walls of tall factories – originally built
there because of the canal's very presence – for $1/2$ mile above the bottom three locks.

NAVIGATIONAL NOTES

1 A British Waterways Leeds & Liverpool type anti-vandal key is needed for all the locks and moveable bridges on the Ashton, and for the first lift bridge on the Lower Peak Forest.
2 Moor only at recognised sites in this area, and do not offer anyone you do not know a ride in your boat.
3 Bridge 21 is very low.
4 Beswick Locks are closed overnight, and *re-open at 08.00.*

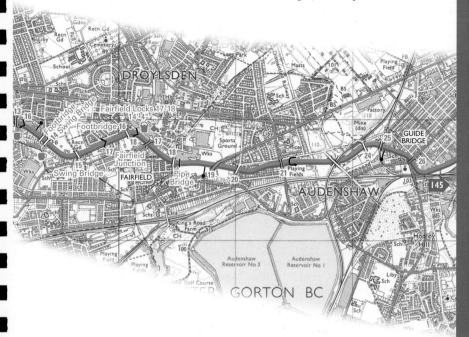

There are moorings, and a sanitary station, at the BW Office by locks 1 and 2 on the Ashton Canal. Large-scale redevelopment has been completed at Paradise Wharf and Piccadilly Village, making this final stretch unusually gentrified, with smart flats, basins and a crane. The Rochdale Canal, which is still privately owned, used to stretch for 33 miles over the Pennines from Manchester to Sowerby Bridge – where it joined the terminus of the Calder & Hebble Navigation. Although undergoing restoration, it is closed to through navigation, and in Manchester much of the canal has been reduced to a shallow, landscaped water channel. However, the bottom mile or so of the canal is navigable, from the junction with the Ashton Canal at Ducie Street down to Castlefield and its meeting with the Bridgewater Canal. This remaining section of the Rochdale Canal is thus a vital link between the Bridgewater and Ashton Canals in the 100-mile 'Cheshire Ring'. Persons wishing to navigate the nine wide locks to the Bridgewater Canal should apply to the Head Office of the Rochdale Canal Company, 75 Dale Street, Manchester (0161 236 2456) for a separate (and quite expensive) licence. The locks can accommodate vessels up to 74ft long and 14ft wide, drawing up to 4ft, with a height above water level of up to 9ft. The Rochdale passage is described on page 31, on the Bridgewater Canal section.

Fairfield

Gt Manchester. Immediately south of Fairfield Junction are a group of neat and tidy buildings around a fine chapel. This is an original Moravian settlement, established in 1785 by Benjamin Latrobe and consisting of tidy rows of cottages built in brick, intended to house the members of a self-contained community.

Velodrome (0161 223 2244). Access from the new bridge, west of bridge 9. In full view from bridge 8, when climbing the locks. A full programme of exciting cycle races is staged.

Manchester

All services. One of Britain's finest Victorian cities, a monument to 19thC commerce and the textile boom. There is an incredible wealth of Victorian buildings surviving in spite of redevelopment – the Town Hall and the surrounding streets being a particularly rich area (north of Oxford Street Bridge). St Peter's Square, by the Town Hall, was the site of the 'Peterloo Massacre' in 1819, when a meeting demanding political reform was brutally dispersed by troops carrying drawn sabres. Eleven people were killed and many more were injured. The Free Trade Hall, once the home of the Hallé Orchestra, is a little further along the road. Built in 1856 on the site of the original Free Trade Hall, it was badly damaged in World War II, but was subsequently re-built to its original Palladian design. It has been converted into a hotel, and the Hallé has moved to the new Bridgewater Hall. The old Central Station has now been converted into a £20 million conference and exhibition centre called GMex. There is theatre, ballet and cinema, art galleries, and a wealth of interesting buildings as well as Victorian shopping arcades, many pubs with an excellent choice of good beer, and many excellent restaurants all a short walk from the canal.

Manchester Tourist Information Centre Town Hall Extension, Lloyd Street, to the north of Oxford Street Bridge (0161 234 3157/8).

Pubs and Restaurants

The Yew Tree South of bridge 14. A traditional pub serving real ale. Garden.

Friendship Canalside by lock 15, Edge Lane, Openshaw (0161 370 2111). Busy popular local serving Chester's real ale and *lunchtime* food. Garden. Children welcome. Free pool games *on certain days* and regular entertainment.

Strawberry Duck Canalside at lock 13, Crabtree Lane, Clayton (0161 223 4415). Traditional two-room pub with regular entertainment. Children welcome *until 18.00.* Holts, Whitbread, Boddingtons and guest real ales and *lunchtime* food. Outside seating.

Jolly Angler Ducie Street, Manchester (0161 236 5307). Near the junction. A small, plain and friendly pub visited by Mike Harding, the folk singer, and offering Hydes' real ale and snacks *at all times.* Regular folk music sessions (*Fri & Mon*). Moorings nearby, but don't leave your boat here overnight.

La Peniche Café-Bar Paradise Wharf, Ducie Street (0161 273 5553). A floating French-style bar offering Brittany pancakes, galettes and crêpes. *L & D (not Sat L or Sun D).*

THE CHESHIRE RING – THEN AND NOW

This route has remained one of the most popular cruising circuits for many years now - a one-week trip encompassing parts of the Trent & Mersey, the Bridgewater, the Ashton, the Peak Forest and the Macclesfield canals, passing through a wide and exciting variety of canalscape. Part of the journey includes a passage through central Manchester, a pleasant experience these days, but it was not always so . . .

The problem used to be timing your passage through the city so that the 'Rochdale Nine' locks were open, and your subsequent overnight mooring was a safe one! Local children preyed upon you as you tackled the Ancoats, Beswick and Clayton flights, leaping across the locks from one side to the other, begging lifts, and 'picking up' *anything* you might have left lying around . . .

The lock machinery was stiff, water supply uncertain, and the things which fouled your propeller defied description . . .

It is, thankfully, very different now, and the city passage is attractive, interesting and enjoyable. Just take the usual precautions.

ROCHDALE CANAL

MAXIMUM DIMENSIONS
Length: 74'
Beam: 14' 2"
Headroom: 7' 6"
Draught: 4'

MILEAGE
SOWERBY BRIDGE to
Hedben Bridge: 5½
West Summit Lock: 13¾
Littleborough: 15½ (present limit of navigation)
MANCHESTER: 32

Locks:
to Littleborough: 47
to Manchester: 91

OPERATING AUTHORITY
Rochdale Canal Trust 01422 844990

The Rochdale Canal Trust produce an excellent set of **Navigational Notes** for boaters using the canal, obtainable by ringing 01422 844990.

The Rochdale Canal is one of three Pennine canal crossings. It was authorised by an Act of Parliament in 1794 and completed exactly 10 years later.

With its wide locks the Rochdale Canal was able to handle barges, Humber keels and even small coasters, the latter sometimes trading between the continent and Irish ports, using the River Mersey and the Irwell Navigation at the eastern end. However, the Achilles' heel of the waterway lay in its requirement for a copious supply of water at the summit pound, together with the sheer physical effort required to operate the 3 locks per mile that are averaged over the canal's relatively short length.

The boom years for the canal were in the 1820s and 1830s before the inevitable railway competition began to make an impression. Passenger carrying Packet Boats (Manchester to Rochdale: 13 miles and 41 locks in 7 hours) and fast, light-goods-carrying Fly Boats (20 tons transported from Manchester to Todmorden in 12 hours) were both successful enterprises in the early 1800s.

In 1887 the canal's fortunes appeared to take an upturn when the canal company bought its own boats.

Traffic included cotton, grain, coal, wool, cement, salt and timber, and whilst end to end carriage steadily declined, shorter journeys continued to thrive. At the outbreak of the Great War the canal company was still ordering new craft (powered by 25 hp. inverted compound steam engines) and capable, loaded, of pulling a further two laden dumb barges. However, in 1921, as competition from the roads took its toll, the fleet ceased operation and traffic became spasmodic. The last loaded boat to trade over the canal's entire length was n.b. Alice, in April 1937, carrying 20 tons of wire from Manchester to Sowerby Bridge.

The navigation was officially closed by an act of 1952, except for the stretch connecting the Bridgewater and Ashton Canals in Manchester. Restoration was commenced 20 years ago and the canal society has not only succeeded in protecting nearly all its original line, but has also re-opened 16 miles of the eastern end. It has also, in conjunction with the local authority based Canal Trust, inspired the construction of Tuel Lane Lock and Tunnel.

Calderdale's network of Tourist Information Centres are among the best in the country and make an excellent starting point for any visitor to the area. Whilst the canal remains incomplete as a through route to Manchester, it makes great sense for the boater to use his craft as a 'moveable base', from which to strike out and (using the excellent rail and bus network) visit the wide diversity of attractions lying within easy reach of the waterway.

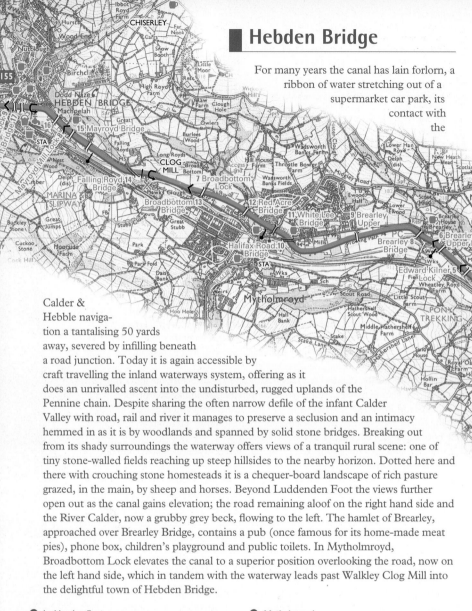

Hebden Bridge

For many years the canal has lain forlorn, a ribbon of water stretching out of a supermarket car park, its contact with the Calder & Hebble navigation a tantalising 50 yards away, severed by infilling beneath a road junction. Today it is again accessible by craft travelling the inland waterways system, offering as it does an unrivalled ascent into the undisturbed, rugged uplands of the Pennine chain. Despite sharing the often narrow defile of the infant Calder Valley with road, rail and river it manages to preserve a seclusion and an intimacy hemmed in as it is by woodlands and spanned by solid stone bridges. Breaking out from its shady surroundings the waterway offers views of a tranquil rural scene: one of tiny stone-walled fields reaching up steep hillsides to the nearby horizon. Dotted here and there with crouching stone homesteads it is a chequer-board landscape of rich pasture grazed, in the main, by sheep and horses. Beyond Luddenden Foot the views further open out as the canal gains elevation; the road remaining aloof on the right hand side and the River Calder, now a grubby grey beck, flowing to the left. The hamlet of Brearley, approached over Brearley Bridge, contains a pub (once famous for its home-made meat pies), phone box, children's playground and public toilets. In Mytholmroyd, Broadbottom Lock elevates the canal to a superior position overlooking the road, now on the left hand side, which in tandem with the waterway leads past Walkley Clog Mill into the delightful town of Hebden Bridge.

● **Luddenden Foot**
W. Yorks. PO, tel, stores, off-licence, take-away, library. Centred around more recent lines of communication in the valley bottom, the village once featured the railway station where Branwell Brontë was booking clerk. Passengers arriving on one of the earliest passenger lines to be opened in Britain, were greeted with the cry of 'Foo-it! Foo-it!' as porters sought to differentiate this upstart settlement from the ancient, textile-producing village, perched on the hillside half a mile above.

● **Mytholmroyd**
W. Yorks, PO, tel, stores, take-aways, hairdressers, station. Since Doomsday the ingredients of a farming and weaving community have existed in the area, confined largely to individual settlements above the marshy valley bottom. The site of the present village was initially a fordable crossing of the River Calder and, with the coming of the canal and the railway, developed as a focus for steam-powered textile production. Initially producers of cotton goods (with the canal as both supplier of raw materials and

shipper of finished goods) the mills went on to manufacture worsted in the late 19thC, which in turn stimulated the growth of local dyeworks. Infamous as the base for the activities of David Hartley and the 'Coiners', Mytholmroyd is also the birthplace of Ted Hughes, the current Poet Laureate, and home to the annual Dock Pudding championships – usually held in May.

The Coiners of Cragg Vale Coining was the illicit manufacture of coins, often using metal filed or 'clipped' away from the perimeter of genuine coins. This was melted down and cast into new coins with an appropriate design hammered onto the face and reverse sides. A new rim was then hammered onto the adulterated coin. On 10th November 1769 an excise man, William Dighton, who had been sent to curtail the activities of the Cragg Vale coiners, was murdered in Halifax by members of the gang. Loyalty was not a notable feature within coiner circles and the miscreants were quickly betrayed to the authorities in return for an enticing reward.

Dock Pudding Championships Dock Pudding is made from the weed Polygonum Bistorta (sweet dock) and is not to be confused with the large coarse cow docks. Mixed with other ingredients and cooked to a variety of secret recipes, the finished product, looking not unlike a slimy, spinach concoction, is entered into a competition and judged on its culinary merits. Believed by many locals to be an essential spring medicine, efficacious in the cure of acne and as a cleanser of the blood.

● **Hebden Bridge**
W. Yorks. EC Tue, MD Wed Thur, All services.
Developed as a settlement in late medieval times providing both a meeting point of pack-horse routes and a river crossing. However it was not until the late 19thC, with the advent of steam power, the building of canal and railway, together with the mechanisation and centralisation of the

NAVIGATIONAL NOTES

1. The canal is operated by an independent trust and charges a licence fee for all craft using it.
2. The towpath is generally good throughout.
3. The use of Tuel Deep Lock is limited by water availability and is operated by a resident lock keeper. Boaters wishing to visit the waterway should first telephone 0860 336750 to check both the keeper's duty hours and the water situation.

textile industry, that the town attained its present size and layout. Displaying a variety and delicacy of stonework – towers, turrets and pediments at every turn – houses and mills peel off from the market square to straggle haphazardly up steep hillsides. The first bridge to cross the River Hebden was wooden, dating from 1477 and replaced by the present stone pack-horse bridge some 30 years later. This solid structure contrasts with the delicate ironwork of the cast-iron Victorian road bridge, sited upstream beside the ornate council offices, which incorporate the original fire station. Double-decker housing and a diversity of religious non-conformism are also characteristic of this strikingly compact mill-town.

Hebble End Works Canal Towpath, Hebble End, Hebden Bridge (01422 843378). The opportunity to study a whole range of craft skills in action. *Open daily.* Free.

Walkley Clogs Burnley Road, Hebden Bridge (01422 842061). Only surviving clog mill where visitors can see clogs being made in the traditional way. Also visit **The Enchanted Wood** and **Victorian Arcades** selling a range of goods. Restaurant. *Open every day except Xmas day & Box. Day, 10.00–17.00 Mon–Fri and 17.30 Sat, Sun & B. Hols. Free except weekends & B. Hols.*

World of the Honey Bee Hebble End Works, Hebden Bridge (01422 845557). Working hives, demonstrations, displays, video shows and microscopes offer answers to the many questions posed about the production of honey. Also Insect World examines the fascinating lives of 'mini-beasts'. *Open daily in summer; telephone for winter opening.* Charge.

Hardcastle Crags National Trust, Hollin Hall Office, Hebden Bridge (01422 844518). Large tract of Trust-managed countryside, 1½ miles north of Hebden Bridge, easily accessible by bus. Regular events and guided walks – telephone for details. *Open all year.* Free.

Tourist Information Centre 1 Bridge Gate, Hebden Bridge (01422 843831).
Metro-Train & Metro-Bus (0113 245 7676). Telephone for all local travel information or selection of free timetables.

● **Heptonstall**
W. Yorks. PO, tel, stores. Extraordinary 'textile village', little changed over the centuries, set high on hills overlooking Hebden Bridge. Walk up The Buttress (beyond the pack-horse bridge) or take a bus and visit this settlement barely touched by time. In one small area there is a ruined 15thC church, its early Victorian replacement and the Octagonal Chapel: the oldest continually used Methodist church in the world, dating from 1764. Also a 16thC cloth market hall, school museum, a dungeon and David Hartley's (the infamous coiner) grave. There is also the grave of Sylvia Plath, American poet and wife of Ted Hughes. The village provides one of the most spectacular viewpoints in Calderdale.

The Old Grammar School Museum Heptonstall, Hebden Bridge (01422 843738). Depicts an old school classroom together with varying local history displays. *Open Easter–Oct weekends & B. Hols, 13.00–17.00.* Charge.

Cloth Hall Heptonstall. Built between 1545 and 1558 as a market for local handloom weavers to sell their cloth to dealers. It is now a *private* house.

Weavers' Square Heptonstall. A unique museum of stone depicting many types of Yorkshire paving.

Boatyards

See Calder & Hebble canal, page 48

THE BEER NECESSITIES

Take an old ice-cream cooler, a scrapyard copper, a home-made cask washer and two locally constructed mash tuns; place them in a canalside mill (once a sweet factory) and what have you got? A family-run brewery – whose proprietor (for many years a joiner) is not short of ingenuity. Always fermenting new ideas for the future, his imagination stretches into the often mind-bending task of naming new brews, tapping into local history with names like 'Luddite' and 'Coiners'. When the ailing sweet factory finally called time on its production it was sold complete with its old manufacturing equipment. Ideas are already brewing as to how it might be pressed into use for ale production. The family are all adept at meeting new challenges, right down to Sooty the brewery cat. Keeping the mouse population in check is a doddle for the four-legged feline; not so easy if you've had the misfortune to lose a leg in a brush with a car.

BOAT TRIPS
Calder Valley Cruising *Gracie Fields, Sarah Siddons* and tug *Oliver* provide a variety of imaginative trips, some horse-drawn, all the year round. Information centre, shop and tearoom aboard barge *Branwell*. Ring 01422 845557 for full details

Pubs and Restaurants

See also Calder & Hebble canal, page 49

🍺 **Puzzle Hall Inn** 21 Hollins Mill Lane, Sowerby Bridge (01422 835547). South of canal before Sowerby Long Bridge. Vaux ales served in a tiny, two-roomed Pub alongside the canal. Food *until 19.00* with curry night *Wed*. Live jazz *Tue* and folk *Thur & Sat*.

🍺 **Old Brandy Wine** Station Road, Luddenden Foot (01422 886173). Timothy Taylor, Boddingtons and Tetley's real ales in this ex-factory and working-man's club, recently refurbished. Discos *Fri & Sat*. Darts, pool and electronic games.

🍺✕ **Coach and Horses** Luddenden Foot (01422 884102). Large, open-plan (originally six rooms) family pub serving an appetising array of inexpensive home-cooked food (including puddings). Also a good fish selection and baguette-based snacks. Theakston and Younger real ales plus guest. Quiz night *Thur*. Food served *lunchtimes and evenings Mon–Sat and all day until 21.30 Sun*. Vegetarians catered for. Children's Menu.

🍺 **Weavers Arms** Luddenden Foot (01422 882241). Open *11.00–23.00* serving Thwaites real ales and sandwiches at the bar. Comfortable pub, once the haunt of Branwell Brontë during his sojourn at the local station. Pub games. Vegetarians catered for. *Take-away next door.*

🍺 **Grove Inn** Brearley House (01422 844650). Cosy, single room pub, beside the main road, serving Tetley's and Boddingtons real ales. Snacks and typical bar food served *lunchtimes and evenings*. Quiz night *Thur*. Vegetarians catered for. Busy in *summer*.

🍺 **White Lion** Mytholmroyd (01422 883131). An interesting range of very reasonably priced bar meals and snacks, served *lunchtimes* in comfortable surroundings, by a friendly, welcoming landlady. Tetley's real ales (including Imperial), moorings outside, pub games, Quiz *Mon & Wed,* live music *Sat*. Vegetarians catered for.

🍺✕ **Dusty Miller** Mytholmroyd (01422 882247). Once the regular haunt of the Cragside Coiners it now offers meals and bar snacks at exceptionally low prices, Vaux real ales and a regular guest beer. Food available *L & D, but not Sun D*. Pool table. Vegetarians catered for. Children's portions.

🍺 **Shoulder of Mutton** Mytholmroyd (01422 883165). Opposite railway station. Award winning pub that takes its beer and food seriously. Ales include Blacksheep, Boddingtons, Flowers, Castle Eden, Hartleys and various guests. There are three cosy eating areas, portions are generous and the price low. Food available *lunchtimes and evenings; no food Tue evenings*. Vegetarians catered for.

🍺✕ **Mayroyd Barn** Mayroyd, Hebden Bridge (01422 846064). Above Mayroyd Bridge. Converted, grade I listed, tithe barn, featuring a central, circular bar dispensing Boddingtons real ale. Emphasis on family eating in comfortable surroundings with many original features of the barn exposed. Snacks and meals available *L & D; not Sun evenings*. Vegetarians catered for. Children's menu and both outdoor and indoor play areas. Patio.

🍺 There are a wide choice of pubs to choose from in Hebden Bridge, together with an even wider choice of real ales.

✕ The selection of tearooms, bistros, pizzerias and restaurants is equally copious.

These two pubs both represent worthwhile walks or bus rides:

🍺 **Hare & Hounds** Billy Lane, Chiserley, Hebden Bridge (01422 842671). Cosy pub serving Timothy Taylor real ales and tasty bar meals (*not Mon*). Families welcome. *Hourly* Halifax service bus No 593 *during day* or mini-bus H3 and H7 *evenings & weekends*.

🍺 **Mount Skip Inn** Heights Road, Wadsworth, Hebden Bridge (01422 842765). Timothy Taylor and Tetley's real ales in a pub with striking views into Cragg Vale and Calderdale. Home-cooked food with vegetarians catered for (*not Mon lunchtimes*). Walk 1½ miles up Birchcliffe Road or take mini-bus H3 – *regular 7 day service including evenings.*

Todmorden

As so often happens with an aqueduct the boater is unaware of its beauty, grandeur or construction. So it is with Black Pit Aqueduct whose four substantial arches squat almost toad-like, close to the bed of the newly-merged Rivers Hebden and Calder. Beyond are Stubbing (meaning a cleared area of woodland) Upper and Lower Locks carrying the canal out of Hebden Bridge, up past gayly painted cottages, washing stretched like bunting across cobbled alleys. The waterway is now tucked tightly under a steep hillside covered by ancient deciduous woodland as the canal hugs the narrow valley bottom interspersed, on the towpath side, by textile mills and dyeworks. Above Callis Lock there is a useful, boater-friendly coal merchant selling just about everything that is combustible. Approaching Todmorden, at Lobb Mill Lock, the waterway breaks out into open ground for the first time since leaving Hebden Bridge. Perched high on the hills to the north of the canal stands the disused Cross Stone church: its badly blackened stonework a reminder of the concentration of local industry. A sweeping bend takes the waterway

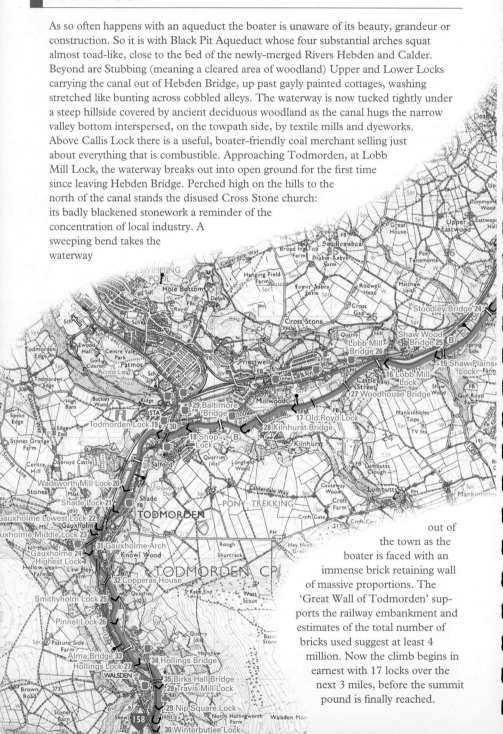

out of the town as the boater is faced with an immense brick retaining wall of massive proportions. The 'Great Wall of Todmorden' supports the railway embankment and estimates of the total number of bricks used suggest at least 4 million. Now the climb begins in earnest with 17 locks over the next 3 miles, before the summit pound is finally reached.

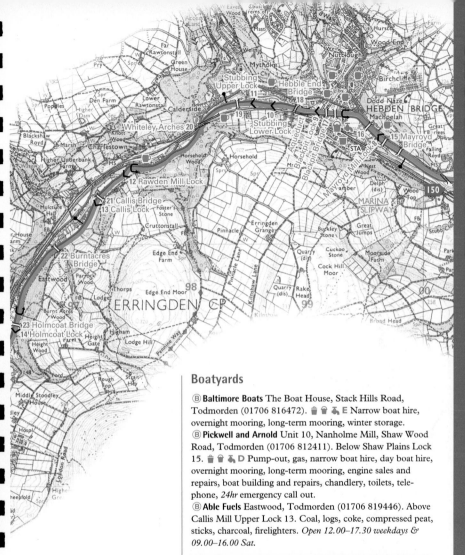

Boatyards

Ⓑ**Baltimore Boats** The Boat House, Stack Hills Road, Todmorden (01706 816472). 🚽 🚿 ♿ E Narrow boat hire, overnight mooring, long-term mooring, winter storage.

Ⓑ**Pickwell and Arnold** Unit 10, Nanholme Mill, Shaw Wood Road, Todmorden (01706 812411). Below Shaw Plains Lock 15. 🚽 🚿 ♿ D Pump-out, gas, narrow boat hire, day boat hire, overnight mooring, long-term mooring, engine sales and repairs, boat building and repairs, chandlery, toilets, telephone, *24hr* emergency call out.

Ⓑ**Able Fuels** Eastwood, Todmorden (01706 819446). Above Callis Mill Upper Lock 13. Coal, logs, coke, compressed peat, sticks, charcoal, firelighters. *Open 12.00–17.30 weekdays & 09.00–16.00 Sat.*

CHARLESTOWN RAILWAY DISASTER

In 1912 there was a serious derailment on the Charlestown curve when the 14.25 Manchester to Leeds express left the track, having effectively shattered the alignment of the rails at this point. The accident, involving a 2-4-2 radial tank engine, occurred on the stretch of line just before the railway crosses the canal on Whiteley Arches. The inspector, Colonel Druit, found at the subsequent enquiry that while the 45 mph line speed at this point was suitable for normal express running, it was too high for tank engines of this type. Indeed, he went on to question the suitability of tank engines per se – with their high centre of gravity and inherent instability – for sustained high speed traction. The de-railed locomotive, together with all its carriages, toppled down the embankment, coming to rest strewn across what is now the camp site of the Woodman Inn.

Todmorden

W. Yorks. EC Tue. MD Wed, Thur, Fri, Sat, Sun. Laundrette, all services. 19thC manufacturing success led to the concentration of wealth in the pockets of a few individuals whose ostentation was often manifested locally in civic and domestic architecture. Todmorden is fortunate, indeed, to have benefited greatly from the philanthropy of the Fielden family, whose legacy of good taste in buildings represents a feast in stone. Their choice of architect, in John Gibson of London, proved most successful. His work both echoes the solid vernacular building from a previous era, while introducing a further wealth of styles, which in turn complement the fine stone railway viaduct that dominates the town's centre. Simple classical building sits side by side with the richly ornate: a striking example of the latter being the elaborately pedimented town hall. Originally built astride the county boundary (moved in a later reorganisation) between Lancashire and Yorkshire, this Italian Renaissance style building is fronted by 6 sturdy pillars, surmounted by statuary depicting, on the one half, the agriculture and engineering of Yorkshire, while on the other various facets of cotton spinning in Lancashire. In contrast the Unitarian Church, erected by Joshua and Samuel Fielden, again to a design by Gibson, is pure Victorian Gothic revival and a fitting memorial to their father, John Fielden MP. His concern for his fellow man extended to Westminster and industrial reform, being largely responsible for the Ten Hours Act of 1847 which limited the maximum working day to ten hours for any person under 18 and any woman over 18.

Craft Centre Lever Street, Todmorden (01706 818170). Small family-run centre: stalls, workshops and a tea room.

Free Library Rochdale Road, Todmorden. Typifies the many individual buildings in the town displaying the skills of the stone mason in conjunction with the philanthropy of local benefactors. The library was a gift from the local Co-operative society in 1897 and its asymmetry is pleasing in a simple way. It gives a second name to Todmorden Lock beside it, namely Library Lock.

Hippodrome Theatre Halifax Road, Todmorden (01706 814875). A striking building of its period, recently refurbished, though seemingly under-used.

St Mary's Church Rochdale Road, Todmorden. Built on land given to the town in about 1476 it still retains its 15thC tower. Subsequently much altered the present Gothic revival chancel bears little relationship to the original, although it contains a pleasing carved oak screen and attractive stained-glass windows.

Stoodley Pike The original monument was erected in 1815 to commemorate the end of the Napoleonic wars. However, weakened by lightning, it collapsed 40 years later and was replaced by the present 120ft high structure. Visible from the canal, as you approach the town, it makes the object of a bracing walk, rewarded by stunning views across Calderdale.

Tourist Information Centre 15 Burnley Road, Todmorden (01706 818181).

ON YOUR TOD

It is said that the only man-made feature distinguishable on the earth, when viewed from the moon, is the Great Wall of China. Clearly this must be due to its length rather than its – relatively speaking – minuscule width. For a guard detachment, patrolling some of its more remote lengths, it must have been a singularly lonely and, in some cases, solitary occupation. The 'Great Wall of Tod' – the name given to the canalside railway retaining wall beyond Library Lock – is unlikely to hold quite such long-standing historical significance. Nor will it become a talking point amongst future lunar cosmonauts. Owing its existence to the less than prosaic function of keeping 'railway out of t'cut' it still remains, nonetheless, one of the wonders of a more local world. Building with brick in the Calder Valley, rather than the local gritstone, was largely down to the advent of the railway: a phenomenon repeated throughout many other areas of the country.

Pubs and Restaurants

🍺 **Fox and Goose** 9 Heptonstall Road, Hebden Bridge (01422 842649). A serious beer drinker's pub dispensing Goose Eye real ale together with 10 guests a week. Home-made bar meals and snacks *lunchtimes and evenings except Tue evening.* A 'conversational establishment' eschewing theme nights. Traditional pub games.

🍺 ✕ **Stubbing Wharf** King Street, Hebden Bridge (01422 844107). Whitbread and Castle Eden real ales in a comfortable, family pub beside the canal. A wide selection of inexpensive food served in the bar and no smoking dining room *lunchtimes and evenings.* Quiz *Tue* and story telling *last Fri in the month.* Pool, moorings outside.

🍺 **Woodman Inn** Hebden Bridge (01422 842458). Below Rawden Mill Lock. *Open all day* for an inexpensive, wide-ranging selection of food (including breakfasts) together with Tetley's and guest real ales. Children's menu and play area. Pub games and camping. Quiz *Tue,* disco *Thur* and live music *Sat.*

✕ ♀ **Calder Bank House** Springside, Todmorden (01706 816188). Originally the home of a prosperous mill owner, the present proprietors serve teas and offer an interesting menu for *dinner if booked in advance.* The garden and smallholding are an attraction for adults and children alike. Mooring out-side. B & B.

🍺 ✕ **Rose and Crown** Todmorden (01706 812423). Opposite Woodhouse Bridge. A squat stone building, originally three cottages built in the late 18thC, entered through a pair of delightful stained-glass doors. This is an original pub with all the traditional trappings run by a landlord with traditional values: for example, he insists that there shall be no drinking out of bottles. Trophy, Boddingtons, Timothy Taylor, Castle Eden, Pedigree and Chester's real ales together with excellent meals available *lunchtimes and evenings, 7 days a week.* Vegetarian and children's menus. Darts *Tue & Thur,* quiz *Wed;* dominoes and chess.

🍺 **Swan with Two Necks** Todmorden (01706 815944). North of canal, between bridges 27 & 28. Neglected for some years, the new landlord intends to create a traditional hostelry and would be happy to collect boaters if they telephone. He serves Worthington, Theakston and guest real ales together with extremely inexpensive bar meals and snacks. *(lunchtimes and evenings, 7 days a week).* Children welcome in beer garden or if eating. Vegetarians catered for. Pool and traditional pub games.

🍺 **Shannon and Chesapeake** Todmorden (01706 813386). North of canal, between bridges 27 & 28. Webster's and Ruddles real ales. *Sunday breakfasts 11.00–14.00.* Pool.

🍺 **Rope and Anchor** Todmorden (01706 816054). North of canal, near bridge 29. Tetley's (including Imperial) real ale. Pub games. *There are a PO, butcher, grocer and 2 take-aways opposite.*

🍺 **Bramsche Continental Bar** Rochdale Road, Todmorden (01706 815117). Close to bridge 30. Bearing the name of Todmorden's twin town this bar not only serves a wide range of continental lagers and fruit beers but also dispenses Timothy Taylor, Theakston and 2 guest real ales. Excellent range of food available *lunchtimes and 12.00–17.00 Sun.* Vegetarians and children catered for. Interesting selection of spirits.

🍺 **Golden Lion** Rochdale Road, Todmorden (01706 813532). Close to bridge 30. Variously post office, armoury and drawing office for Stoodley Pike this 300 year old coaching house now concentrates on serving Boddingtons, Flowers and Timothy Taylor real ales and bar food (*always available*). Children and vegetarians catered for. Outside seating. Quiz *Wed.*

🍺 **White Hart** Station Road, Todmorden (01706 812198). Imposing mock-Tudor building replacing the 1728 original that once housed the local court. Market place and focal point of the town's development it now dispenses Tetley's and guest real ales. *Lunchtime food (not Tue or Fri)* and discos *Thur & Fri.* Pool and pub games.

🍺 **Mason's Arms** 1 Bacup Road, Gauxholme (01706 812180). Close to bridge 31. Almost lost under the railway arches this pub serves Marston's, Thwaites and John Smith's real ales together with *evening food and Sunday lunch. Useful PO and stores through railway viaduct and turn left.*

Summit

The transition between sheltered valley bottom, with its compact, functional towns, and the open moorland that the waterway now winds towards, is fairly abrupt. Rapidly extending views, both behind and in front, take over from the navigation's former intimacy. At Longlees Lock the remote summit pound is reached; although this was once the site of both a chemical and a brick works. Now reverted to coarse grasses, rushes and mosses this section of the waterway is a haven to birdlife that can include meadow pipit, snipe, sandpiper, wheatear, dunlin, curlew and redshank. The typical moorland of the area is an acid peat overlying gritstone, poor draining and therefore agriculturally unproductive. Two contrasting, though striking features, planted on the landscape are the Steanor Bottom Toll House (at the intersection of two roads to the west) and the 763 yd span of the high-voltage line totally straddling the valley here. Beyond West Summit Lock the canal begins its descent, past the strung-out Courtaulds factory, towards Littleborough and the industrial chimneys of Rochdale beckoning beyond.

● **Walsden**
W. Yorks. EC Tue. PO, Tel, stores, garage, take-aways, station. Meaning 'Valley of the Welsh' this textile village, just outside Todmorden, offers the boater all the important forms of sustenance.

● **Summit**
Lancs. PO, Tel, Stores. Once a bustling woollen weaving community, the village has played an important part in three very different forms of transport. It sits beside the summit level of the canal; a place of sustenance to the thirsty

boater and source of the much needed water supply for locks descending east and west. The railway burrows underneath in a tunnel 2869yds long: the longest rail tunnel in the world when built in 1839. In 1984 a petroleum-carrying goods train caught fire and burnt uncontrollably in the tunnel for several weeks; smoke and flames belching from the ventilation shafts.

Steanor Bottom Toll House Just to the north of the village and built in 1824 at the junction of the old and new routes to Littleborough, this is considered to be the finest example of a turnpike toll house in England.

Pubs and Restaurants

⚓ ✕ **Hollins Inn** Walsden (01706 817105). Comfortable, family pub resurrected from the ashes of the original which burnt down in 1978. Theakston and John Smith's real ales together with at least 2 interesting guests. Excellent selection of reasonably priced à la carte and bar food *available lunchtimes, evenings (not Sun & Mon evenings) and all day Sunday.* Good vegetarian menu. Outside seating and bowling green. Quiz *Thur* and cabaret *Fri.* Pool.

⚓ **Cross Keys Inn** Walsden (01706 815185). A homely, welcoming establishment serving a wide range of real ales including Black Sheep, Tetley's and Buchanan's together with traditional, home-cooked food *lunchtimes, evenings and all day Sunday.* Vegetarians and children catered for. Canalside patio and moorings. B & B.

⚓ **Border Rose** Rochdale Road, Walsden (01706 812142). Thwaites and Tetley's real ales together with bar snacks served *lunchtimes except Tue.* Children and vegetarians catered for. Outside seating, and entertainment *Sat.*

⚓ ✕ **Waggon and Horses** Rochdale Road, Walsden (01706 813318). A smartly refurbished pub that welcomes boaters and families with an extremely inexpensive menu served *lunchtimes and evenings.* Also Worthington and Bass real ales; darts; pool and *Tue* quiz. The landlord operates an excellent *lending and exchanging library:* ideal for the boater stranded in a low pound!

⚓ ✕ **Bird I'th Hand** (01706 378145). Between Walsden and Summit, near Warland Upper Lock No 35. Food orientated establishment offering anything from snacks to a gourmet meal *(lunchtimes and evenings, 7 days)* in a warm, cosy 3-roomed pub. Dating from 1823 this coaching house (once owned by a pigeon fancier) now serves Whitbread real ale and caters for vegetarians, children, and quiz fanatics on a *Wed.*

⚓ ✕ **Summit Inn** Summit (01706 378011). Canalside at West Summit Lock No 37. Thwaites real ale and a wide range of interesting à la carte and bar food (generous portions)

● **Littleborough**
Lancs. EC Tue. All services. Laundrette. A bustling little town, busy with visitors in summer though, strangely, without a market. Opposite the solid stone parish church is the excellent **Coach House Heritage Centre** – a local initiative to provide tourist information established in a Grade II listed building. Just round the corner, in Victoria Street, are a good butcher and baker.

Coach House Heritage Centre Lodge Street, Littleborough (01706 378481). *Open summer Tue–Fri & Sun 14.00–17.00; Sat 11.00–17.00. Winter closed at 16.30.* Exhibits and gifts.

available *lunchtimes and evenings (not Tue evening in winter).* Vegetarians and children both well catered for. Outside seating. Music *Thur & Fri* and quiz *Sun.* Pub games. *Telephone for details of special, pre-booked, ethnic menus.*

⚓ **Gale Inn** Gale, Littleborough (01706 377664). Footpath from Windy Bank Bridge. Theakston real ale and bar food served *lunchtimes and evenings (except Mon)* in a comfortable, welcoming pub whose safety-conscious ghost (a one-time serving wench) keeps turning off the gas. Children and vegetarians catered for. Quiz *Mon* and pub games.

⚓ ✕ **Waterside Inn** Littleborough (01706 376250). Boddingtons and Flowers real ales together with a varied menu served *lunchtimes and evenings (less frequently in winter).* Vegetarians and children catered for. Quiz *Mon* and singer *Thur.* B & B.

⚓ **Queens Hotel** Church Street, Littleborough (01706 379394). Thwaites real ale and *lunchtime* snacks.

⚓ **Falcon** Littleborough (01706 378640). Walkers, Tetley's, Boddingtons and guest real ales together with *lunchtime (not Wed)* bar meals served in this early 19thC coaching inn. A large, comfortably furnished, family pub with disco on *Thur & Fri* and folk group on *Tue.* Pool.

✕ **Coach House Coffee Shop** Lodge Street, Littleborough (01706 378481). Inexpensive home-made snacks and cakes, teas and coffees served in this friendly annexe to the Heritage Centre. *Open Tue–Sat 10.30–16.30 & 14.00–16.30 Sun.*

⚓ **Royal Oak** Littleborough (01706 371346). Robinson's and Hartleys real ales and an inexpensive range of snacks and bar meals served *lunchtimes (not Tue).* Darts and pool.

⚓ **Wheatsheaf** Littleborough (01706 377695). A comfortable, family pub serving *lunchtime* bar food and Boddingtons and Flowers real ales. Disco *Fri.*

Narrow boats on the Trent & Mersey Canal

TRENT & MERSEY CANAL

MAXIMUM DIMENSIONS	MILEAGE
North end of Harecastle Tunnel to Croxton Aqueduct	HARDINGS WOOD, junction with Macclesfield Canal to King's Lock,
Length: 72'	Middlewich, junction with
Beam: 7'	Middlewich Branch: 10$^1/_2$
Headroom: 7'	Anderton Lift, (for River Weaver): 22$^3/_4$
Croxton Aqueduct to Preston Brook Tunnel	PRESTON BROOK north end of tunnel and
Length: 72'	Bridgewater Canal: 29$^3/_4$
Beam: 9'	
Headroom: 6' 3"	Locks: 36
MANAGER:	
(0161) 427 1079	

This early canal was originally conceived partly as a roundabout link between the ports of Liverpool and Hull, while passing through the busy area of the Potteries and mid-Cheshire, and terminating either in the River Weaver or in the Mersey. One of its prime movers was the famous potter Josiah Wedgwood (1730–1795). Wedgwood was greatly assisted in the promotion of the canal by his friends, notably Thomas Bentley and Erasmus Darwin. Pamphlets were published, influential support was marshalled; and in 1766 the Trent & Mersey Canal Act was passed by Parliament, authorising the building of a navigation from the River Trent at Shardlow to Runcorn Gap, where it would join the proposed extension of the Bridgewater Canal from Manchester.

The ageing James Brindley was appointed engineer of the new canal. Construction began at once and much public interest was excited in this remarkable project, especially in the great 2900yd tunnel under Harecastle Hill.

Once opened in 1777 the Trent & Mersey Canal was a great success, attracting much trade in all kinds of commodities. Vast tonnages of china clay and flints for the pottery industry were brought by sea from Devon and Cornwall, then transhipped into canal boats on the Mersey and brought straight to the factories around Burslem, taking finished goods away again. Everyone near the canal benefited: much lower freight costs meant cheaper goods, healthier industries and more jobs. Agriculture gained greatly from the new supply of water, and of stable manure from the cities.

The Trent & Mersey soon earned its other name (suggested by Brindley) as the Grand Trunk Canal – in the 93 miles between Derwent Mouth and Preston Brook, the Trent & Mersey gained connection with no fewer than nine other canals or significant branches.

By the 1820s the Trent & Mersey was so busy that the narrow and slowly-sinking tunnel at Harecastle had become a serious bottleneck for traffic. Thomas Telford was called in; he recommended building a second tunnel beside Brindley's old one. His recommendation was eventually accepted by the company, and a tremendous burst of energy saw the whole tunnel completed in under three years, in 1827. A much-needed towpath was included in this new tunnel although this has now been removed so that boats can use the headroom in the centre of the channel.

Although the Trent & Mersey was taken over in 1845 by the new North Staffordshire Railway Company, the canal flourished until the Great War as a most important trading route. The entire waterway is covered in Book 4.

The section Derwent Mouth to Great Haywood is covered in Book 3.

Trent & Mersey Canal Introduction

Harding's Wood Junction

At the north end of Harecastle Tunnel (2926yds long) the navigation passes Kidsgrove station and a coal yard: beyond is Harding's Wood Junction with the Macclesfield Canal, which crosses the T & M on Poole Aqueduct. The canal continues to fall through a heavily locked stretch sometimes called 'heartbreak hill' but known to the old boatmen as the 'Cheshire Locks'. Two minor aqueducts are encountered, but the locks are all pairs of narrow locks, side by side. At Hassall Green are a *PO, tel, and stores* incorporating a canal shop, restaurant and boatyard services.

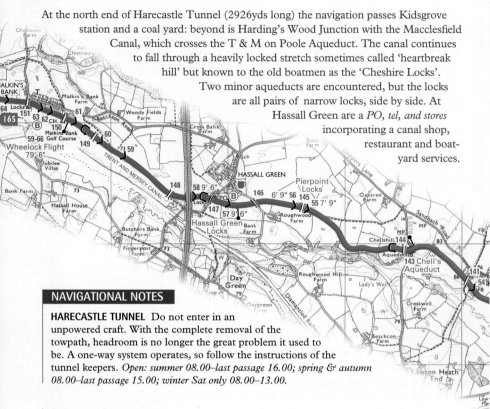

NAVIGATIONAL NOTES

HARECASTLE TUNNEL Do not enter in an unpowered craft. With the complete removal of the towpath, headroom is no longer the great problem it used to be. A one-way system operates, so follow the instructions of the tunnel keepers. *Open: summer 08.00–last passage 16.00; spring & autumn 08.00–last passage 15.00; winter Sat only 08.00–13.00.*

Pubs and Restaurants

◗ ✕ **Harecastle Hotel** Kidsgrove (01782 773925). A family pub close to bridge 132. Reasonably priced food (*available L & D, 7 days a week*), accompanied by their own traditional Mowcop gravy. Burtonwood and guest real ales. Vegetarians catered for. B & B.

◗ **Blue Bell** (01782 771371). At the junction with the Macclesfield Canal. Friendly one bar local serving Boddingtons real ale. Bar meals and snacks *lunchtimes only*.

◗ **Tavern** (01782 775382). Opposite the Blue Bell. Basic lockside pub offering Tetley's real ale and a guest. Bar food *lunchtimes and evenings*. Garden area.

◗ **Red Bull** (01782 782600). Canalside by the Red Bull flight. Robinson's and Hartleys real ales. Bar food served *lunchtimes and evenings, 7 days a week*. Vegetarians catered for. Canalside seating. *Thursday* quiz night.

✕ ♀ **Mrs B's Victorian Supper Rooms** Congleton Road, Butt Lane, Kidsgrove (01782 775654).

Enchanting period establishment offering a choice of dishes in a friendly atmosphere. Choose from the à la carte menu or enjoy the 7 course dinner. *19.30 for 20.00 – reservations essential. Closed Sun.*

◗ **Broughton Arms** (01270 765202). Canalside at Rode Heath. A friendly family pub, with comfortable bars and canalside seating. A range of Marston's real ales and food in the bar and dining area *lunchtimes and evenings*. Vegetarians catered for.

✕ ♀ **Lockside Restaurant** Hassall Green (01270 762266). Canalside at the Canal Centre. *Open Tue–Sat at 19.00*, last orders 21.30. Appetising range of reasonably priced dishes served. Children's menu and vegetarians catered for. Canalside seating. B & B.

◗ **Romping Donkey** Hassall Green (01270 765202). A pretty country pub. Tetley's real ale, and bar meals and snacks *lunchtimes and evenings*. *Sunday* roasts and regular barbecues. Children welcome. 'Bouncy castle'.

The Three Harecastle Tunnels

There are three parallel tunnels through Harecastle Hill. The first was completed in 1777, after 11 years' work. Since there was no towpath in the tunnel the boats had to be 'legged' through by men lying on the boat's cabin roof and 'walking' along the tunnel roof. (The towing horse would have to be walked over the top of the hill.) This slow means of propulsion made Harecastle a major bottleneck. In 1822 the Trent & Mersey Canal Company called in Thomas Telford, who recommended that a second tunnel be constructed alongside the first one. The new tunnel was completed in 1827, with a towpath (now removed). An electric tug was introduced in 1914 to speed up traffic through Telford's tunnel; this service was continued until 1954. The third tunnel was built after the other two, and carried the Stoke-Kidsgrove railway line. This tunnel was closed in the 1960s.

Kidsgrove

Staffs. MD Tue. All services. Originally an iron and coal producing town, Kidsgrove was much helped by the completion of the Trent & Mersey Canal. James Brindley is buried here.

Rode Heath

PO, tel, stores. A useful shopping area right by bridge 140. There is a butcher's shop at bridge 139.

Rode Heath Rise Once the site of a salt works, it has now been landscaped and restored as a wildflower meadow. Ring 01477 534115 for further information

Boatyards

Ⓑ **David Piper** Red Bull Basin, Church Lawton, Kidsgrove (01782 784754). By Red Bull Aqueduct. 🚽 ♨ **D** Pump-out, gas, overnight mooring, long-term mooring, winter storage, slipway up to 60ft, chandlery, books and maps, boat building, boat sales, engine sales and repairs. Breakdowns welcome.

Ⓑ **Smithsons Solid Fuel and Caravan Centre** Kidsgrove (01782 787887). Near bridge 132. **D** Calor gas, solid fuel, lubricants and caravan fittings which can be used as chandlery.

Ⓑ **BW Red Bull Yard** North of bridge 134. (01782 785703). 🚽 ♨

Ⓑ **Canal Centre** Hassall Green, Sandbach (01270 762266). ♨ **D** Pump-out, gas, overnight and long-term mooring, winter storage, groceries, books and maps. Also post office, general store, off-licence, gifts, licensed restaurant and tea room, B & B, paraffin, coal.

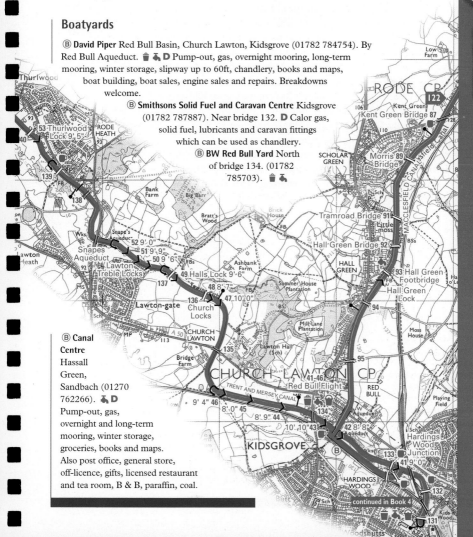

Wheelock

The canal now descends the Wheelock
flight of eight locks, which are the last
paired locks one sees when travelling northwards. The countryside continues to be
quiet and unspoilt but unspectacular. The
pair of locks halfway down the flight is situated
in the little settlement of Malkin's Bank, overlooked by terraced houses. The boatman's co-op used
to be here, in the small terrace of cottages. The adjoining
boatyard now specialises in the restoration of traditional working boats. At the bottom of the flight is the village of Wheelock;
west of here the navigation curls round the side of a hill before
entering the very long-established salt-producing area that is based on
Middlewich. The 'wild' brine pumping and rock-salt mining that has gone
on hereabouts has resulted in severe local subsidence; the effect on the canal
has been to necessitate the constant raising of the banks as lengths of the canal
bed sink. This of course means that the affected lengths tend to be much deeper
than ordinary canals. Non-swimmers beware of falling overboard. The navigation
now begins to lose the rural character it has enjoyed since Kidsgrove. Falling
through yet more locks, the canal is joined by a busy main road (useful for fish and
chips, west of Kings Lock; and Chinese take-away, west of bridge 166) which
accompanies it into an increasingly flat and industrialised landscape, past several
salt works and into Middlewich, where a branch of the Shropshire Union leads off
westwards towards that canal at Barbridge. The first 100 yards or so of this branch
is the Wardle Canal, claimed to be the shortest canal in the country. There is a
useful shop at bridge 166.

- ● **Wheelock**
  *Ches. EC Tue. PO, tel, stores, garage, fish and
  chips.* Busy little main road village on the canal.
- ● **Sandbach**
  *Ches. EC Tue. MD Thur. PO, tel, stores, garage,
  bank, station.* 1½ miles north of Wheelock.
  An old market town that has maintained its
  charm despite the steady growth of its salt and
  chemical industries. After walking from the
  canal you can refresh yourself with a pint of real
  ale from any of the seven pubs visible from the
  seat in the market place.
  Ancient Crosses In the cobbled market place on
  a massive base stand two superb Saxon crosses,
  believed to commemorate the conversion of the
  area to Christianity in the 7thC. They suffered

severely in the 17thC when the Puritans broke
them up and scattered the fragments for miles.
After years of searching for the parts, George
Ormerod succeeded in re-erecting the crosses
in 1816, with new stone replacing the missing
fragments.
St Mary's Church High Street. A large, 16thC
church with a handsome battlemented tower.
The most interesting features of the interior
are the 17thC carved roof and the fine chancel
screen.
The Old Hall Hotel An outstanding example of
Elizabethan half-timbered architecture, which
was formerly the home of the lord of the
manor, but is now used as an hotel.

Boatyards

ⓑ **Malkins Bank Canal Services** (01270
764595). 🛁 Overnight mooring, long-term

mooring, slipway, chandlery, boat building and
restoration. Breakdown service.

Pubs and Restaurants

🍺 **Nags Head** Wheelock (01270 762457). 1/4 west of bridge 154. A small black and white pub serving Boddingtons and Chester's real ales. Traditional bar food *every lunchtime and weekday evenings.* Garden and aviary. Barbecue *summer Sats.* Children and dogs welcome. Pool and traditional pub games. Chinese take-away opposite.

🍺 **Commercial** Wheelock (01270 760122). Near bridge 154. Set in a Georgian house with an old fashioned and spacious feel this pub serves Marston's, Cains and Thwaites real ale, together with a guest. *Closed lunchtime Mon–Sat. No children.*

🍺 **Cheshire Cheese** Wheelock (01270 760319). Heavily-beamed, canalside pub serving Marston's and Banks's real ale and a wide range of meals and snacks *lunchtimes and evenings.* Vegetarians catered for. Large beer garden.

🍺 **Market Tavern** The Square, Sandbach (01270 762099). Opposite the crosses. Lively, old, traditional town pub serving Robinson's real ales and home-cooked bar food *lunchtimes Wed–Sat.* Children's menu and beer garden. One of the seven real ale pubs in, or close to, the square.

🍺 **Kinderton Arms** (01606 832158). Close to canal 1 mile south of Middlewich, by lock 70. Ignore its dour appearance and walk in to enjoy Tetley's and Boddingtons real ales and a friendly welcome. Excellent pub grub (large portions) served *lunchtimes and evenings, 7 days a week,* at remarkably low prices. Traditional *Sunday* lunches, children and vegetarians catered for, tea and coffee.

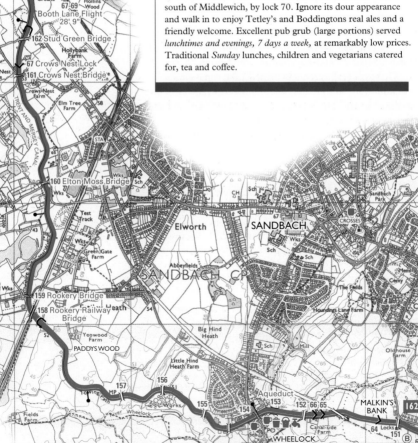

Middlewich

The Trent & Mersey skirts the centre of the town, passing lots of moored narrow boats and through three consecutive narrow locks, arriving at a wide (14ft) lock (which has suffered from subsidence) with a pub beside it. This used to represent the beginning of a wide, almost lock-free navigation right through to Preston Brook, Manchester and Wigan (very convenient for the salt industry when it shipped most of its goods by boat), but Croxton Aqueduct had to be replaced many years ago, and is now a steel structure only 8ft 2in wide. The aqueduct crosses the River Dane, which flows alongside the navigation as both water courses leave industrial Middlewich and move out into fine open country. Initially, this is a stretch of canal as beautiful as any in the country. Often overhung by trees, the navigation winds along the side of a hill as it follows the delightful valley of the River Dane. The parkland on the other side of the valley encompasses Bostock Hall, a school for children with learning difficulties. At Whatcroft Hall (privately owned), the canal circles around to the east, passing under a derelict railway before heading for the industrial outskirts of Northwich and shedding its beauty and solitude once again.

NAVIGATIONAL NOTES

There are several privately owned wide 'lagoons' caused by subsidence along this section of the Trent & Mersey, in some of which repose the hulks of abandoned barges and narrow boats, lately being salvaged. Navigators should be wary of straying off the main line, since the offside canal bank is often submerged and invisible just below the water level.

Boatyards

Ⓑ **Andersen Boats** Wych House, St Anne's Road, Middlewich (01606 833668). Pump-out, gas, narrow boat hire, books and maps.

Ⓑ **Middlewich Narrowboats** Canal Terrace, Middlewich (01606 832460). 🛒 🚽 ♿ D Pump-out, gas, narrow boat hire, overnight mooring (*not Fri*), long-term mooring, dry dock, groceries, chandlery, books and maps, engine repairs, toilets, laundry service, breakdown service. *Closed Sun.* Useful tool hire shop next door.

Pubs and Restaurants

🍺 **Kings Lock** Middlewich (01606 833537). Overlooking the lock. Bar food *lunchtimes and evenings. Canalside seating. B & B.*

🍺 ✕ **Boars Head** Kinderton Street, Middlewich (01606 833191). Large rambling pub offering Robinson's real ale and bar snacks *from 12.00–21.00.* Children's room in hotel next door together with restaurant serving meals *lunchtimes and evenings.* Patio. B & B.

🍺 **Cheshire Cheese** Lewin Street, Middlewich (01606 832097). Basic but welcoming traditional pub offering Cains, John Smith's and Burtonwood real ales (plus 2 guests weekly) together with inexpensive bar snacks *lunchtimes and evenings.* Beer garden. Children welcome.

🍺 **Newton Brewery Inn** Middlewich (01606 833502). 1/4 mile south of Big Lock. Marston's real ale served in a small friendly pub with an attractive garden running down to the towpath. Selection of meals and snacks *lunchtimes and evenings (not Sun evening).* Children welcome.

🍺 ✕ **Big Lock** Middlewich (01606 833489). Canalside. Variously a bottle-making factory and canal-horse stables this pub now serves Ruddles, Courage and Webster's real ales (and guests) together with bar snacks and an à la carte menu. Food available *L & D, 7 days a week.* Children and vegetarians catered for. Garden area and *weekend music in winter.* There is a canal shop selling gifts, maps, soft drinks, etc. adjacent.

● **Middlewich**
Ches. EC Wed. PO, tel, stores, bank, garage. A town that since Roman times has been dedicated to salt extraction. Most of the salt produced here goes to various chemical industries. Subsidence from salt extraction has prevented redevelopment for many years, but a big renewal scheme is now in progress. The canalside area is a haven of peace below the busy streets.

St Michael's Church A handsome medieval church which was a place of refuge for the Royalists during the Civil War. It has a fine interior with richly carved woodwork.

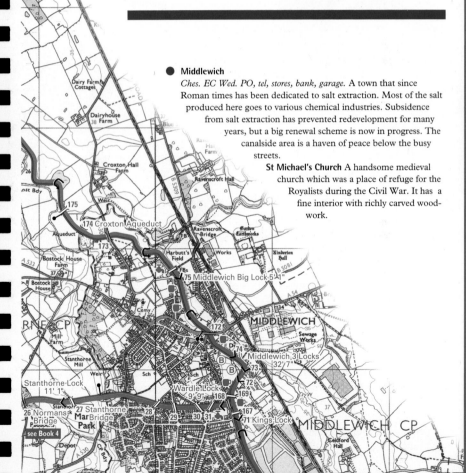

Anderton Lift

The outlying canal settlement of Broken Cross acts as a buffer between the beauty and solitude of the Dane Valley and the industrial ravages around Northwich. Beyond is another length in which salt mining has determined the nature of the scenery. Part of it is heavily industrial, with enormous ICI works dominating the scene; much of it is devastated but rural (just), some of it is nondescript, and some of it is superb

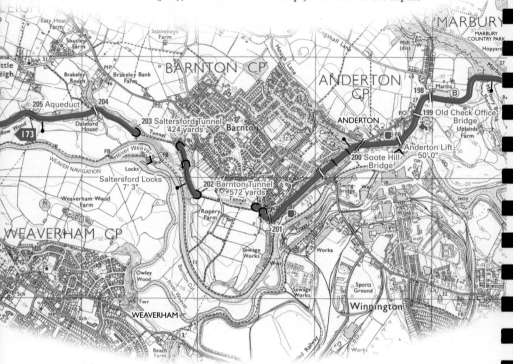

countryside. Donkey engines can still be seen in surrounding fields pumping brine. Leaving the vicinity of Lostock Gralam (*licensed grocer 100 yds east of bridge 189 open every day until 22.00*) and the outskirts of Northwich, one passes Marston (*late opening stores and tel*) and Wincham (*PO, tel, stores*). Just west of the village, one travels along a 1/2-mile stretch of canal that was only cut in 1958, as the old route was about to collapse into – needless to say – underground salt workings. Beyond the woods of Marbury Country Park (attractive short stay moorings) is Anderton (*PO, tel, stores*) – the short entrance canal to the famous boat lift down into the Weaver Navigation is on the left. The main line continues westward, winding along what is now a steep hill and into Barnton Tunnel. At the west end one emerges onto a hillside overlooking the River Weaver, with a marvellous view straight down the huge Saltersford Locks. Now Saltersford Tunnel is entered: beyond it, one finds oneself in completely open country again. There are good moorings in the basins to the east of both tunnels.

NAVIGATIONAL NOTES

Saltersford Tunnel is crooked, affording only a brief glimpse of the other end. Two boats cannot pass in this or Barnton Tunnel, so make sure they are clear before proceeding.

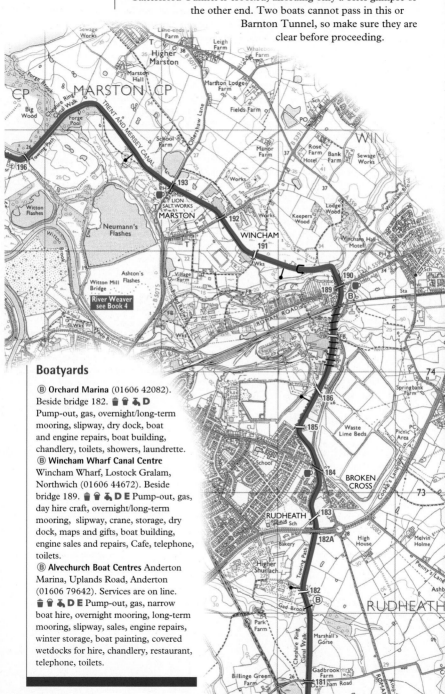

Boatyards

ⓑ **Orchard Marina** (01606 42082). Beside bridge 182. 🚾 🚿 ⚓ D Pump-out, gas, overnight/long-term mooring, slipway, dry dock, boat and engine repairs, boat building, chandlery, toilets, showers, laundrette.

ⓑ **Wincham Wharf Canal Centre** Wincham Wharf, Lostock Gralam, Northwich (01606 44672). Beside bridge 189. 🚾 🚿 ⚓ D E Pump-out, gas, day hire craft, overnight/long-term mooring, slipway, crane, storage, dry dock, maps and gifts, boat building, engine sales and repairs, Cafe, telephone, toilets.

ⓑ **Alvechurch Boat Centres** Anderton Marina, Uplands Road, Anderton (01606 79642). Services are on line. 🚾 🚿 ⚓ D E Pump-out, gas, narrow boat hire, overnight mooring, long-term mooring, slipway, sales, engine repairs, winter storage, boat painting, covered wetdocks for hire, chandlery, restaurant, telephone, toilets.

● Marston

Ches. Tel. A salt-producing village, suffering badly from its own industry. The numerous gaps in this village are caused by the demolition or collapse of houses affected by subsidence. Waste ground abounds.

The Lion Salt Works Offershaw Lane, Marston (01606 41823). Beside the canal at bridge 193. The Thompson family established an open pan salt works in Marston in 1842, producing fishery salt, bay salt, crystal salt and lump salt. The salt was pumped as wild brine from 45 yds beneath the works and evaporated in a large iron pan. The crystals thus formed were raked into tubs to form blocks, and subsequently dried in brick stove houses, before being exported (with the first part of the journey by canal) to India, Canada and West Africa. The works closed in 1986 but is currently being restored and is well worth visiting. Excellent audio visual and many exhibits. *Open 13.30–16.30.* Charge. Also information on the attractive countryside of Vale Royal and its rich industrial heritage.

Marbury Country Park A 200 acre park occupying the landscaped gardens of the former Marbury Hall and estate, once the home of the Barry and Smith-Barry families. Overlooking Budworth Mere, the house was demolished in 1968 and the much neglected gardens restored to their former glory by Cheshire County Heritage and Recreation service. The Information Centre ($1/2$ mile north of bridge 196) houses a display of Marbury's wildlife and history, including its use as a POW camp during World War II. Visitor's moorings and picnic area.

● Anderton Lift

An amazing and enormous piece of machinery built in 1875 by Leader Williams (later engineer of the Manchester Ship Canal) to connect the Trent & Mersey to the flourishing Weaver Navigation, 50ft below. As built, the lift consisted of two water-filled tanks counterbalancing each other in a vertical slide, resting on massive hydraulic rams. It worked on the very straight-forward principle that making the ascending tank slightly lighter – by pumping a little water out – would assist the hydraulic rams (which were operated by a steam engine and pump) in moving both tanks, with boats in them, up or down their respective slide. In 1908 the lift had to have major repairs, so it was modernised at the same time. The troublesome hydraulic rams were done away with; from then on each tank – which contained 250 tons of water – had its own counterweights and was independent of the other tank. Electricity replaced steam as the motive power. One of the most fascinating individual features of the canal system, it draws thousands of sightseers every year. Restoration depends upon raising the necessary funding – currently estimated at £10,000,000.

● Northwich

Ches. EC Wed. MD Fri, Sat. All services. Regular buses from Barnton. A rather attractive town at the junction of the Rivers Weaver and Dane. (The latter brings large quantities of sand down into the Weaver Navigation, necessitating a heavy expenditure on dredging.) As in every other town in this area, salt has for centuries been responsible for the continued prosperity of Northwich. The Weaver Navigation has of course been another very prominent factor in the town's history, and the building and repairing of barges, narrow boats, and small sea-going ships has been carried on here for over 200 years. Nowadays this industry has been almost forced out of business by foreign competition, and the last private shipyard on the river closed down in 1971. (This yard – Isaac Pimblott's – used to be between Hunt's Locks and Hartford Bridge. Their last contract was a tug for Aden.) However, the big BW yard in the town continues to thrive; some very large maintenance craft are built and repaired here. The wharves by Town Bridge are empty, and are an excellent temporary mooring site for anyone wishing to visit the place. The town centre is very close; much of it has been completely rebuilt very recently. There is now an extensive shopping precinct. Although the large number of pubs has been whittled down in the rebuilding process, there are still some pleasant old streets. The Weaver and the big swing bridges across it remain a dominant part of the background.

Tourist Information Centre. This service can be accessed via the local council by ringing 01606 862862.

Dock Road Edwardian Pumping Station Weir Street, Northwich (0161 794 9314). Intriguing listed building housing unique pumps and gas-powered engines fully restored to working order. Building open and engines working *Easter–end Sep on Sat, Sun & B. Hols 14.00–17.00.* Charge.

Salt Museum Weaver Hall, London Road, Northwich (01606 41331). The history of the salt industry from Roman times to the present day, housed in the town's former workhouse. Look out for the remarkable model ship, made from salt of course. *Open all year Tue–Fri 10.00–17.00; Sat & Sun 14.00–17.00; B.Hol Mon 10.00–17.00.* Audio visual introduction. Charge.

BOAT TRIPS
Canal Explorer operating boat trips from Wincham Wharf *Easter till the end of Sep.* Group and party bookings. Ring 01606 44672 for details.
Aquarius based beside the Anderton Lift and running trips north through the tunnels and south to The Lion Salt Works. Boat also available for private charter (maximum 40 people). Refreshments. Ring 01606 76204 for further details.
Weaver Sovereign offering trips to various destinations along the River Weaver. *All trips leave from the Town Quay, Northwich and include a commentary, food and bar.* Weston Docks, Runcorn is also visited. Boat also available for private charter (maximum 60 people). Details from 01606 76204.

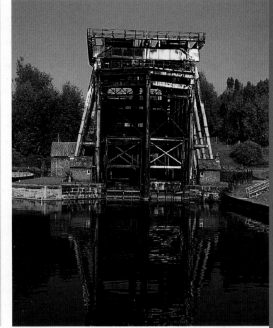

Anderton Lift

Pubs and Restaurants

🍺 **Old Broken Cross** (01606 40431). Canalside, at bridge 184. A very attractive old pub serving well kept Greenalls and guest real ales. A selection of snacks and meals are served *lunchtimes and evenings (not Sun evening)*. Vegetarians catered for. Small canalside garden. Chemist, grocer, laundrette and other shops are 1/2 mile past pub, towards Northwich.

🍺✕ **Sweet Waters** Wincham Wharf (01606 46099). Canalside by bridge 189. A tastefully renovated warehouse building (reputed to be the oldest on the T & M) with waterside seating and regular *Fri night* blues evenings. Boddingtons and guest real ales together with an interesting and varied bar and restaurant menu, served *lunchtimes and evenings (not Mon L & D)*. Children and vegetarians catered for.

🍺 **Salt Barge** Marston (01606 43064). Opposite the Lion Salt Works, beside bridge 193. A deceptively large pub with a friendly atmosphere, neatly divided into cosy areas, and with an inviting family room. Burtonwood and Chester's real ale and good food *lunchtimes and evenings*. Children's menu and *Sunday* lunch. Garden with play area.

✕♀ **The Moorings** Anderton Marina (01606 79789). Part of the Alvechurch Boat Centres complex. Open for *lunchtime snacks 10.00–16.00 and evenings 18.00–22.00* for full à la carte menu. Children and vegetarians catered for. Canalside seating. Boaters please moor outside the basin.

🍺 **Stanley Arms** (01606 75059). Canalside, right opposite the Anderton Lift (*also PO, stores*). A friendly real ale pub (Tetley's and Greenalls) with a lovely family room, where children are welcome. An excellent selection of good bar food is served *lunchtimes and evenings – not Tue evenings* (including regular Indian food nights). Outside seating and children's play area. Vegetarians catered for. The landlord keeps a collection of local Tourist Information.

🍺 **Red Lion** Barnton (01606 74817). Just east of bridge 201. A very wide range of inexpensive bar food, including pizzas and curries served *lunchtimes and evenings, 7 days a week. Open all day Sun.* Garden and children's room.

Dutton

This, the northernmost stretch of the Trent & Mersey, is a very pleasant one and delightfully rural. Most of the way the navigation follows the south side of the hills that overlook the River Weaver. From about 60ft up, one is often rewarded with excellent views of this splendid valley and the occasional large vessels that ply up and down it. At one point one can see the elegant Dutton railway viaduct in the distance; then the two waterways diverge as the Trent & Mersey enters the woods preceding Preston Brook Tunnel. There is a stop lock south of the tunnel just beyond a pretty covered dry dock; there are often fine examples of restored working boats moored here. At the north end of the tunnel a notice announces that from here onwards one is on the Bridgewater Canal (see page 23). There are good moorings north of bridge 213, and to the south of Dutton stop lock.

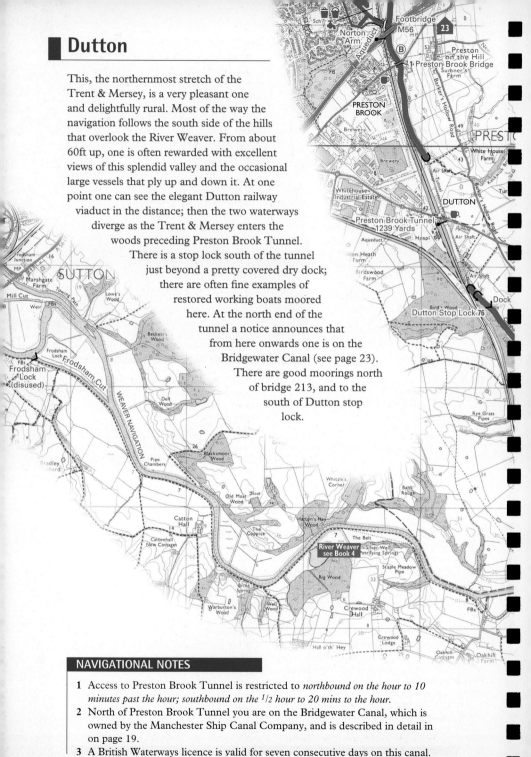

NAVIGATIONAL NOTES

1. Access to Preston Brook Tunnel is restricted to *northbound on the hour to 10 minutes past the hour; southbound on the 1/2 hour to 20 mins to the hour.*
2. North of Preston Brook Tunnel you are on the Bridgewater Canal, which is owned by the Manchester Ship Canal Company, and is described in detail in on page 19.
3. A British Waterways licence is valid for seven consecutive days on this canal.

Pubs and Restaurants

🍺 ✕ **Leigh Arms** (01606 853327). ¼ mile south of bridge 209, overlooking the Weaver and Acton Swing Bridge. Burtonwood and Forshaws real ale in an attractive old coaching inn with stained glass windows in the bar. Good food from an interesting menu available *12.00–21.00, seven days a week*. Vegetarians well catered for. Restaurant and outside seating area. Barbecue *summer weekends*. Children's play area.

🍺 ✕ **Horns** (01606 852192). 200yds south of bridge 209 on the A49, by Acton Swing Bridge. Friendly, roadside pub serving Greenalls real ale together with bar food *lunchtimes, evenings and all day Sunday*. Cosy bars, large garden and children's play area. Folk night *1st Tue in month*.

🍺 ✕ **Hollybush** Acton Bridge (01606 853196). ¼ mile north of bridge 209. One of the oldest farmhouse pubs in the country having a unique charm and character. Four cosy rooms, including traditional tap room, make up the bar area together with the tasteful addition of a new restaurant all set in this listed, timber-framed building. Wide range of interesting, home-cooked food served in the bar and restaurant *L & D, seven days a week*. Children and vegetarians catered for. Tetley's and guest real ales. Traditional pub games. Accommodation.

🍺 **Talbot Arms** Dutton (01928 718181). Burtonwood and Flowers real ales served in this comfortable pub atop Preston Brook tunnel. Traditional bar food available *lunchtimes 7 days a week and evenings Thur, Fri & Sat*. Outside seating and discos *Fri & Sat*. Quiz nights *Wed*.

Boatyards

Ⓑ **Black Prince Holidays** Bartington Wharf, Acton Bridge, Northwich (01606 852945). 🚽 🛢 ♿ **D** Pump-out, gas, electric boat recharging, narrow boat hire, day hire craft, overnight mooring (*not Fri*), long-term mooring, engine repairs, groceries, chandlery, books and maps, boat sales, toilets, gifts, laundry, telephone.

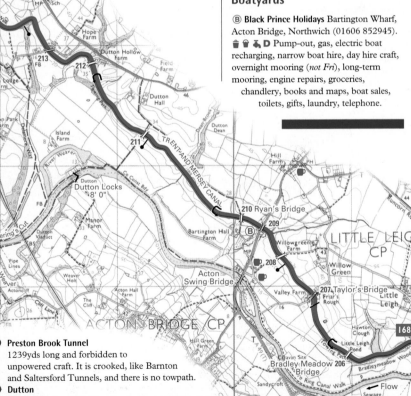

● **Preston Brook Tunnel**
1239yds long and forbidden to unpowered craft. It is crooked, like Barnton and Saltersford Tunnels, and there is no towpath.

● **Dutton**
Ches. Tel, garage. Small settlement on top of Preston Brook Tunnel, at the end of the lane uphill from the south end of the tunnel.

INDEX